BOYCHIKS IN THE HOOD

Boychiks in the Hood

TRAVELS IN THE HASIDIC UNDERGROUND

Robert Eisenberg

HarperSanFrancisco
An Imprint of HarperCollins*Publishers*

A TREE CLAUSE BOOK

HarperSanFrancisco and the author, in association with The Basic Foundation, a not-for-profit organization whose primary mission is reforestation, will facilitate the planting of two trees for every one tree used in the manufacture of this book.

An earlier version of chapter 1 previously appeared in the *Village Voice*. Portions of chapter 7 appeared in the *Forward*.

HarperCollins®, 🏭®, and HarperSanFrancisco™ are trademarks of HarperCollins Publishers Inc.

FIRST EDITION

Library of Congress Cataloging-in-Publication Data
Eisenberg, Robert.
Boychiks in the hood : travels in the Hasidic underground / Robert Eisenberg.
p.   cm.
ISBN 0–06–251222–6 (cloth)
ISBN 0–06–251223–4 (pbk.)
    1. Hasidism–United States.   2. Hasidim–United States.   I. Title
BM198.4.U6E37   1995   95–9838
296.8'332–dc20   CIP

95 96 97 98 99 ❖ HAD 10 9 8 7 6 5 4 3 2 1

FOR YOSHU

CONTENTS

BOYCHIKS IN THE HOOD

A Map of the Hasidim

AN INTRODUCTION

Imagine: It is the year 2075, and the only Jews left in the United States, aside from a few old-timers, are Hasidim and other Orthodox Jews. Impossible, you say? Actually, it's quite likely.

With a skyrocketing intermarriage rate and a low rate of retention of the offspring of these unions, the established Jewish community is beginning to crumble. There are some encouraging countertrends, to be sure, such as the Reform movement's success in outreach to the unaffiliated, but how long this will continue is anyone's guess. In the meantime, the ultra-Orthodox Hasidic population grows by leaps and bounds. Today there are about a quarter million Hasidim in North America. They are growing at a rate of 5 percent a year, a trajectory which, if anything, is on the upswing, as new generations have ever more children per family. Moreover, the Hasidim are attracting a steady stream of Jews from other sectors. A 5 percent annual increase translates into a doubling of population every fifteen years. This means that the

250,000 Hasidim of today will number between 8 and 10 million in the year 2075. Not only is this biologically possible, it is economically feasible, as more and more Hasidim find themselves on firmer financial footing, having made the leap from dazed immigrant to success story in the Golden Land.

The Hasidim are not surprised by this growth. They have a saying, *Toireh iz de besteh sroire.* Torah is the best merchandise. They say this not only when comparing the spiritual pursuit of studying Torah to more mundane mercantile activities, but also when dealing with the question of Jewish continuity, much on the minds of American Jews today. What they are saying is simple: Study Torah, follow its precepts, and continuity will take care of itself. Abandon Torah, and all the federation committees, all the Hadassahs, all the United Jewish Appeals and B'nai Briths, will not be able to staunch the hemorrhage.

Who are the Hasidim? To most observers, they seem strikingly anachronistic and somewhat mysterious. Dressed in the garb of eighteenth-century Poles–fur hats and black overcoats for the men, wigs and long skirts for the women–they seem almost otherworldly. The ultra-Orthodox of today, however, are not remnants of another time; they are the green shoots of a vibrant tradition that has its roots deep in the soil of Judaism. But it would be a mistake to think of them as monolithic. International Hasidism– there are about 650,000 worldwide–consists of a number of groups, each with its own unique perspective.

The founder of modern Hasidism, Israel Baal Shem Tov, was born in 1698 on the Russian-Polish border. He breathed life into a Judaism that had become ossified with punctilious observance of ritual and devoid of any emotional content, and his influence spread to millions of Jews over the next two centuries.

One of his followers, Elimelech of Lisensk, an early Hasidic leader of southern Poland, spawned a number of Hasidic dynasties that are still in existence today, either directly through his descendants or through his disciples. One of them is the Sanzer Hasidim, whose nineteenth-century founder expounded ecstatic expression in prayer. On the eve of World War II, there were between 2,000 and 3,000 living descendants of the Sanzer Rebbe. By the end of the war, fewer than 300 had survived.

Solomon Halberstam, the Bobover Rebbe, is one of them. Today he is arguably the most influential individual in New York City politics, with a powerful ability to deliver votes. As the senior figure in COJO, the Council of Jewish Organizations, his influence extends into Boro Park, the largest Orthodox neighborhood in Brooklyn and indeed the entire country. Rabbi Halberstam can rally a turnout of Hasidim and their sympathizers that can produce at least 50,000 and perhaps 100,000 votes for the favored candidate. It is no wonder that so many politicians, including the mayor of New York City and the governor of New York State, pay allegiance to him.

Israeli Rabbi Yissacher Dov Rokeach, the Belzer Rebbe, is also part of a line emanating from Elimelech of Lisensk. At his son's wedding, Rabbi Rokeach's guests included Mayor Teddy Kollek of Jerusalem, former U.N. Ambassador Benjamin Netanyahu, and Shimon Peres, Israel's foreign minister. The rabbi's wedding guests caused an outcry in the Hasidic world, where overly close ties with Zionists can provoke cries of traitor because the Torah is interpreted as saying that there shall be no Jewish state until the Messiah arrives. Some Hasidim from the Satmar sect even engaged in an organized campaign to take down wall posters congratulating the bride and groom. But none of this should be interpreted as any indication that the Belzer Rebbe is a Zionist; he is simply more pragmatic.

And it is pragmatism that the Satmar disdain. Because of a fortuitous draw of the card in the geopolitics of World War II, they are the largest Hasidic group in the world today. Located in

Hungary, they were spared the bloody grasp of Eichmann until the waning weeks of the war. The Satmar are most obstreperous in their refusal to accept the Zionist state, and although perhaps half of them live in Israel, they exercise a highly disciplined shunning of all state funds for education, no small feat considering that the average Satmar family has eight to ten children.

The Satmar Rebbe springs from the Teitelbaum line, which originated in Hungary in the eighteenth century. They drew an iron gate between themselves and any rabbinical authority willing to bend on the *Halakha,* or Jewish law.

The best-known contemporary Hasidic leader is the late Rabbi Menachem Mendel Schneerson, the Lubavitcher Rebbe, who died in the summer of 1994 at the age of ninety-two. His network of Chabad Houses in places as far-flung as Bangkok and Katmandu work vigorously to bring Jews back into the fold. And they have their work cut out for them, because 90 percent of Jews are not Orthodox, and the intermarriage rate is approaching 70 percent in some cities. Rebbe Schneerson was a descendant of Shneur Zalman of Lyadi, who authored the *Tanya,* a widely read mystical book. It is some of Schneerson's more voluble followers who are proclaiming him the Messiah. Others do more quotidian street work from Mitzvah tanks, large RVs in major cities where Jewish passersby are ushered in to recite a few prayers and reaffirm their *yiddishkeit,* or Jewishness.

Aside from the Bobovers, Belzers, Satmar, and Lubavitchers, the other major Hasidic groups are Vishnitzers, Gerers, Klausenbergers, Skverers and Bratslavers, along with a smattering of smaller sects. Slightly more than half live in Israel, primarily in the cities of Benei Berak and Jerusalem. In addition, there are sizable communities in Antwerp (about 15,000), London (at least 15,000, together with Manchester), Paris, Sydney and Melbourne, and smaller colonies elsewhere in Europe, South Africa, and Latin America.

The major Hasidic centers in North America are in Brooklyn, with a total of 150,000, of whom about 80,000 live in Boro Park, 45,000 in Williamsburg, 15,000 in Crown Heights, and 10,000 scattered in other neighborhoods, primarily Flatbush. There are perhaps 25,000 in the rest of New York City, together with Long Island and New Jersey. In the northern suburbs of New York, they number a minimum of 20,000 and are growing rapidly. Hasidim are also a presence in Los Angeles, Chicago, Baltimore, Detroit, Cleveland, Miami, St. Louis, Philadelphia, Pittsburgh, and Denver. Canada is the home to about 20,000 Hasidim, the vast majority of whom reside in Montreal or Toronto.

In the United States and Canada, Satmar, with 50,000, is by far the largest group. It is followed by Bobov and Lubavitch, with between 20,000 and 25,000 members each. Belzers, Gerers, and Vishnitzers trail farther behind. Many other groups are unaffiliated, or they are Mitnaggedim—technically not Hasidim, since they emphasize rigorous textual study over emotive prayer, and do not follow any rebbes. In terms of strictness of observance and outward appearance, however, Hasidim and Mitnaggedim are all but indistinguishable.

All of this is not to imply that Hasidim are into a numbers game; they are not. They rarely talk about the size of their group, and have to be prodded into disclosing how many children they have. Quality—of education, of commitment, of adherence to the strictures of the Mosaic law—is of much greater importance than quantity.

Hasidim have no need for the appurtenances of the modern world unless it advances their cause of getting closer to God. They have no use for restaurants, although they occasionally go to kosher ones, nor for movie theaters, television, secular education, professional skills beyond basic craftsmanship, opera, symphony, rock music, literature (other than that spawned from the Torah), or conspicuous consumption. Most of them have no more than a passing interest in politics, and their credo can be summed up in the aphorism "Is it good for the Jews?" or more specifically, for Orthodox Jews. They wish the best for Israel—not Israel the state, per se, but the Jews living in it. They couldn't care less about United Jewish Appeal or other mainstream charities, and those who can give to *yeshivot,* Jewish schools of higher learning, or other educational centers. They are insular, isolated, and when they look outside their world, they see AIDS, crack, promiscuous sex, and a general breakdown of morals. In general, they don't feel a scintilla of regret that they are "missing out."

My interests in Hasidism are manifold. I first became interested in Hasidism when I learned that a distant branch of my family, which was not particularly religious, were Satmars. Intrigued, I wanted to learn more.

I soon found that surprisingly little has been written about the Hasidim, particularly those outside of Israel. Each colony, as it were, of Hasidim has a unique profile, just as each group does. To say that the Hasidim are unaffected by the outside environment would be inaccurate. Therefore, it was my intention to investigate their communities, which have been widely dispersed. I fell into this plan when I went to Williamsburg on a Saturday afternoon in 1992 and ended up in the warm embrace of a family of Satmar Hasidim. The Satmar are often viewed as unapproachable; their last write-up in the press, other than small blurbs in newspapers, was a 1975 feature in the *National Geographic* that treated them as some sort of anthropological curiosity, which in some ways they are. But in other ways they are surprisingly conventional and far from monolithic, as I soon found out.

In general, precious little literature exists on the state of contemporary Hasidim. There is *Defenders of the Faith,* by Samuel Heilman, which examines their lives through the lens of an American social scientist in Israel. There is *Holy Days,* written by Lis Harris, a staff writer for the *New Yorker,* who consorted with the Lubavitchers in Crown Heights. In addition there are a few other scattered works, including Solomon Poll's now classic *The Hasidic Community of Williamsburg,* published in 1962, and Egon Mayer's *From Suburb to Shtetl,* an analysis of Boro Park in the late seventies. Why there is such a dearth of literature is inexplicable to me. There is so much to write about, either in sociological or narrative form, from rules of dress to aberrant behavior. An entire book could be written just about Hasidic garb.

This book, however, is something of a cross between a travelogue and a cohesive introduction to Hasidism today. Each place I went, each individual I encountered, had something unique and admirable to show for themselves.

The Hasidim, like other small and devout groups such as the Amish and the Hutterites, stand as a rock against the incursions of the modern world. Their idiosyncrasies, their lore, their love for their fellow men and women, are preserved in pristine form. The waves of contemporary life may lap at this boulder, but to no avail. In this sense, by looking at them, we see what we were, and–for better or worse–what we've become.

CHAPTER I

Boychiks in the Hood

WILLIAMSBURG, BROOKLYN

*S*everal years ago, crossing the English Channel from Belgium, I encountered a strange apparition: two gaunt *yeshiva* boys floating across the deck, their earlocks, or *payess,* swinging wildly. On an impulse, I called out to them in Yiddish, which I had learned as a child from my grandmother, one of the few people over age forty to have survived the concentration camps. I had extremely long hair, and they stared at me as if I were some sort of extraterrestrial. After a charged moment, they responded warmly, inviting me to their cabin, which had four beds but only two occupants. To the gentle lulling of the ship, the two pimply religious school lads—on their way home from a trip to Antwerp to get advice from a well-known sage—offered me a Judaic version of brimstone and hellfire, something I'd never encountered in the suburban Reform Sunday school I'd attended as a child.

Hell most certainly exists, they assured me. It is a place where the *neshuma,* the soul, is tossed back and forth like a hot potato, for eternity. This they began to act out, passing an imaginary basketball with the nimbleness of the Harlem Globetrotters. For eternity, one repeated, waving his finger at me. Not just the soul, the other added with a touch of drama, but the entire body. One is tossed into a vat of ordure and left to stew, also for eternity. They continued in this vein throughout much of the night, rocking back and forth on their beds, sometimes faster, sometimes slower. Every so often, a bony hand would appear in front of my top bunk from somewhere below, clutching a piece of fruit. "Eat! Eat!" one of them commanded.

This was my first introduction to the Satmar Hasidim. Before the boat docked in England, they gave me their address in Williamsburg, Brooklyn, and told me to stop in if I was ever in the neighborhood.

What Pat Buchanan is to the Republican Party, Satmars are to other Hasidim. In the ultra-Orthodox world, it just doesn't get any more religious than this.

To many, the word Satmar conjures up an amorphous mass of black protoplasm, 100,000 strong, gobbling up everything in sight. When Judaism struggles with assimilation, Satmar eats *Haskala,* the Enlightenment, for breakfast. When European Jewry succumbed, Satmar survived. Satmar takes on all comers—Hitler, acculturation, Zionist opprobrium—and prevails: Chasing down Lubavitchers with nunchakus. Burning the Israeli flag at anti-Zionist rallies. Greeting drivers on the Sabbath in Jerusalem with a brick through their windshields. Hogging the public trough in Williamsburg, to the distress of their Hispanic neighbors. Engaging in violent internal struggles. And even, according to some Hasidim, kidnapping gifted children in order to inculcate them with the Satmar's unique brand of Orthodox Judaism.

About 50,000 Satmars live in North America, three-quarters of them in the Williamsburg section of Brooklyn, New York. There are also communities in Boro Park, upstate New York, Los Angeles, Montreal, Toronto, Antwerp, and Israel. Williamsburg is easily one of the most densely packed neighborhoods in the United States, and the Satmar are by far the largest Hasidic group in America. The more visible Lubavitchers are a distant second or third, in a colorful constellation consisting of Bobovers, Belzers, Gerers, Vishnitzers, Munkaczers, Bratslavers, Klausenbergers, and Skverers, among others.

Almost all these groups participate in Israeli civic life by way of religious parties, but not the Satmar. Until the Messiah comes, they refuse to take any part in the Jewish state. Given their militant anti-Zionism, intense insularity, and inbred distrust of outsiders, it is understandable that very little has been written in English about the Satmar. This self-imposed pariah status is reinforced by their almost exclusive use of Yiddish, a language few American Jews actually speak. The most minute aspects of their lives—from which shoe to put on first in the morning, to which side of the bed to sleep on at night—are rigidly ritualized.

The Satmars originated in what many early-twentieth-century Jews considered the intellectual Appalachia of Europe—remote Transylvania, straddling the Hungarian-Romanian border. From the very beginning, the Satmar movement was a violent reaction to any sort of accommodation to the modern world.

A large proportion of the Satmar Hasidim perished during World War II, but not to the same extent as did Polish Jewry. Adolph Eichmann's liquidation machine didn't get around to the destruction of Hungary's Jews until the final months of the war, and then they found little official enthusiasm for the project among their Hungarian allies. The ragged survivors managed to transplant themselves to the streets of New York. The neighborhood they ended up in was Williamsburg, already a religious quarter and a home for Jewish immigrants from the Old World.

Some of my relatives ended up here too. Many years ago, in Hungary, my father's family were Satmars. Well before the war, however, part of the family broke from the group and went on to live largely secular lives in Budapest and the United States. The others seemed to disappear into a haze. Some, I'd heard, were in Brooklyn–the Williamsburg branch, my family called them. Although I had never given them much thought, after encountering those boys on the channel-crossing I felt compelled to go there: not so much to search out this phantom offshoot of my family, but to see how my life might have been had my grandfather's father not turned away from Hasidism.

I begin my travels in the Hasidic world on a warm Saturday afternoon in 1992, walking down the empty streets of Williamsburg. I have no idea what I will find, or even if it is possible to make any substantive contact. I have only a crumpled piece of paper with the addresses of the two *boychiks* from the boat. But after a few discreet inquiries, I learn that they are spending their summer in the Catskills, so I am left standing in front of a brownstone on Lee Avenue, reading raffle posters for a yeshiva written entirely in Yiddish. At this moment I enter a world that seems to exist in a parallel universe.

The posters boldly promise cars and cash to winners. One has a drawing showing a Hasidic couple and eight children getting out of a new Oldsmobile. Another advertises a clothing store. A short, dumpy Hasid greets another on the street: "Three hundred dollars I paid for this heavy suit and it's killing me," he says, perspiring. "I was smarter," replies the other, "I bought this light suit for half the price at G & G Clothing." "All suits *shatnes* tested," reads the tag line. Shatnes is the biblical injunction against mixing wool and linen, which Hasidim avoid at all costs. Above the posters loom the huge low-income housing projects where Hispanic families are squeezed next to Hasidic families in an uneasy coexistence.

As I read the posters, a man sticks his head from out of a doorway and looks at me quizzically. I gesture to my yarmulke, but he isn't impressed. He has buck teeth, wears thick glasses and a Sabbath overcoat. Peeking inside, I see rows of heavy wooden benches and walls lined with books. This building is a *cheder,* a day school, and he is a *melamed,* a schoolteacher. I stand in the doorway examining the empty classroom. He knows that the general perception of the Satmar is one of insularity, and he tries hard to present a different face. "Don't worry," he smiles, "we don't bite."

We engage in small talk. But when I shift my weight, he hears the jingling of coins in my pants pockets and stirs uneasily. I have violated a basic precept by carrying money on Shabbos. "How do I know you're not from the FBI?" he asks suddenly. Rather than trying to convince him otherwise, I wish him good Shabbos and move on.

A few blocks away, I come upon a young couple. The wife wears an elegant print dress and the husband sports a double-breasted suit over his ample belly. Their children play at the curb. The streets are empty, the neighborhood frozen in a Brooklyn tableau of Joe DiMaggio and Neil Simon. I ask the couple, in Yiddish, for directions to the main synagogue, and the husband answers my question with a question: "Have you eaten?"

"Not really," I reply.

"Come with me," he smiles, and leads me effortlessly into his world.

We turn the corner and enter a brownstone through the open front door. Inside, there are maybe six young couples, a middle-aged

couple, and an elderly woman, all relaxing around an opulent dining set, their feet propped up casually on chairs. To my surprise,
the kitchen is spacious and modern with an island counter. Modern art covers the walls. A wrought-iron handrail leads upstairs. I
walk in with my ponytail, a two-day growth of beard, and a suede
yarmulke. My guide introduces me as someone who hasn't eaten
yet. Before a word is spoken, a plateful of meat, chicken, kishke,
and kugel is placed in front of me. A second plate of gefilte fish,
tender and sweet, is placed to my right, and a bowl of fruit is set in
the center of the table. A paper plate of baked delights—apple
strudel, rugelach, and coffee cake—waits in the wings.

A young man with playful eyes and black payess takes the lead
in introducing me to everyone. The food is copious, the room
well-appointed, the lady of the house, the *balebustah*, elegant in
turban and pearls.

"I fell into a gold mine," I exclaim. They all laugh. The lady of
the house, fluent in English, without the intonations of the ghetto
or even a New York accent, introduces herself. She is a travel
agent, she says, and her husband is in the uniform business. Someone else adds that it is a misperception that most Satmars are in
the diamond trade—they are mostly in garments and electronics.

I am plied with vodka and Budweiser as we jabber away in Yiddish. They throw out nuggets of information: Satmars will marry
each other and other Ungarishe, or Hungarian Hasidim, such as
Munkaczers, and occasionally even other non-Hungarian Hasidim,
but never Lubavitchers. Lubavitchers are damaged goods, idol-
aters. They worship the Lubavitcher Rebbe, Menachem Mendel
Schneerson, who was at that time hospitalized in Manhattan after
suffering a stroke. It's not the rebbe's fault that his followers regard
him as *Moshiach*, the Messiah, my hosts insist. Satmars follow the
issue closely. A recent *New York Times Magazine* story on the

Lubavitcher Rebbe was read and reread by virtually every Jew in Williamsburg.

Satmars love Ronald Reagan, "a *yiddishe goy*," one tells me, but they're not too crazy about the current president, George Bush, who is perceived as anti-Israel. When I ask why they should care if Bush is ostensibly anti-Israel when they themselves are, a young man pipes up, "Bush is anti-*Israeli*, we are anti-*Israel*."

The Satmars' policies toward the Jewish state are contradictory. Informally, they are avid supporters of the most hawkish political parties in Israel. But if they lived there, they wouldn't vote. At the same time, most Satmars strain to distance themselves from Neturei Karta, a Hasidic movement that is virulently anti-Zionist and takes it upon itself to advise the Palestinians at the peace talks. Yet this splinter group accommodates itself to the influence of the Satmar and their leader, Rabbi Moishe Teitelbaum.

My hosts produce a copy of the Satmar house organ, *Der Yid*, and I am asked to read it. Impressed at my ability to decipher Yiddish, they ask me where I learned it.

"My *bubbe*."

"Your grandmother knows Yiddish?"

"*Yah*, she is a survivor of Auschwitz."

"Your grandmother, she is a Jew? All your grandparents? You look like a flower child from the Village. So how do you know so much?"

I list two or three books, the secular Jewish press, the Lubavitcher *Algemeiner Journal*, as well as *Der Yid*, as regular reading, but I warn them not to put a page of Talmud in front of me. "I would stare at it like a blind cow." They laugh appreciatively.

Leafing through *Der Yid*, I find an account of the latest Hasidic mega-wedding at the Javits Center. An offspring of the Munkaczer

Rebbe got married and invited 25,000 guests. Thousands of bearded faces are squeezed into the picture, a huge black monolith snubbing its nose at Hitler.

Newlyweds go on to have huge families. Three of the young men at the table come from families of thirteen or more. "What's the largest family you know?" I ask. "Seventeen," one says. "No, twenty-one," another reminds him. How can they handle so many children? "It is easier to deal with seventeen than with three," the balebustah says, from personal knowledge. But few Satmars live as well as this family. Most are crowded into three- or four-room apartments. The Satmar Rebbe strenuously encourages his people to move to the suburban Hasidic community of Kiryas Joel in the town of Monroe, where each family can have its own subsidized bungalow. But most are as excited at this prospect as Eva Gabor was about moving to Hooterville in *Green Acres*. Nevertheless, 1,200 families have heeded the rebbe's call.

Since so many cousins marry one another, an enterprising Hasid in Monroe has set up a confidential computer bank detailing the blood characteristics of every eligible young Satmar. The result has been a drastic decline in Tay-Sachs and other hereditary diseases. When I express surprise that cousins are allowed to marry one another, I am given a lecture on who can marry whom. "You cannot marry your own aunt," one says in a talmudic singsong, "but you can marry your niece."

Being on the dole is fairly common in Williamsburg. Many families are on food stamps, and the Satmar are notorious for their ability to pull political strings and take advantage of every conceivable government program. Yet this is not an entirely poor community. Multimillionaires abound. The most famous of these are the Goldsteins of 47th Street Photo, which went bankrupt.

"Bad real estate investments. The real estate they didn't put in a separate shell from the stores," says one young man.

"Nah, nah, it wasn't so simple," says another with roguish eyes, who looks like he could be a drummer for Alice Cooper. This fellow, Shraga, works in the garment district for a huge importer of underwear, also a Satmar. Shraga reads the *New York Times* an hour a day, and his knowledge of the outside world is formidable.

The Satmar operate a food bank that is a model of discretion. Vans drop boxes of comestibles on the doorsteps of the disadvantaged late every Thursday night. The vans are camouflaged as legitimate grocery-store delivery trucks so as not to embarrass anyone. The elderly stay with their families. Homes for the aged are considered an abomination. A person who is hospitalized is never at a loss for visitors. At school, which children start at age three, there are no sports, no swimming, and no secular subjects other than state-mandated courses in civics. "Sure we know the difference between Washington and Lincoln. Lincoln had a beard, Washington didn't."

The Satmar are absolutely uninterested in recruiting other Jews or even getting them to be more religious. "This Lubavitcher preoccupation with getting every Jew to put on *t'fillin* [phylacteries, two small leather cases holding inscriptions from the Scriptures, fastened to the forehead and an arm by leather straps during morning prayers] once and then letting them go is very strange," someone says. "We have a few new people, but they are from Persia, Russia, and other Hasidic groups, not the mainstream." All the recruiting makes the Lubavitch seem tainted. "You go to a Lubavitch wedding, you look at the family, you see an uncle, a Lubavitcher, another is with a shaved face, another a Reform. We don't have any of that here."

After this encounter, I am taken on a tour of the community. "Shraga will show you around," the lady of the house says. "You two are both 'dissidents.' Birds of a feather . . . " On the street, the few people who are not inside taking their Shabbos afternoon naps are oblivious to me, except for a boy who, having seen the notebook peeking out of my pocket, runs up to me and yells to his father, *"Er trugt! Er trugt!"* meaning that I'm carrying something. On the Sabbath, one is not supposed to carry anything, not supposed to tear anything, not even supposed to comb one's hair. "Go put your book under those bleachers there until we are finished with our walk," Shràga tells me. Another boy invites me over for dinner.

My guide stops to point out the rebbe's house, a boxy affair. The current rebbe, Moishe, inherited the mantle from his uncle Joel Teitelbaum, known affectionately as *Der Yoilish,* a figure of monumental significance. Before he died, Der Yoilish established the institutional framework that carried the Satmar from a few thousand dazed survivors to where they are today.

Moishe, however, is treated with ambivalence, at least by the people I meet. His approval rating seems to hover around that of George Bush. Not that he is actively disliked; he is just not considered charismatic enough to be at the helm. A dissident movement has sprung up. Known as *Kagners,* or opponents, they have their own leader with a house catty-corner from the rebbe's. He is Nachman Brach, a successful electronics wholesaler, and he is backed by Der Yoilish's second wife, Feige. While Brach himself does not claim to be a successor, he is said to be bankrolling the widow, who is revered by the insurgents.

"I have a brother, a Kagner, and one brother with Moishe, but they get along," Shraga says. Where things really heat up is in Monroe, where the most *farbrente,* the most dedicated, go to live. Beatings have been reported, along with torchlight marches to the homes of dissidents. But in Williamsburg things are relatively mellow. In a surprising number of ways, the Satmar, although more religiously strict than the Lubavitchers, are far less dogmatic. "We question the rebbe," says Shraga, "and are free to challenge him in many ways."

"What about Zionism?"

"There is no difference of opinion here–not until Moshiach comes. But, for example, this guy here"–Shraga points to an acquaintance who is listening to our conversation as we stand on the street corner between the homes of the two adversaries. "This fellow is with Brach, aren't you?" The man nods. "He is also a Litvisher." A Litvisher, or Mitnagged, is part of a non-Hasidic approach to Judaism that puts more emphasis on the study of the law, and less on expressive prayer.

"And he's still a Satmar?" I ask.

"Sure. Unlike Lubavitch, there can be Satmar without the Satmar Rebbe."

That sounds heretical, so I ask the man in Yiddish, "What do you think of the rebbe?"

"We need a new rebbe. You want to be our rebbe?" he jokes.

My guide feels compelled to dispel common misperceptions. "This hole-in-the-sheets business [when a husband and wife can only come in contact through a tear or cut in the sheets], I don't care where it came from, maybe another rebbe. Our job is to give our wives pleasure."

"That's one stereotype," I say. "But another one is that you burn the Israeli flag; that you advise Arafat."

"I want to tell you one thing about Israel: Mishpat Kasztner." The case of Kasztner is well known in the early history of the Jewish state. A Hungarian Jew, Kasztner was accused of collaborating with the Germans, thereby hastening the destruction of Hungarian Jewry. His name was subsequently cleared by the Israeli Supreme Court, but not before a young zealot from Tel Aviv blew him away.

Since Kasztner was a Zionist and many of the Hungarians were anti-Zionist, the case is used by Satmars to justify their anti-Zionism. But as Shraga insists: "I don't need to justify. The Torah justifies." Before I leave, he invites me to a wedding on Monday.

On my way out of the neighborhood, I encounter a Sephardic Israeli with a scraggly beard, dressed in the style of a Hasid. It's a strange combination, like mixing falafel and gefilte fish. Sephardic Jews are largely from Arab countries and are influenced by that culture.

"No, I am not a Satmar," he says. "I'm a Lubavitcher. I became a Lubavitcher."

"So what are you doing in Williamsburg?"

"I'm on my way back to Crown Heights after visiting the rebbe in the hospital in Manhattan." Making the rounds of the Hasidic neighborhoods on a hot Shabbos afternoon, I muse. He continues, "My ex-wife and children are Satmars, though."

"How's that?" I ask tersely, like Sergeant Friday on *Dragnet.*

"She and her Satmar husband kidnapped my children. Satmars are dangerous, I tell you."

As we're talking, a retarded man, like the village idiot out of a Shalom Aleichem story, comes up and asks, "Are you with the new rebbe or the old rebbe's wife?" As the Israeli begins to explain himself, I slip away.

The wedding hall is on a seamier edge of Boro Park, where all Hasidic groups, including Satmar, coexist. It sits in the shadow of the elevated tracks and across the street from a discount emporium offering everything for seventy-nine cents. The crowd begins to arrive, pouring out of station wagons—huge families with ten to twelve kids, the children pushed up against every nook and cranny of the car.

To enter the premises, the guests must pass through a gauntlet of *schnorrers,* an audacious cross between beggar and jive-artist.

The lead schnorrer holds out a crusty piece of paper that has been folded a couple of hundred times. It shows an ample Hasid administering the Heimlich maneuver to a skinnier man. Underneath, something is scribbled in Hebrew.

"Lady, you can help me maybe with a quarter?" The scrappy schnorrer has planted himself squarely in the doorway of the wedding hall. He is unavoidable.

"I'm sorry, I don't have any money," a matron replies.

"Okay, okay, next time."

Another schnorrer approaches guests with a tin can and repeats like a mantra the line, "Easy! Easy! Take it easy." He is a young Israeli with a ponytail, dressed entirely in white. He has the aura of Carlos Santana. This *sabra* enters the wedding chapel and roams about like he owns the place, which throws the chubby young manager into a tizzy. "This guy I don't like."

"Why not?" I ask. "Because he went in the building?"

"No. That's okay. It's a Jewish tradition. Beggars are free to wander anywhere."

"Then why not?" I implore.

"This guy, he's never happy with anything. He gets a quarter, he asks for fifty cents; gets a dollar, asks for five."

Weddings are held here almost every day, except Shabbos. A squat Russian woman who serves as assistant manager told me that when she first got here, she couldn't believe how little Hasidim drink. "In Russia even the Jews drink at weddings."

I am seated at a long table with five or six younger men. Sure enough, a bottle of slivovitz is scarcely touched. Not only is drinking out, but smoking, so long associated with Hasidim, has fallen out of style. I ask the fellows if they are all Satmar. Four readily identify themselves as such. One demands that I ask him to multiply any two numerals. I give him two three-digit numbers. He looks at me for a moment like a goat from a Chagall painting, blank-eyed. Then he blurts out the answer.

The fifth fellow at my table doesn't say that he is a Satmar, so I ask what he is. "A closet Satmar," he replies in English.

"Maybe we should out him," one of them recommends.

Switching subjects, I ask, "Who do Satmars marry, besides each other?"

"Under no circumstances will we marry Bobovers, Klausenbergers, Lubavitchers, or Israeli Vishnitzers—but American Vishnitzers are okay. They have their own rebbe."

"Why won't you marry into these groups?"

"Because they say bad things about the rebbe. How could I be married to someone like this? The in-laws would be at war and I would be in the middle."

I ask about the Israeli elections. "I realize you can't vote for two reasons. A, you're not in Israel. B, You wouldn't vote anyway. But who do you support?"

Chagall's goat looks at me directly and says, "I have my opinions and I have my beliefs. My beliefs keep me from expressing my opinions."

"What do you mean?"

"Well, in my opinion, I would kill them all."

"Who?"

"The Arabs."

I sense he doesn't mean this literally.

"But I thought you were an anti-Zionist."

"That is my belief. I was expressing my opinion."

The actual marriage ceremony takes place on the sidewalk in front of the wedding hall, in keeping with the custom of being married under the stars. Hasidim crowd around as the bride circles the groom seven times. Meanwhile, the elevated train roars overhead, and a Hispanic couple argues on the opposite street corner.

Inside, the band has begun to play, accompanying a famous Hasidic singer, David Werdyger. The pint-sized Werdyger belts it out like Ethel Merman. He is wearing a *spodik,* a fur hat shaped like a bishop's miter that makes him look like an escapee from a Moose Lodge initiation. The hat stands out in a sea of *shtreimels,* the less flamboyant hats made out of pelts of sable. Shtreimels often cost more than a thousand dollars.

The men shuffle round and round in a circle. Several vigorously invite me to join. Soon we are circumambulating the groom, who charges back and forth against the inner edge of the circle arm-in-arm with his ninety-year-old grandfather. "Ninety years old and ninety grandchildren," somebody says.

The groom is hoisted up on a chair and the bride is brought out from behind the panels separating the women and the men. She too is hoisted up on a chair. The chairs are brought together, then apart, together, apart. Everyone is encouraged to dance. I am treated no differently than anyone else.

Meanwhile, a disheveled Hasid makes his way through the crowd, passing out Lubavitch literature without inhibition. The pamphlets proclaim that the Lubavitcher Rebbe is the Messiah.

"What's this?" I ask.

"He's a former Bratslaver Hasid who became a Lubavitcher. He shows up at all the weddings."

A Bratslaver Hasid is the follower of Nachman of Bratslav, a nineteenth-century mystic. The Bratslaver Hasidim are known in Israel for their newly religious ex-convicts and for retreating to the woods on some nights and howling their obedience to God.

"You don't mind that he's passing out Lubavitch literature?" I ask a Satmar.

"Maybe I mind. Maybe I don't," he replies. "It doesn't matter. It's his right."

I don't know what is more amazing, the audacity of the intruding Messianist, or the equanimity with which he is received.

Shraga introduces me to his brother, a precocious twelve-year-old. "Ask him any primary score. He knows them all."

"How did Jerry Brown do in Connecticut?"

"Thirty-seven percent," he replies.

"How about Clinton?"

"Thirty-six percent."

"Tell me," one of my tablemates leans over, "Do you believe?"

I reply with the Yiddish word *efshaw,* sort of the Platonic essence of "maybe."

"What about you?" I ask.

No reply. He begins absentmindedly to hum a *niggun,* a Hasidic melody, which I take to be his way of dodging a tough question, or perhaps refusing to answer something so obvious.

Belief may not be a prerequisite to being a Hasid, but behavior certainly is. There seem to be cracks in the wall, not strong enough to cause serious decay, but strong enough to cause a redoubling of efforts to keep the world out.

"I watched *The Chosen* on the VCR," Shraga tells me. *The Chosen,* by Chaim Potok, is the story of a Hasidic youth who questions his beliefs. In this environment, *Deep Throat* would be far less subversive.

Yet the Satmar are on a Malthusian roll, growing by 5 percent a year, doubling every fifteen. Each new generation is more religious than the last, and each generation has more children than the last. In 100 years, the Satmar—by then conceivably 2 million strong—along with other Hasidic groups, may very well be the only Jews left in America, given the trend toward intermarriage and low birth rate among the Chosen. A movement that has always been on the periphery of Judaism could well become the dominant strain. Time will tell.

CHAPTER 2

Boss of the Bobovs

BORO PARK, BROOKLYN

Out of the wreckage of the Second World War emerged Bobov, today the second or third largest Hasidic group in America. Bobov had the sorry misfortune to be located at Ground Zero of the Final Solution, Galicia, in southern Poland. Before the war, Bobov was a dynasty, with a line of rabbis stretching back to the mid-nineteenth century, its Grand Rabbi living in grand style, and marriages and other life-cycle events attracting followers in the tens of thousands. About one-quarter survived the war, including its junior leader, Solomon Halberstam, son of the grand rabbi, Ben Tzion. For this reason Bobov is called the largest living memorial to the Holocaust. Other Hasidic groups had it worse—not in percentage terms, because that's virtually impossible—but because they were spiritually decapitated by the murders of their rabbinic leaders. To this extent, at least, Bobov was fortunate. Solomon, its current Grand Rabbi, was a young rabbi before the war and is at present the only surviving Hasidic rebbe of prewar Europe.

Halberstam's own tribulations are of epic proportions. He lost his wife and two children, barely escaping Poland himself. Yet he came to America undaunted and began, upon his arrival, to reconstruct his shattered dynasty: He married again, had six children, and gathered together the tattered remnants of those other leaderless groups. Today there are about 25,000 Bobovers in the United States.

The Bobover Rebbe survived by a combination of luck and resourcefulness. At the outbreak of the war, his father, Ben Tzion, fled to Lemberg, or Lvov, in the western Ukraine. The Germans eventually overtook Lemberg, and Ben Tzion was caught and murdered by the Nazis. Solomon, who had accompanied his father, escaped and made his way through occupied Poland back to his native Galicia, where his mother, sisters, wife, and children were being held in the Bochnia ghetto. Using false papers, he lived outside the ghetto and smuggled innumerable ghetto-dwellers, including his own family, from Poland to relative safety in Hungary. In 1943, when the Germans rounded up all Polish and non-Budapest Hungarian Jews to take them to the concentration camps, he and his wife and children escaped once more to Oradea, on the Romanian border. But fate finally caught up with them, and the Germans snatched his wife and two of his children, while he and his Bar Mitzvah-aged son, Naftali, managed to escape into Romania, and eventually to the United States.

Naftali is now a great-grandfather, and Solomon took on the mantle of his father and became the Bobover Rebbe, a task for which he was well suited, having served as the Chief Rabbi of the town of Bobov before the war under his father's tutelage.

Despite his spiritual status, Rebbe Halberstam is very much of this world. He influences a formidable voting bloc numbering in the tens of thousands, and his *kehilla*, or community organization, consistently endorses conservative positions and political candidates. Courted by visiting dignitaries such as Lech Walesa, as well as local politicians (his picture has appeared on the front page of the *New York Times* with a deferential Mayor Rudolph Giuliani), he has the smooth and glowing visage of a *tzaddik,* or holy man, a face that belies his personal suffering. He is said to be a *sadeneh mensch,* a silken personality, exuding compassion and sensitivity, yet at the same time almost rugged in his constitution.

Bobovers are the largest Hasidic sect in Boro Park, the preeminent Orthodox neighborhood in America. It is a veritable Golconda of religious bookstores, Jewish travel agencies, kosher pizza shops, gold and silver emporiums, matchmaking bureaus, and countless *shtiebelachs,* or prayer halls, catering to its 100,000 residents. Yet Bobov is not nearly as well known as Lubavitch, with approximately the same number of adherents.

Bobov's position on Israel is ambivalent. While professedly anti-Zionist, Bobovers are conspicuously absent from Satmar-inspired anti-Israel rallies at the United Nations, or from the occasional pandemonium in front of the Waldorf when certain Israeli politicians come to town. In addition, Bobov has developed good relations with the more ambiguously Zionistic Klausenbergers and Belzers, two large Hasidic groups that accept educational stipends from the Israeli government, something that would be anathema to Satmar. Yet Bobov still claims adherence to the ultra-Orthodox credo embraced by most Hasidim that the State of Israel has no right to exist until the Messiah comes.

Theologically, Bobov does not stand out in the Hasidic firmament as do the Lubavitchers, many of whom preach the imminent arrival of the Messiah in the form of their recently deceased Rebbe, Menachem Mendel Schneerson. But what makes Bobov distinctive is the quantum of sheer pound-for-pound suffering its members experienced during the war and its hale-and-hearty comeback, a comeback not just physical but seemingly psychological as well.

At Bobov's Boro Park headquarters, a huge marbled synagogue on 48th Street, depression does not hang over the place like a thundercloud. The war is more of an ontological toothache than a diffusely felt insurmountable event. It is localized.

Although my father's family came from Hungary, my mother's side was Polish. My maternal grandfather was a Bobover *mitschlepper*–not a full-fledged member, but a sort of fellow traveler. He was a Hasid with a well-groomed beard who fell under the sway of modernism in the big city of Krakow before the war–a *moderne yid*, as he would refer to himself, not assimilated, but accommodating to the undercurrents of twentieth-century life, reading books in German and the Polish press, and attending plays where women appeared on stage. But his father and uncles were all Bobovers. I had no knowledge of this until my grandmother once offhandedly remarked that we come from Bobovers. And since all my known relatives were secular, it never occurred to me that I might have relatively nondistant Hasidic family members.

It is my determination to approach the Bobov community to see if I have any relatives who are Hasidim. It seems highly improbable, since they were all starting to drift away from religion before the war. To the best of my knowledge, my relatives are all lie-on-the-beach-on-Yom-Kippur sorts. Now, however, I decided to seek out any relatives I might have in the Bobov community.

The optimal way to gain entrée to a Hasidic community is not through a bureaucratic channel or some arcane petition to the rebbe. It is to show up on the doorstep of a given sect's main synagogue, and that's exactly what I do.

At the threshold of the imposing structure, I announce to a group of *yungerleit*, young men, who are milling about, that I am looking for relatives of my grandfather, Wolf Meyer Nichtborger of Liminowa, Poland. I only know that he operated a bakery and read a lot of newspapers, and that he was an *ideleh neshuma*, a saintly sort more given to good philosophical conversations than haggling over the price of a bismarck.

Actually, he went by the family name Nichtborger on some occasions, and Ableser on others. This was because nomenclature among Eastern European Jews was often convoluted due to the fact that Jewish babies were usually registered under the family names of their mothers as well as their fathers. There is also a sort of pecking order from the Napoleonic era, when the Jews were given names by the German authorities. The names range from the pristine to the pejorative, and where one stood on this aesthetic spectrum was often a function of one's ability to pay *protektzia*, a bribe, to, or at the very least win the affection of, the local *Beamte*.

Bakshish often resulted in names such as Edelstein (precious stone) and Rosenberg (rose mountain), whereas the less fortunate were tagged with unflattering sobriquets such as Schmalz (grease), Eselkopf (donkey's head), and, well, Nichtburger, as in alien or "not a citizen." Somewhere along the way this metamorphosed into Nichtborger, or "not a borrower." This name, which would do Ben Franklin proud, is highly uncommon. For example, the Manhattan phone book lists only one. There are a few others elsewhere, but they are spelled Nichtberger, the equally inoffensive "not a mountain person."

Nichtborger, the young men in front of the synagogue muse. Yes, there is a Nichtborger, they say, and lo and behold, he comes from my grandfather's *shtetl* in Poland. And where do you live? they ask. Nebraska, I reply.

In the meantime, a tribal elder approaches me, and hearing my Yiddish, invites me to his apartment a block away for a cup of coffee and a perusal of his grandchildren's photos. I find myself unable to decline the offer, so we head toward his place. My host, Mr. Rosenberg, has three children and twenty-three grandchildren, and he's barely seventy–not too extreme by Hasidic standards, but enough to set Paul Ehrlich's hair on end.

One son teaches in a day school and the other sells Jewish ritual items, such as *tallisim,* prayer shawls, yarmulkes, and spice boxes used in the Havdalah ritual at the end of the Sabbath. The punchline to an old Yiddish joke, "From this he makes a living?" passes through my head.

He tells me that his daughter is married to a diamond merchant. This statement elicits a cagey smile on his part, one that seems to evoke not innuendos of illegal activities, but rather highly remunerative ones. The diamond industry is one of the motherlodes–and surely the best-known one–of Hasidic occupations, along with nursing home ownership and electronics retailing.

It turns out that Rosenberg and my grandmother were denizens of the same concentration camp, Plaszow, the one that figures prominently in *Schindler's List.* I don't know if Rosenberg had family before the war–I can't bring myself to ask–but it isn't at all unusual for septuagenarians in the Bobover sect to have lost their spouse and all their children and to have valiantly started over again.

Rosenberg takes me to a nearby *shtiebl* run by the Klausenbergers, where a group of retirees gathers around a table full of leather-bound books and study a page of the Gemara. This is the Talmud, and it is absorbed along with other commentaries including that of the eleventh-century French rabbi, Rashi, and the ancient and penultimate Torah commentator, Onkelos, an early convert. This analysis is abruptly concluded with the evening prayers. It's a far cry from a life of pinochle and condo association meetings, but they seem to have achieved some sort of happy equilibrium.

I wander back to the Bobov *shul,* where by now I have achieved minor celebrity status, something I estimate to have a half-life of about ten minutes. Nevertheless, my Yiddish and my family's geographical origins have obtained me some sort of warped cachet.

And now, brought before me like some latter-day slave in a Cecil B. DeMille biblical epic, is none other than Mr. Nichtborger, sales rep for a chemical company, with a shy smile on his diffident face.

I see no mutual resemblance. But after a half hour of going back and forth in front of a roomful of yungerleit, who watch the proceedings with the intensity of a cockfight audience, we discover we have a cousin in common whom we both know. He lives in Holon, a nondescript middle-class suburb outside of Tel Aviv, and I recall meeting him once for five minutes when I was ten. All I remember is that he had a sixth sense for insects. He could lean across a room like the elongated man and slap a fly into oblivion without even looking at it. Somehow, for a Jew to be this remorseless, even with flies, made me uneasy. Other than that, he was totally unremarkable. I think he was some kind of Labor Party apparatchik. He had the thick lips of a Der Sturmer caricature and wore a short-sleeved double-knit white shirt that shimmered in its acrylic glory.

Upon this fortuitous discovery indicating some proof of kinship, in the same way that a bloody sheet indicates proof of consummation of a marriage, a bottle of brandy is produced and we toast each other. Everyone, including myself, is amazed. Here I am, much removed from my Hasidic roots by the Holocaust plus 2,000 miles of American prairie, mountains, and farmland, not to mention a Jewish upbringing that can only generously be categorized as Reform—except for the singular quirk that my Holocaust-surviving grandmother lived with me until I went to college and insisted that I speak Yiddish. Other than that, she made a mockery of Jewish customs and laws, labeling them *bubbe mantzes,* granny tales, and *narishkeiten,* drollery.

No one in this particular group has ever seen a secular Jew show up and express some putative relationship with them.

"Something, something, impelled you to go this far," someone says, looking at me as if this could be the start of something big, i.e., religious conversion. I don't hesitate to inform him that unfortunately, try as I might to believe otherwise, my religious views are much closer to my grandmother's than to my newly discovered third cousin's. But as for Jewish peoplehood, that's a completely different story. "*Am Yisrael Chai.* The People of Israel live," I toast. We raise our glasses and down the brandy in unison.

I still desperately want to meet the rebbe, who, after all, was my grandfather's spiritual leader, but who unfortunately is taking a summer break with his wife and one or two lieutenants in Saratoga Springs, about 150 miles north of the city near the Adirondacks. He would not be returning till later on in the week, for the commemoration of his father's *yahrzeit,* or the anniversary of his death. I resolve to drive up to Saratoga the following day.

By now my fellow brandy-drinkers are drifting away, and the cavernous study hall is practically empty. I say good night to my cousin and leave. About three blocks away, on my way to the car, I see a pudgy young man in his early twenties pacing back and forth on the main thoroughfare of 13th Avenue with a cloth pouch slung over his shoulders. He approaches me and asks if I am Jewish. Yep, I reply.

"You look young and healthy," he says, appraising me like an animal in a feedlot. "We could use you in the Jewish Defense League." He hands me a card imprinted with a clenched fist and the letters JDL.

"Now I know what you're thinking," he tells me, with the elan of Professor Harold Hill in *The Music Man.* " 'This is Meir Kahane's group. They are troublemakers.' Let me tell you, we're not the same as we were under Kahane. We're not focused on Arabs and international affairs. Our goal is very simple. When someone sees a Jew on the street, they'll think twice before they give him a *klopp,* a punch. Hey, when someone sees a black on the street, do they think they can beat him up? Of course not. Well, we want the same for Jews."

I thank him for the card and get in the car. He presses his face up against my window. "We have lawyers to take care of you if you're arrested, doctors to take care of you if you're hurt. Hey, have you ever been to a karate lesson? That's what it's like. If you're interested, give me a call."

As I begin to drive away, he pulls out a minuscule bottle of gin-seng juice and downs it in one slug. "Good for the energy level," he says. "All roots are."

The next day I set out for Saratoga thinking how incongruous it is for such a quintessential urban character as the rebbe to be spending his summer far removed from the nation's biggest metropolis and center of Jewish life, in a town of 26,000 people only twenty-five miles from the Vermont border. But rebbes have a long tradition of taking cures in the mountains. Just before the war, for example, Krynica in the Carpathians was a big spot for rebbes to take the cure. There they had their pictures taken on their way to the mineral baths by enterprising paparazzi who sold the photos to the masses. At the time cameras were scarce, and ambitious photographers set up their tripods just outside the baths. Not only did the Bobover Rebbe's forbears visit Krynica, but all the other great rabbis of Galicia did as well.

Just past the Saratoga Performing Arts Center, with its big sign welcoming the New York City Opera, the New York City Ballet, and the Philadelphia Orchestra, I come across an elderly woman trudging along with a grocery cart in a trench coat and thick stockings in the 90-degree heat. She is wearing a wig with the consistency of straw that seems to be tilted to one side. Pulling up beside her, I lean out my window nonchalantly and ask in Yiddish if she knows where the Bobover Rebbe is. Without missing a beat, she replies that I must go to Lafayette Street. There I will find the shtiebl he prays at. Then she smiles. "Are you interested in long-distance service?" she asks sweetly, as if she's offering me a piece of strudel. "My husband is in the business."

I decline politely.

"Where is your father from?" she asks.

"Budapest."

"What is your name?"

"Eisenberg."

"Are you one of the Williamsburger Eisenbergs?" she inquires, oblivious to my shorn face and ponytail. "There is such a family, you know."

I reply that I am sure there are several hundred, wish her a good day, and make my way in the direction of Lafayette Street.

The edge of the block where the rebbe's shtiebl is turns out to be a ramshackle cluster of rundown triple-deckers within spitting distance of downtown. As I get out of the car, a vigorous Hasid in his sixties with a bulbous nose and blond *payess* wound around his ears comes at me with the ferocity of a bull. "*Nu*, so, who are you looking for?" he asks.

"I am looking for the Bobover Rebbe," I answer in Yiddish. Somewhat placated, he smiles and asks why I am not religious. He looks at my notebook. "A Jew carries a *siddur* [a prayer book], not a notebook," he says. Clearly, the man wants to talk *tachlis,* get down to business, not beat around the bush with conversational niceties. Eschewing any sort of middle-class discretion, he burrows on. What is my income? he asks. My marital status? Before I get a chance to answer, he launches into a story. He had Aryan papers during the war. I could see that because he looks like a Danish dairy farmer at an anti-EEC barricade. He was caught by the authorities and put into jail with a Jewish lawyer who was not very religious–or rather, not religious at all.

"He was an *apikoros*. You know what that is? That's someone who studies the law but still doesn't believe. A Reform rabbi is an apikoros. You, on the other hand, you're probably just ignorant."

As they were waiting to be carted off to a concentration camp, my narrator felt compelled to convert the lawyer back to *yid-dishkeit*. In the cell the lawyer asked him how, in these environs, he could possibly believe in God. My narrator takes one step back for dramatic effect, and plants his feet firmly on the ground.

"How can I believe in God?" he says hoarsely, shaking his head back and forth, as if this question is the height of heresy (which it is). "How can I believe in God?" he repeats. "You see this hat?" he asks, alluding to his black Fedora. "Is it black or white? Black, the lawyer tells me. So I look at him and say, 'If everyone told you the hat is white, you would believe it's white, would you not?'" He pauses, raises his eyebrows, and lifts his hands like a reverend getting a congregation to stand. "*Then* the lawyer begins to understand." He looks at me triumphantly, as if he just shitcanned Spinoza. If this is his explanation for the existence of God, he's up there with Descartes in succinctness.

"Listen," he says in a lighter vein. "I know all about modern life. Two businesses I have, tie manufacturing and men's suits. One of my longtime salesmen, Irv Blatt, I always ask if he goes with other women. 'My wife is old,' he tells me, 'how can I not?' But we," he says referring to the Orthodox and their purity practices, "we have two weeks off—two weeks every month." He makes a wall with his hands. "It's not pleasant, but it's a good idea. It keeps things fresh."

Just then, a woman in her late thirties wearing a print muumuu appears, trailed by four children. She has heard our conversation, and she informs me that she and her husband are caretakers of the shtiebl for the summer. "So you want to talk to the rebbe," she says in English. "Come back at nine."

"But at nine I have a plane to catch."

"Okay, so call him on the phone." She leads me into her kitchen where there are three more children, all in high chairs. Dialing the number, she hands me the phone, into which I proceed to tell the person at the other end the Nichtborger saga, all the while thinking that I'm talking to the Bobover Rebbe. But it turns out to be one of his assistants, who says I have to wait until evening services. So I change my plane reservations and wait.

The Yiddish I hear all around me is distinctively Polish. There are actually three or four dialects of this thousand-year-old language, an offshoot of German. Speakers of each dialect can understand one another, just as a Bostonian can understand an Alabaman, yet each version is distinctive. The two major ones are Polish and Lithuanian. Bobovers embrace Polish Yiddish, which has an earthier, more colloquial tone, while Lubavitchers tend to sound more Lithuanian, whose hallmark is precision. Before the war, each group had a propensity to mildly needle one another. The Litvishers were considered dry and humorless, while their Polish counterparts were derided as corner-cutters and con artists.

About an hour before nine after kicking around town, I go to the shtiebl to wait for evening services, but am almost immediately commandeered under the arm by a cousin of the Bobover Rebbe, who insists I come over to his house for dinner. Apparently, he has heard about me from the tie manufacturer.

The Bobover Rebbe's cousin stands out from the group of Hasidim milling about the courtyard in between the triple-deckers and the modest synagogue building—he is the only one wearing white stockings that come up to his knees. This is a privilege reserved for rabbis. He is also arrayed in a black silk *bekishe,* a long robe that almost looks like a kimono with a wide *gardle,* a type of belt. Different gardles signify different things. For example, Belzers wear narrower gardles, while Gerers wear wider ones. And within each Hasidic group, gardles of different widths are worn on the weekday and the Sabbath.

After a short walk, we arrive at his house, the interior of which can only be described by the Yiddish word *hegdesh,* which means a mess to an exponential degree. Chipped linoleum floors in the hallway, chipped linoleum everywhere. In fact, chipped linoleum, burnt linoleum, cracked linoleum, all seem to be the unifying theme. To the right of the entryway, in a large room, a makeshift synagogue is set up to accommodate an overflow Sabbath morning crowd from the shtiebl around the corner. At the front of the room is an imposing wooden ark housing an almost-Lilliputian Torah scroll swathed in blue velvet. Dominating the scene is a long conference table covered with a plastic tablecloth and flecked with cigarette burns. At the table sits the rabbi's son, about age thirty, his face six inches from a prodigious tome. He is wearing a jarring golden bekishe and has long payess. He bears a striking resemblance to Tiny Tim.

Peering through thick glasses, he sways back and forth at the dizzying pace of a metronome set on allegro. Every few minutes, he emits a high-pitched blast, like a trumpet, followed by long periods of silence. Sitting across from him is his chunky *chaver,* or study partner, a man with beaver-like incisors, who intermittently pronounces barely comprehensible phrases in Yiddish. Each word seems to embody some arcane legal principle, and the brevity of expression is itself elegant, as if this is some highly evolved mode of communication, somewhere between the verbal and the telepathic. The phrases are barked out with the verve of a quarterback.

At some point he turns around to shake my hand. This too is accomplished with a characteristic economy of movement, for although he swivels his torso, his head stays focused on the book. I ask them if they have families. Neither of them are married, my host tells me. The son is a lifelong bachelor, and his study partner is divorced. The divorced one shifts a bit uncomfortably.

These two boys—and if they're unmarried, even when they're old they're called *boochers,* or boys—wake up at seven every morning and study almost nonstop until eleven at night, my host assures me. "My son has been through *shas* three times." Shas is the entire cycle of the Talmud, which if studied at the fairly intense rate of one page a day, takes seven years.

We continue on into the kitchen, where he introduces me to his wife, a birdlike woman with narrow nostrils and a perpetually tense expression on her face. As stressed out as she is, he is almost unbearably calm. She immediately produces a bowl of vegetable soup, a plate of chopped liver, and a loaf of challah.

This man, the Bobover Rebbe's cousin, is himself a rabbi in the religious exurb of Monsey, north of New York. He has his own small shtiebl and a modest coterie of followers. Most of his children live in Israel. He is what's known as a *shtikl rebbe,* a minor rebbe, who has a few followers in the face of a greater benign presence, in this case, the Bobover Rebbe.

His wife comes out of the kitchen every five minutes and asks why I am not eating the soup. I can't bring myself to tell her that, smother it as I might in Rokeach oyster crackers, I find it unsavory. Finally, the rabbi tells her to leave me alone. She then suggests that I take the soup with me in a plastic bowl. All the while, the rabbi is telling me an amazing story of the war. All the stories I've heard so far are amazing, but this one is statistically exceptional. He and his family survived the war intact, living openly under three years of German occupation in Transnistria, a section of the Ukraine. In the waning weeks of the war, they were going to hang his father, a noted rabbi. The family was forced to watch. The SS Kommandant slipped a noose around his neck, and the father began fervently to pray Tillim (psalms). Two junior officers saw him as a holy man and refused to continue. This was the end of the war, and discipline was breaking down. They thought it would be better to refuse to follow orders now than to be punished in the hereafter.

The Kommandant stepped up to the rabbi and threw the Tillim on the ground, asking him what he was doing. He replied that he was praying to God. "You think God will save you?" the Kommandant asked.

"My father looked the Kommandant in the eye and said, 'Yes.' Then the Kommandant took the noose off and walked away." The father is still alive, living in Benei Berak, a religious suburb of Tel Aviv.

After a few moments of silence, the son enters the room, tilting his head from side to side like a cockatoo.

"Have you ever tried eyebright?" he blurts out. "No," I reply. He begins to describe it as the pharmaceutical equivalent of the Swiss Army knife. It helps with everything from incontinence to acne. But what it helps with most is to see colors more brightly and letters with greater clarity. I can understand his interest in this, because his lenses look like glass brick. Young Hasidim seem enamored with folk cures–health food stores sprinkle the ultra-Orthodox neighborhoods of Israel.

Here is the trend in action. He produces a horse capsule filled with what looks like finely ground grass clippings. "Take it," he implores. I oblige. Nothing happens. Red is still red, blue is still blue, and the tiny black characters of Rashi in his book are still largely invisible without the aid of a magnifying glass. Yet every few minutes he asks, "Do you feel anything? Do you feel anything?" After a while I begin to feel like Aldous Huxley on his first acid trip if he were accompanied by a *nudnick*. All the while, the mother is coming in and out of the kitchen with increasing frequency and asking why I haven't finished the soup. Between mother and son, I fear that if this goes on much longer the placebo effect will take hold and I will begin to hallucinate. Fortunately, the rabbi waves them both off.

Twilight descends, and the rabbi says it's time to go to the shtiebl. We say our goodbyes and walk arm in arm to the synagogue. Inside, about twenty Hasidic men and boys are preparing to pray. It's a very modest room, with makeshift furniture and a simple podium for a pulpit.

On the wall is a poster admonishing against gossip: "Don't talk *loshon hora*, don't. In your house or school or shtiebl guard your lips from speaking evil. Don't talk *loshon hora*, don't." It shows a stout Hasid gleefully gossiping into the phone with a salacious glint in his eyes as he is being ground up by a meat grinder. His bottom half is already missing, and the rest of him is sinking as if into quicksand. The drawing is crude but effective.

I am simultaneously approached by a child with a *pushke*, a box for making charitable contributions, and a middle-aged man with mutton chops and a sparse growth of beard on his chin who is bearing a receipt pad. The pad is for recording donations to a fund for the poor. As I make my contributions and give my name to the man, who insists on giving me a receipt, a white-haired gent with a Hungarian accent sidles up to me and says, "You are one of the Budapester Eisenbergs. My wife met you today." I remember the encounter. "So what long-distance service do you use? I can offer you a better price." Prayers are about to begin, so I give him my number and tell him to call me later. "What about copier toner?" he asks. "Does your office need this?"

I turn my attention to the podium. Seemingly from out of nowhere, the Bobover Rebbe has materialized. "That's the Bobover Rebbe," a child tells me. He too is wearing long white stockings and has the childlike countenance of an innocent, all the more amazing considering his personal tragedies. He sports wire-rim glasses and is of medium height with an almost perfectly round face. He begins to lead the services in free-form fashion. Some men pace and others chat with one another between prayers. After services, two *ba'alei teshuvah,* newly religious young men, approach him respectfully. They are dressed in modern clothing. The rebbe's young lieutenant approaches me and says, "The rebbe will see you now."

The rebbe grasps my hand and beams radiantly. "So your grandfather was a Bobover," he says to me in Yiddish.

"Yes," I reply, "they were Nichtborgers."

"Yes, yes, I remember." His eyes roll back into his head as if he is plumbing the recesses of his memory. "There were five brothers. Baruch, Mortke, Herschel, Leibl, and Yankel." He smiles at me impishly, like a spelling bee contestant who has just spelled a particularly difficult word. Perhaps he has cribbed for this, but even so, it is amazing. To have plucked the names of these five brothers, one of whom is my great-grandfather, from the abyss of millions of Holocaust victims gives me a sense of genealogical rootedness I never had. Alex Haley couldn't have put it better.

He blesses me.

"Yeverechechah veyishmerechah, yaer panav adonai eilecha vechuneka. May the Lord bless you and watch over you, may he shine his countenance upon you and be gracious onto you."

As I am about to leave, one of the rebbe's assistants pulls out a piece of paper. "The Bobover Rebbe wants your address to invite you to the weddings of his grandchildren." I give it to him.

As I walk out the door, a ba'al teshuvah approaches me, and with the intensity of an acolyte, says, "His wife and children were killed in the war. It's amazing he gets up in the morning. But what keeps him going is what no drug, no therapy, no amount of money can do. It's faith. And whether you believe it or not, you've got to admit it's a powerful thing."

CHAPTER 3

Leave It to Tcheeva

ST. PAUL, MINNESOTA

*E*ver since the advent of the *Haskala,* the Enlightenment, in Europe two hundred years ago, Jews have become less observant with each passing generation. But a few, like salmon swimming upstream, defy the odds. By all accounts this is the first generation in modern history where a sizable number of children are more religious than their parents. The prophet Malachi predicted that there would come a time when "the heart of the father will be turned to the children and the heart of the children will be turned to their fathers." To some, that time is well nigh, and it signals the approach of the Messiah.

About 2,000 American Jews become religious every year. This is a movement that began in earnest in the late sixties, when guitar-toting rabbi Shlomo Carlebach set up the House of Love and Prayer in the vicinity of San Francisco's Haight Ashbury district. Since then, about 50,000 Jews from all backgrounds have turned the corner. In the colorful patois of Hasidic Yiddish, they have *gemacht a tcheeva,* or made a repentance. Together with their children and grandchildren, these *ba'alei teshuvah,* or returnees to the faith, constitute one-third of Orthodox Jewry in America today.

Hannah is one of them. She lives in a minuscule bungalow in a blue-collar neighborhood of St. Paul, Minnesota, where about twenty families of Lubavitcher Hasidim have set up a community. Their presence is a slice of pumpernickel in a sea of Wonder Bread.

A curious incident impelled Hannah to become religious at age thirteen. One day she brought a book home from school and accidentally ripped it. She frantically searched the house for tape but to no avail. Upon returning to the book, she discovered that it had miraculously repaired itself. This she interpreted as a sign of God, and from that day on was a believer.

She went away to a Jewish girl's high school in Denver but soon became disappointed. It was modern Orthodox, and therefore not religious enough. The differences between the modern Orthodox and ultra-Orthodox Hasidim can be of seismic proportions. Although both are rigorously vigilant in their observance of Jewish law, the modern Orthodox dress like members of the general public, although women may wear slightly longer skirts. They like to point out that nowhere in the Torah does it prescribe that anyone wear a long black coat. Moreover, the men lack beards. But more important, unlike the Hasidim, who shun secular education, the modern Orthodox embrace it. They have a disproportionately high number of doctors, lawyers, and other professionals. As a general rule, modern Orthodox families have three or four children, not eight or nine. On a Saturday night after the Sabbath, when a Hasid might crack a volume of the Talmud, a modern Orthodox Jew might take his wife to a Broadway show, or switch on *Saturday Night Live.* By contrast, a Hasid wouldn't watch an entertainment program on network television unless he was forced to, and would never attend a theatrical production that featured a woman on stage.

Hannah found the girls at the Denver school too fashion oriented. To her, the whole place reeked of status symbols. They came from massive homes in the suburbs with the luxury of two kitchen sinks, one for milk and one for meat, vacationed in the best hotels in Miami Beach, and ended up in schools such as Barnard or Stern College.

Then on a trip home the local Chabad emissary told Hannah about the Machon Chana school in Crown Heights, Brooklyn, for girls from secular families. Chabad Hasidim are followers of the proselytizing Lubavitcher Rebbe, the late Menachem Mendel Schneerson. Unlike other Hasidic groups, they are actively involved in bringing the secular majority of Jews back to the Bible. They have always met with varying degrees of success, but the late sixties and early seventies was a golden era, when a bumper crop of Jewish ex-hippies and disillusioned radicals deposited themselves on Chabad's Brooklyn doorstep for a crash course in Jewish spirituality. Many stayed.

Hannah spent her last year of high school at Machon Chana. Her roommates there included a yoga devotee and a vegetarian. "The late sixties was a spiritual time," she explains, "and my Jewishness was very much in line with it. But Chabad gave me everything I needed—spiritually and emotionally—and I didn't need to look outside my religion for anything else."

To support herself, she worked in a factory on the Lower East Side, sewing rims on yarmulkes. Despite its close proximity, she had no problem resisting the allures of the Village. In Crown Heights she was introduced to her future husband, Nochum, the son of Argentinean Jews of Turkish origin. Nochum grew up in a Jewish orphanage on the outskirts of Buenos Aires, where his mother did laundry; he became religious when a visiting Chabad rabbi took him under his wing and encouraged him to go to *yeshiva* in Israel. After that he moved to Crown Heights.

Today Hannah is a pear-shaped thirty-nine-year-old who could easily pass as a subject for Archimboldo, the sixteenth-century artist who used food to depict his characters—but a Jewish version, with cheeks like matzo balls, complexion the consistency of challah, and the eyes of a smoked whitefish. She has ten children. Her father, an alcoholic, faded out of her life early on. Her mother works as a secretary. One brother is a Chabad rabbi in Marin County. Another is a Los Angeles–based drifter who occasionally shows up at his mother's house, driving his beat-up van. He comes in for milk and cookies and rails at the television set.

Hannah feels she was sold a bill of goods with regard to her future husband. "When I was first introduced to Nochum, the Chabadniks told me that he was a scholar, the type who goes around with a *sefer*, a holy book, cracking it every chance he gets. That's not my Nochum."

In the Hasidic world, one's provenance, or *yichus*—one's pedigree or ancestry—is frequently inquired after. In this sense, ba'alei teshuvah are starting out with a clean slate. They are genealogical tabula rasas whose roots cannot be traced back to some great eighteenth-century rabbi. For this reason, it is only on rare occasions that a ba'al teshuvah is allowed to marry a born Hasid. So it made sense for Hannah to be matched up with Nochum, at least in the eyes of her sponsors.

"At first it was okay. We went for walks after the Sabbath, he rented a car and took me for rides. When he showed up at my apartment with gifts, my roommate hid in the next room so we shouldn't be alone."

The courtship lasted three months.

"After the marriage, we moved to Buenos Aires, where he got a job as a *schochet*, a ritual slaughterer. The pay was good because a schochet gets paid in dollars. We lived in Argentina for five years and I had my first three children there. But I cried every day. I wasn't allowed to come home. Finally, my mother found Nochum work as a schochet in St. Paul, and she bought tickets for us to come back." She sighs. "I am the victim of a *shiduch* scam."

A shiduch is an arranged marriage, and in the early seventies the locals in Crown Heights were eager to bring newly religious young people together. So eager—according to Hannah—that they didn't bother to check individual backgrounds and temperament before making a match.

"It was an epidemic. People wanted to earn brownie points for making a shiduch." She shrugs stoically.

"I'd like to say we've had mostly good times, but I would be lying. I love him, but he blocks my potential. I've sold Amway, and right now I sell watches that I buy at postal auctions." She produces an antediluvian Longines from the bookshelf. "About four or five years ago, I could have bought the local kosher butcher shop. The owners were ready to retire and they liked me. They said, 'Hannah, you will be good at this.' They offered to lease it to me, no money down. But Nochum said no."

I ask Hannah if she feels any discrimination as a woman. In response, I hear an explanation of the traditional Jewish view of women's roles. God created the world in ascending order, and his last creation, she tells me, was woman. God took Adam's rib, not his toenail or a lock of hair, to create woman, and that is because the rib is in the center of the body. This makes a woman man's equal, not his inferior or superior. Respecting women is a cornerstone of the Jewish religion. The Talmud commands, "Clothe yourself according to your means, but clothe your wife above your means."

"But aren't these all stock answers?" I ask. Women can't be rabbis. They can't be called to the Torah. They are seated separately in the synagogue.

"Who says women can't be rabbis?" she says with uncharacteristic fierceness. "That's not law, that's custom. A woman can even be called up to read the Torah, as long as it's only in front of other women and not a mixed crowd. We are seated apart from men not because of any inferiority, but because of the psychological effect we have on them."

Hannah's oldest son, Baruch, enters the house. He is a delicate-looking seventeen-year-old with a scraggly beard and black velvet *yarmulke*. Accompanying him is Micah, his best friend. Tall and blond, Micah looks like Gary Cooper with *payess*. He is chewing sunflower seeds and spitting out the shells. About twenty years ago, his mother studied at the Crown Heights yeshiva with Hannah.

Micah is in Minneapolis visiting his extended family, none of whom is religious. His father is a Hasidic optometrist in downtown Brooklyn, his mother a Seven Sisters graduate who converted to Judaism. Modernity oozes through his pores, but when it comes to religion, he is utterly serious. His two oldest brothers are studying at a yeshiva in Montreal. "Not only do the boys come out of there *edel*, refined, but very *gelernt*, learned," he says in an almost matronly fashion. He swivels his lanky frame and goes into the kitchen.

"This is a kid who comes from a very tough background," Hannah tells me. Micah's mother, Judy, married a Jew and moved to Israel in the late sixties. The couple became religious and soon discovered that the husband was a *Kohan*, or a descendant of the priestly class, and therefore forbidden from marrying a convert. They had to choose between a commitment to the faith or each other, and they chose the former, breaking up an otherwise happy marriage. She returned home and commenced study at Machon Chana, the girl's yeshiva in Crown Heights. There she was introduced to another ba'al teshuvah and encouraged to marry him.

She dutifully complied. Hannah unequivocally describes their marriage as a nightmare. In recent years, her friend has moved to New England to get away from her husband. Yet she has remained religious.

"She has a close connection to the One Above," Hannah says, sounding like a smitten schoolgirl whenever she mentions God. References to his name sprinkle her conversation like an exotic condiment. If someone asks her how she is, she'll reply, *"Baruch Hashem,* blessed is the Lord, I am fine." If she is expecting someone at a certain hour, she'll say, *"B'ezrat Hashem,* God willing, he'll be here."

Dominating Hannah's living room—above a tableful of half-eaten peanut butter sandwiches and bowls of petrified egg salad—are five rabbinical portraits, each more somber than the last. These are the five heads of Chabad since its inception 200 years ago. (Actually, there were seven, but the likenesses of two have been lost.) The first is the saintly Schneerson, who peers down with benign intensity. Next to him is his father-in-law, Joseph Isaac, whose date of release from Soviet prison is commemorated as a Chabad holiday. The room itself is a sort of shrine to the Chabad movement. There is literature from Tzivos Hashem, the Chabad children's organization dedicated to turning little privates into generals by getting them to do good deeds. Hanging on the wall among family photos is a framed dollar bill handed out by the rebbe at one of his regular *farbrengen,* or get-togethers, in Brooklyn. In George Washington's place on the dollar bill is a picture of the rebbe.

Baruch strolls out of the kitchen. He is a yeshiva dropout who now earns $20 an hour as a *mashgiach* in a slaughterhouse in northern Minnesota. A mashgiach is entrusted by rabbis with the supervision of the koshering process and is given the mandate to ensure that meat sold in shops and restaurants comply with the dietary laws. He works with his father, who is a more highly skilled schochet.

Baruch expresses no regrets over his decision to quit yeshiva, and is working part time on his high school diploma in the quiet hamlet of Long Prairie, where the slaughterhouse is located. Next week he goes to New York on vacation—not to Manhattan or the mountains, but to Crown Heights. "If I hang around long enough, I might catch a glimpse of the rebbe," he says, popping a bubble.

He has put his considerable earning power to use buying rollerblades and getting HBO for his studio apartment in Long Prairie. "There's nothing to do there. We are very isolated and there are no other Jews in town," he complains. He frets that his religious commitment is eroding. "Even though I lay *t'fillin* every day, my praying doesn't have the same *kavoineh*, the same spirit."

He longs to return to New York, not to go to yeshiva, but to attend auto body repair school. In the meantime, he makes do with his job as a mashgiach.

The St. Paul Chabad community of which Hannah's family is a part is primarily composed of ba'alei teshuvah families. It supports a day school of about a hundred children, yet is dwarfed in size by the modern Orthodox presence in the Minneapolis suburb of St. Louis Park. But St. Louis Park lacks the funky feel of St. Paul, where swarms of Hasidic children run past nondescript tract homes and plastic toys litter the front lawns. It is here that Hasidim have taken over an Orthodox synagogue that served a dwindling congregation and turned it into a vibrant community center. Secular Jews show up from all over the Twin Cities to partake in boozy all-nighters on Purim and Simchat Torah, the two holidays on which the Orthodox traditionally allow themselves to get mildly inebriated.

Many of the Hasidic men work in the Jewish community. Nochum himself is something of a Jewish jack-of-all-trades. Besides being a schochet, he is also a *soifer*, or scribe, qualified to check for flaws in *mezuzot*, the tiny scrolls on the doorposts of religious Jews. And not only does he slice, he carves. As his Hyundai plates attest, Nochum is a *mohel*, or ritual circumciser, who spent a month in Israel practicing on Arab babies to learn the craft. Each mohel job brings in about five hundred dollars. But his main source of income comes from being a schochet.

I ask Baruch if I can visit the slaughterhouse.

"Sure. Why not tomorrow? Come tomorrow," he says eagerly. "I'm sure it's okay with the owner."

"Who is the owner?"

"The plant is owned by *goyim*, non-Jews, but the kosher section is leased out to two Jewish businessmen. They lease kosher sections all over the Midwest. They wouldn't care if you showed up."

The next day I drive out of the Twin Cities and into Minnesota farm country. The radio is tuned to a public station broadcasting a lecture by a black militant from Minneapolis, informing a rapt audience of rural Minnesotans that this is the third whitest state in the nation. The rhetoric is straight out of the sixties. I drive past Sauk Center, home of Sinclair Lewis and his cringing conformist, Babbitt. In Sauk Center there is a Sinclair Lewis Arts Center and a Main Street, but no mention of Babbitt. About twenty miles away is Long Prairie, population 2,786.

Finding the meatpacking plant is easy, but getting in is not. I enter the office, and a matronly Midwestern receptionist behind a glass panel sizes me up.

"Who do you want to see?" she asks suspiciously.

There has been a recent network exposé on dirty meatpacking plants, and I get the feeling she thinks I am here to do a latter-day version of *The Jungle*.

"I'm here to see the koshering section."

"Bud," she turns around and yells at a string bean of a man with bushy eyebrows and Scandinavian features, "he's here for the rabbis."

She seems agitated. Bud emerges from a cubicle. He eyes me like a fleck of dirt.

"So you want to see the rabbis?"

I nod affirmatively.

"Well, they're on break in the rabbi's room. Now what do you want to see them for?"

Just as I am about to elaborate, I see Baruch floating by on a pair of rollerblades.

"Oh, look, there's Rabbi Baruch now!" the receptionist says excitedly, pointing at the Hasidic apparition.

I flag him down.

"Rabbi Baruch, this young man is looking for you," she announces.

"It's okay, I know him," he says. "Come with me."

He leads me inside the plant.

"Don't they know you're too young to be a rabbi?" I ask.

"They call all of us here rabbis," he smiles. "Shhh–don't tell them any differently."

Although visitors are not allowed on the killing floor, Baruch promises to take me there. But first he leads me into a dingy antechamber where the *shochtim* take their breaks. There, sitting at a table studying psalms from an open prayer book, is Nochum.

With his tinted reading glasses and swarthy complexion, he could be a Peronista politician on an Argentinean banknote. His huge belly is cantilevered over his belt, and somewhere near the bottom of his gut *tzitzis* emerge like two rip cords on a parachute. These are the *Arba Kanfot*, or four corners of string that hang out from under the shirt and serve as a reminder to observe all of the Torah's commandments.

He looks up from his book and asks in his thick South American accent, "Hey, you put on t'fillin today?"

"Marriage has been good to you," I reply evasively.

"My Hannah is a wonderful cook," he announces in his nasal inflection. "Listen, you got any good investments? I lost a chunk of money on a heating oil futures contract."

Guilt pierces me like an icicle. The man has ten children.

"At the beginning of winter, I bought it at fifty-two cents. It's supposed to go up in winter but it went down."

I reluctantly suggest silver.

"Silver. That's long-term. I want something seasonal, like unleaded gas. That should go up for the summer."

"Do you need anything?"

"Need? I have needs as long as a roll of toilet paper," he says, sounding like a dejected Speedy Gonzalez. "You call this living?" He looks around the room at the fake wood paneling and dented lockers. It is devoid of anything except packs of generic cigarettes and a refrigerator full of rows and rows of Coke cans.

"How much do you need?"

"Four or five thousand would be nice. I got laid off from my last job and took a 40 percent pay cut. I need to send my kids to camp."

"But you get scholarships," I insist, alluding to the Chabad fund-raising juggernaut that takes in tens of millions of dollars in donations annually from nonreligious Jews. Surely this munificence filters down to people like Nochum.

"I don't get scholarships for camp or for sending the kids to school. Together it costs me nearly $20,000 a year."

My mind suddenly stops working. A $40,000 annual income, no scholarships, ten children. How does he do it? I'd have an easier time trying to figure out a Newtonian equation.

A buzzer sounds. Time to go back to work. Baruch takes me into an adjacent deep-freeze holding dozens of carcasses, as

Nochum prepares to go on the killing floor. Then Baruch leads me through the boning room, a big room where cattle are picked clean for beef. A huge pyramid of ribs and sternums is piled up ignominiously in one corner. At the other end is a conveyor belt of overhead metal trays, alternatively carrying tongues and livers. Tongue, liver, tongue, liver. The effect is mesmerizing. Disembodied organs glide by as if to the imaginary strains of "The Blue Danube."

I am nudged in the back. It is a bisected cow carcass moving toward me on a hook.

Baruch takes me up a ramp and opens a fire door. There, on a small platform of corrugated metal, is the Jewish Torquemada, Nochum, wielding his sword with the dexterity of a matador. With his rotund belly and blood-soaked smock, he looks like a cross between Jeffrey Dahmer and Jerry Garcia. The smock is bright yellow, the color of a school-crossing guard's raincoat.

His knife, a *chalev,* costs about $250 and is imported from Israel. Between each kill he sharpens it on a whetstone, then methodically runs the blade across his thumbnail and skin. If there is so much as a minuscule bump on the blade it cannot be used because the animal could feel pain before its death.

"A rip is much more painful than a cut," Nochum tells me.

A candidate to become a schochet has to jump through a few hoops. First, he must demonstrate to a rabbi that he can identify even the tiniest nick on a blade. This is *hargisha,* the feel test. Then he must *schecht* three chickens–two hens and one rooster–in front of the rabbi, to prove that he will not faint at the sight of blood. Schechting a rooster is very tricky and easily botched. It requires the agility of a surgeon and the anatomical knowledge of Frank Purdue. Finally, he must convince a schochet that he is qualified to schecht. Only then is public notice of his qualification given. But before any of this, he must study the relevant sections of the

Talmud and the *Shulchan Arukh,* the code of Jewish conduct, in yeshiva. Not everyone who attends yeshiva studies the laws of *schechita,* or ritual slaughter, only those preparing to enter the field or planning to become a rabbi. But any religious Jew, male or female, can be a schochet, provided they are not imbeciles or under the age of majority.

A schochet is obligated to follow ethical guidelines. He cannot be paid by the piece. This would create the presumption that a conflict of interest exists, since he might feel tempted to declare nonkosher cattle kosher. For the same reason, he may not get paid more for slaughtering kosher cattle than nonkosher ones. Nor may he own the cattle he schechts.

Treatises have been written arguing that shechita is the least painful form of death. At the turn of the century, in response to a public movement calling for the outlawing of schechita, German-Jewish scientists demonstrated with Teutonic exactitude that 50 percent of a cow's blood is lost in the first minute after slaughter. They drew up a number of sophisticated charts purporting to prove that the beast was almost instantaneously incapable of feeling any pain once the carotids and jugulars were severed.

Yet Jewish lore stresses that shochtim are partners of Amalek, the murderous enemy of ancient Israel, who have turned their innately evil inclinations into something useful. Moreover, the Torah commands *Tsa'ar Ba'alei Chaim,* compassionate treatment of animals, and does not encourage the consumption of meat. Certain liberal Jewish scholars have even gone so far as to insist that Judaism favors a vegetarian diet, but most authorities dismiss this as bunk.

On the killing floor, the cows go through a loading ramp and get hoisted up by a chain attached to their ankles. Some go to their deaths quietly, some kicking and mooing. Nochum deftly runs his blade across their throats and blood rushes out in torrents, buckets of blood from the torso. There can be no pressure on the knife and the cut must be continuous.

A number of the cows are found to be nonkosher. If there is a lump on the neck or skin disease, two non-Jewish assistants take over, hitting the beast on the head with a stun gun that forms an almost perfect circle of blood on the prefrontal lobe. Then, as the animal is suspended by a hook, a dagger is plunged into its chest. The result is the same, torrents of blood from the torso.

I ask one of the assistants if the cow feels any pain.

"No way," replies the typically taciturn northern Minnesotan. He picks up the gun and hits five cattle–bing, bing, bing–on the forehead as if he's stapling down a piece of fabric. One by one they crumple to the floor.

"See any pain there?" he asks.

A trio of bulls emerges from the chute. Two are shoved back in accordance with the Jewish rule that no animal may be slaughtered in front of another. Nochum estimates that the biggest bull weighs 3,400 pounds. It is hoisted up on the chain and lets loose with a protracted death moan when its throat is slit. As the carcass is led away, Nochum turns to me and smiles sweetly. "That's a lot of hamburger," he says.

The parallel here is as obvious as it is absurd. This is a bovine Belsen. There is blood everywhere, puddles on the floor, streaks on the wall, and the odor is interspersed with the overwhelming redolence of ammonia, as if we are immersed in a giant vat of Mr. Clean. Behind a nearby window is an almost surgically antiseptic room of alabaster cow skulls suspended on hooks from the ceiling. They glide by in a macabre rumba. A procession of stomachs and intestines drop with assembly-line precision into the back of a semi. The slaughterhouse is busier than a Lord and Taylor's display window on Christmas Eve.

The kosher cattle are skinned and have a purple Hebrew letter stamped on them. The letter corresponds to the day of the week.

Then they are boned, chopped up, and put into huge cardboard boxes called combos. The combos are sent to processing plants in the East, where they are cut into smaller pieces, soaked, and salted, in a continuation of the kosher process. Baruch, the mashgiach, signs his name to each box. He tells me that his busiest day was when 2,000 pounds of testicles came by on a conveyor belt and he had to affix a *plombe,* or plastic tag certifying kosher, to each one.

I express amazement that testicles are kosher. Baruch shrugs philosophically, "If the cow is kosher, the balls are kosher."

The entire koshering process is rife with controversy. Satmar Hasidim, for example, will not eat meat that has been slaughtered by a Lubavitcher. About half of all Satmar won't eat any meat at all, because they do not trust their own butchers to be rigorous enough. Even the most commonly sold kosher meat, such as Hebrew National, is shunned by Hasidim because the meat is not *glatt,* or conforming to a more demanding level of purity.

Nochum takes his break in the rabbi's room, surrounded by his co-workers—a Moroccan Jew from Emanuel in the West Bank, sidelocks wound tightly around his ears in Yemenite fashion, another Lubavitcher from Montreal, and a Mirrer from Petach Tikva, a thirty-eight-year-old bachelor who lives full-time in Long Prairie. The Mirrers are a group of Mitnaggedim, non-Hasidic Orthodox Jews, who followed their yeshiva head across Russia to Kobe and Shanghai during World War II. Eventually, the entire yeshiva arrived intact in San Francisco, where some dispersed to Flatbush and others to Jerusalem. It was Senpo Sugihara, the heroic Japanese envoy to Lithuania, who managed to save the Mirrers, while the vast majority of Lithuanian Jews were wiped out in the forests around Vilna by mobile Nazi machine-gun squads. The Mirrer's specialty is *bedicka,* looking at the lungs of the cattle after each kill to make sure there are no blemishes or flaws. He sticks his head deep into the torso of each decapitated beast. He is not responsible for discovering imperfections other than in the lungs, but if he happens to come across one, the animal is declared nonkosher.

Nochum kills over a hundred cattle a day. During his break, I ask him if he feels any remorse. "Remorse?" Nochum asks in reply, plunging a cocktail-size bagel into a container of sour cream and stuffing it in his mouth. "Why should I feel remorse? It is all *kidusha,* holiness. When we schecht we are doing God's will. God put everything here for us. The *behayma,* the cow, is here for us. People have to eat, and the butcher and schochet have to have *parnassah,* a living, for their families."

He makes a circle in the air as if to illustrate this economic gestalt.

"Besides, I say a blessing."

"Before you kill each cow?" I ask.

"No, in the morning, for all I will schecht that day."

He licks the sour cream off his fingers.

After work, we descend on Baruch's apartment. There Nochum gets into a protracted telephone conversation with the Montreal Lubavitcher over scheduling hassles. Baruch ducks into the bedroom, where he flips on HBO. On the screen a woman is unbuttoning her blouse. He doesn't seem particularly interested.

"I don't want my father to know we're watching this," he says, turning it off and slipping a cassette of Hasidic crooner Mordechai Ben David into his tape deck.

We soon depart for St. Paul for the Sabbath, passing Bible camps and truck stops along the interstate, a carload of Hasidim jabbering away in Hebrew and English and smoking up a storm. The fact that Nochum is a ba'al teshuvah precludes the use of Yiddish, since most ba'alei teshuvah don't speak this lingua franca of the Hasidic world.

We pull in front of Nochum's house, where Hannah is standing with her brood of immaculately attired children. The interior of the house is equally pristine. Nochum takes his place at the head of the table like some benign potentate, and the children begin to crawl all over his lap. Hannah disappears into the kitchen for a minute and returns with a pair of candleholders. The look on her face is intermittently ethereal and bittersweet. Nochum smiles at her, and Baruch throws me a meaningful glance. It's a system, he seems to be saying. And like any system, it isn't perfect, but somehow it works.

Suicide, child abuse, divorce, the litany of modern problems, all are relatively rare occurrences in the Hasidic world. But this lifestyle exacts an equally high price. The demographic revival of Hasidism—once a frayed rope about to snap—has been nothing less than astonishing. Hannah herself plans on having as many more children as possible. When I ask how they will manage, Nochum rolls his eyes toward the sky. Hashem will take care of it, he says. And with that, the family, twelve strong and counting, plus numerous in-laws and friends, crowd around the much abused dining room table and commence the blessing over the Sabbath wine.

CHAPTER 4

Fairfax Fandango
LOS ANGELES, CALIFORNIA

Of the half-million Jews in Los Angeles, about 2 percent are Orthodox. The observant minority mostly resides in or around the Fairfax district, conveniently accessible to Hollywood, Beverly Hills, and much of the West Side. Fairfax Avenue itself is bifurcated by Melrose to the north, which leaves its hip imprimatur on the district, creating a confluence of the avant garde and the retrograde, something unseen anywhere else except perhaps South Beach in Miami or the Lower East Side in New York.

In recent years, due to a high birthrate and a steady influx of the newly religious, the Orthodox population of Fairfax has exploded. Street life there is a warm alternative to the often tacky and evanescent anonymity of the rest of the city. Old Bolsheviks coexist side-by-side with punks. Sephardim, or Eastern Jews, interact freely with Ashkenazim, the European variety, and secular Jews with Hasidic store owners. This bonhomie extends to the ultra-Orthodox community itself, which in other cities is often beset by intense intergroup rivalry.

Pushy Israelis with thick forearms who could pass as hit men for Bugsy Siegel stuff their faces with falafel and schwarma. A Persian-owned boutique with racks of Jewish records and tidbits of Judaica for sale blasts out Israeli rock. A woman with a thick Polish accent pulls her son in front of a fishmonger. "This is my new boyfriend," she announces with a wink.

This is clearly no isolated Hasidic enclave, no Williamsburg West. There are no naïfs untainted by the rude intrusion of modernity. Here modernity weaves its way through communal life like a golden thread through a tallis. Posters on every street corner promote seminars for instant Jewish spiritual enlightenment in the breathless cadence of a Scientology commercial. The community is simply not large enough or insulated enough to be unaffected by contemporary life. At its core are mystics and hip visionaries, many of whom turned on, tuned in, and dropped out in the sixties, only to reemerge a few years later as virtual replicas of their grandfathers. Easily identifiable on the streets, they look like Hasidim but walk like Mr. Natural, the Keep On Truckin' mascot in Zap Comix.

This is where Lubavitch is a forceful presence, running an annual telethon for California Chabad that takes in millions and is hosted by the likes of Jon Voight and Whoopi Goldberg, where a Mrs. Weinberg of Beverly Hills, shutting her immediate family out of her will, left everything to the Lubavitchers, resulting in a $21 million windfall. This indomitable army of Hasidic fund-raisers, whose efforts benefit scores of day schools, halfway houses, and *yeshivot,* knows how to tap deeply into the emotional reservoirs of wealthy West Los Angeles Reform temple members, whose children increasingly seem to go in one of two directions: complete assimilation, or a fervent return to the fold. It is this latter group that feeds the steady trickle of new bodies into the pews of the prayer halls that dot Fairfax.

Their style may seem strangely incongruent with the traditional Yiddish-speaking Hasidim, largely children of Holocaust survivors, but style doesn't matter here. As long as the *mitzvot,* the commandments of the Torah, are rigorously adhered to, one can create one's own style. The result is an exotic morphology: a seething protoplasm of pious misfits surrounded by an unbreachable wall of hard-core, bred-to-the-bone true believers.

At Canter's Deli, a waiter who looks like a model for a truss advertisement in the Yiddish *Daily Forward* takes my order. "Go to Kinko's," a would-be record mogul in the next booth tells a white Rastafarian, "run off a proposal, and I'll float it around the industry." Canter's, a venerable L.A. institution, has recently become chic, perhaps because it offers up tattered remnants of authenticity in a sea of impermanence. All sorts of Jews at the ragged edges of the community hang out here: racing aficionados, guys with fat stogies seemingly glued to their mouths, kids just out of drug rehabilitation programs, not to mention rock 'n' rollers, *Rolling Stone* reporters, and movie directors.

If Canter's is the gastronomic epicenter of the neighborhood, Congregation Mogen Avraham on LaBrea, a few blocks to the east, is the spiritual one. It is clearly the largest and, by modest Hasidic standards, the most lavish of a series of synagogues lining LaBrea. The others are mere *shtiebelach,* prayer rooms, by comparison. It is also the site of a scandal that has rocked the congregation for several years. As chronicled on the front pages of the *Los Angeles Times* and picked up by the wire services, Mogen Avraham's rabbi, Avraham Low, was arrested for trying to pass a stolen cashier's check to an FBI undercover agent. In addition, the rabbi assured the agents on tape that he could launder vast sums of cash through a network of spiritual institutions in the United States and Israel.

In the basement social hall of the synagogue, three men huddle over mishnaic tomes, rocking back and forth in the ancient study posture known as *schokling*. It is believed that swaying intensifies the learning experience by heightening the ability to concentrate.

I ask an old man with bleary eyes about the rabbi.

"Oy yoy, yoy, yoy, yoy," the gnome-like creature replies, shaking his head. "You want to know about Low? He ruined many, many people. Low borrowed money from the members and plowed them into investments that went sour, mostly real estate. People trusted him. But you know, the funny thing is, no one says anything bad about him. He kept nothing for himself. He has nothing, absolutely nothing."

"You've never heard anything negative about him?" I ask.

"Once I heard in the back of the *shul*, the synagogue, someone muttering that he was unfit to lead."

A rotund young Hasid with squiggly *payess* and eyeglasses halfway down his nose walks into the room and begins to unroll a paper tablecloth for the Sabbath. I ask him about Low. He replies by flipping a lapel on his *kapoteh*, the long black coat modeled after the coats of medieval Polish noblemen, which Hasidim wear even in the heat of summer. Under the lapel is a crudely printed button that reads "Don't Ask," followed by three exclamation points painted in red nail polish. He casually turns over the other lapel to reveal another button. It says, "I don't have any idea."

"Too many people asking too many questions," he huffs. "Journalists don't look for the truth–they look for trouble." He states this as if he were uttering some undeniable talmudic truth.

Suddenly, he is struck by the epiphany that this conversation is being carried on in Yiddish. He looks me up and down.

"So how do you know Yiddish?" he asks. Before I can answer, a sympathetic glint appears in his eye. "At least you are a Jew. We've had *goyishe* journalists crawling around here like flies. They don't know an arm from a leg. So how do you know Yiddish?"

"My grandmother," I reply.

"From her you learned Yiddish?"

"*Yah*. She came after the war."

"Where was she?"

"Auschwitz, Plaszow."

"Ah hah." The men in the room pull on their beards in unison, as if they have collectively unraveled some talmudic *pilpul*, a brain teaser. Secular Jews conversant in Yiddish are about as rare as dodo birds unless they are residents of a nursing home.

Suddenly, I am distracted by a tall, almost patrician cross between Timothy Leary and Baba Ram Dass who is crossing the adjacent hall. He opens a door, kisses a *mezuzah,* and disappears.

"Where is he going?" I ask.

"Into the men's *mikveh*."

The mikveh is the ritual bath where men prepare for the Sabbath. There is a separate one for women.

The exact dimensions of a kosher mikveh are painstakingly detailed in rabbinic texts, along with prescriptions for what sort of water to use, how the water should enter and exit, and what constitutes a proper piping system. The Torah commands *taharat mispacha,* or purity of the family, of which a corollary is a woman's immersion in the mikveh after menstruating. Adherents of the command to use the mikveh note that its purpose is to cleanse women spiritually, not physically, although the thirteenth-century commentator Nachmanides stated that "the glance of a menstrual woman poisons the air . . . she is like a viper who kills with her glance . . . the dust on which she walks is impure like the dust defiled by the bones of the dead." While this sounds wildly misogynistic to modern ears, Hasidic women argue that comments like these are taken grievously out of context. To them, the mikveh represents a requisite step in the sanctified act of marital sexual relations. On a more mundane level, it serves as a place to engage in social discourse and get one's hair done. This social function is also significant for men, who try to go every morning if possible, or at least before the onset of the Sabbath.

The door to the mikveh in the basement of the shul slams shut. "Can I go in?" I ask.

"Sure. Just ask the attendant."

The attendant is a squat Russian émigre with a five o'clock shadow. He has a bemused expression on his face. I don't know if the look is due to some profound sort of Buddhistic detachment achieved as a result of his modest station in life, or a reaction to the chaos swirling around him. He hands me a towel.

Just inside the mikveh is a locker room. About a dozen men are in various stages of undress. Clothes are strewn on benches.

"What's with the rabbi?" I hear someone say as I enter the room. Apparently, this refers to Low. But before the door shuts they see me and clam up. I am clearly an intruder, someone who has invaded this normally uninhibited sanctum of free-wheeling conversation and male bonding.

"Hi," I say. I feel like the Flying Nun on the day she entered the convent. Eyebrows are raised. I murmur a few words in Yiddish.

Nobody is impressed.

Beyond the locker room is a series of showers. Into one a young boy executes a trajectory of urine in an arc so perfect it would make the Mannequin Pis proud. Adjacent to the showers is a deep pool of water reminiscent of the cement pits that Finns plunge into after a sauna. Men mumble a prayer there before ritualistically submerging themselves for a few moments, repeating the process several times. I climb in.

"Your *yarmulke*," a boy says, pointing to my skullcap and indicating that I should take it off. I rest it on a rail.

"How many times should I go under?" I ask the boy.

"I think it's three," he says. "No, maybe it's nine. It's some multiple of three."

The water looks murky. I decide to dispense with the ritual and take a shower instead. Although the shower is otherwise clean, the drain is clogged with Ivory soap wrappers.

I scrub myself and return to the locker room. There the Baba Ram Dass look-alike is drying off. Smiling idyllically, he introduces himself. He is Avraham Greenbaum, resident of Jerusalem, graduate of Oxford, Harvard, and Columbia, former BBC reporter, and Bratslaver Hasid. He is here to deliver a series of lectures on Jewish meditation. Bratslaver Hasidim are nature lovers and meditation freaks, considered something of an anomaly in other Hasidic communities, but very much the mainstream in L.A. They follow the teachings of Nachman of Bratslav, who died nearly 200 years ago, and unlike other Hasidim, pay no fealty to any living rebbe.

I follow Greenbaum outside of the mikveh and onto the street, where we come across a frail man who is acquainted with him. Greenbaum soon departs to prepare for the Sabbath, and I am left in the company of this middle-aged ragamuffin, who is dressed in a frayed work shirt and corduroys bunched together at the waist by a worn-out belt. He invites me into his vintage Toyota for a cigarette.

He lights up and inhales greedily. His skin seems gray from too much smoking, and his eyes burn with a sort of Levantine intensity. We drive a few blocks to a corner somewhere between Fairfax and LaBrea, where he parks the car and begins to tell me his life story. Looking at me deeply, he announces that he spent ages eight to ten in a shallow pit under a barn in southeastern Poland. The dimensions of the pit were roughly the size of the back of his station wagon. This he shared with his mother, father, and aunt, who had bought their way out of a ghetto and sought refuge with a non-Jewish acquaintance. The Polish friend willingly obliged and put them in his basement under the kitchen. But there were holes in the floor and visitors could hear them, so the farmer dug a pit under the barn, intending to put them up for a short period. This turned into two years, during which time my narrator left the pit only once: One night he climbed out but was immediately kicked by a horse and went back in.

He looks at me with smoldering eyes, this homunculus with a hunched-over posture and a body gnarled into some perverse personification of Jewish history, and tells me his story with an extraterrestrial intensity wholly at odds with the carloads of teenagers whizzing by on Beverly Boulevard. Two years in a pit. A pit in southern Poland. Saintly peasants bringing him food and taking his nocturnal turds out in a copper pot. A mother threatening to suffocate him if he makes any noise. And then suddenly California, a Ph.D. from the University of Southern California in the sixties, a stroll down Sunset Boulevard. A surreal life, lived like some cubist masterpiece. No wonder he's only worked one and a half years out of the last twenty.

"I'm below subsistence," he says. "My mother has Alzheimer's. It is only now, in this evolved state, that I can truly communicate with her."

On the windshield of his car is a Stanford faculty sticker. His current wife–he has had three, he tells me–was a professor of philosophy there. He was living in remote Bolinas when Avraham Greenbaum called him up and encouraged him to move to L.A. and enroll his seven children in a Jewish school.

Looking at him, I begin to get a feel for the community. It is chock full of renegades and rejects, survivors of psychoanalysis and worse. It is unlike any other Orthodox Jewish community in the world, and carries the brand of Los Angeles on its back with the stark simplicity of a concentration camp tattoo. If it were a face, it would be a Picasso portrait: two eyes on one side of the head or one eye way up and one way down like some cracked caricature of Jean-Paul Sartre. It is a teeming cauldron of fringe elements and the mainstream, all percolating peacefully under the hot California sun.

It's Friday night, and Mogen Avraham is packed with swaying, schokling Hasidim. Women overlook the entire scene from the balcony like benign archangels. Yet the head rabbi is missing. After being released from thirty-one days in the Federal Detention Center, he prefers not to show his face. The magistrate would not grant bail. Finally, a second judge agreed to a $500,000 bond.

"The rabbi rotted in jail," sighs his chief lieutenant, Elchonon Tauber. Tauber is a tall, graying talmudic scholar in his late thirties. He has the oblong features of an El Greco character and the sedate mien of a well-bred greyhound.

Tauber knew Rabbi Low as well as anybody, but only in the spiritual realm. Low kept his business affairs to himself, dealing out of a locked study with a personal computer and a stream of low-profile visitors. After his arrest, the press made Low out to be a Hasidic Charles Keating, doing business deals at a frantic pace with a variety of partners. That is simply not the case, maintains Tauber. Low merely took part in a few big transactions.

"Av Harahamim," Tauber intones. "Father the merciful one. If only the first judge had been a man, he would have shown *rachmones,* compassion, and granted bail, but since she is a woman, she had to show the world how tough she is."

"But," I protest, "didn't Low get taped promising an FBI undercover agent that he could get people across the border into Canada and smuggle millions of dollars into Europe?"

Tauber gives a talmudic shrug and goes back to his prayers. He is well known and respected as a *rav,* an authority on Jewish law and a leader of the Fairfax community. During one telephone conversation, he was interrupted by another call and put me on hold. When he got back to me, he explained that the call was from a local doctor with an Orthodox patient who would be risking her life if she got pregnant. The doctor wanted to know what birth control was acceptable.

Birth control is certainly acceptable to save a mother's life, I learned, or if she could be severely harmed through pregnancy. The preferred method is oral contraception, since the sages spoke approvingly of a "cup of roots" that induced temporary sterility. Men, however, are forbidden from using contraceptives or ejaculating for any reason other than procreation. The line of authority behind this injunction runs straight to the Torah, where in Genesis 38:9 Onan is punished by death for spilling his seed in order to prevent the conception of a child. The Talmud, expanding on this, castigates the "bringing forth of seed in vain" as a cardinal sin and vigorously inveighs against it.

Abortion is only permitted in order to save the mother's life, but what constitutes a life-threatening condition is open to interpretation. In the Kovno ghetto in 1942, Rabbi Ephraim Ohry issued a blanket ruling permitting abortions on the basis of a German decree that every pregnant Jewish woman should be killed with her fetus.

Yet, under normal circumstances, the fetus is accorded a great deal of respect. The *Zohar,* the mystical Jewish *Book of Radiance,* derides the killer of a fetus as a desecrator of that which was built by the Holy One; and the Talmud says that the fetus is believed to study Torah from beginning to end while in the mother's womb.

A few houses down from Rabbi Low's synagogue is the *kollel,* an advanced institution of talmudic learning affiliated with Mogen Avraham. If a *yeshiva* is a college, a kollel is a graduate school, where Jewish law is examined with punctiliousness.

Before the war, kollels were only for the academic crème de la crème, because about the time a young man was ready to attend a kollel he was expected to get married and start a family. In order for him to do this, he had to pursue a livelihood instead of continuing full-time studies. So only a small elite of brilliant students went on to study in kollels, subsidized by wealthy patrons. But today virtually everyone would prefer study to working in an electronics warehouse or cutting diamonds. So the demand for places in the kollel has exploded, and with it a sort of fiscal crisis has developed. There is an ever greater demand on the productive elements of the community to underwrite the burgeoning cadre of kollel students.

In Israel this has manifested itself in protests among nonreligious parties over state subsidies going to advanced talmudic studies. But the Talmud is the watchword of the Jewish people, the Orthodox retort. And so for now, at least, as a result of the convoluted Israeli electoral system that gives inordinate clout to small parties, the state subsidies continue.

In the United States and Canada, hugely successful financiers such as the Reichmanns of Toronto gave astounding sums to yeshivas and kollels. But the Reichmann fortune went south, going the way of the commercial real estate market. Likewise in Los Angeles, some of the biggest investors sustained severe blows from the real estate recession. Rabbi Low was not immune. But during the good years, Low had grandiose plans and implemented them, buying real estate and plowing the cash-flow back into community institutions such as the kollel and a thousand-pupil *cheder,* or day school, on LaBrea named after his father-in-law, Rabbi Judah Isacsohn.

The most stunning of Low's projects was the construction of a state-of-the-art mikveh for women. Comparing the men's mikveh in the basement of Mogen Avraham to the women's mikveh elsewhere in the neighborhood is like comparing a Volkswagen to a Rolls Royce. The women's mikveh is adorned with Mexican tiles and boasts Jacuzzis, private suites, and powder rooms. It is famous in the Orthodox world.

In the kollel, men sit, yarmulkes tilted toward the back of their heads, scratching their brows and discussing the fine points of Jewish law in Yiddish, English, and Hebrew codewords. Even someone well versed in all three languages could not make out what is being said.

"We're discussing contract law," one of them tells me. "Specifically, a quitclaim deed. What if a husband gets a wife to sign a blank piece of paper and he writes a quitclaim deed around her signature disavowing her ownership in a piece of property. Is it valid?"

I shrug like an ignoramus.

"The answer is no, unless the wife had at another time refused to sign a similar empty sheet of paper. This would show that she has backbone and therefore had no reason to do it this time without clear intentions."

These millennia-old conundrums are tackled with the immediacy of a law school seminar. But soon the conversation turns to Low.

"Sure we've lost members," one of them tells me. "The kollel is now half the size it used to be. And the worst part is, Low brought over maybe a dozen scholars from Israel along with their families to teach us here. He had to send them back. It was a catastrophe. Families with eight to ten people uprooted themselves to come here, and as soon as they arrived they had to return. This kollel is a million-dollar project that went *farblonzhet*–belly-up."

"Is it Low's fault?" I ask.

"Listen, Low is no *tzaddik* [holy man], but he is a very ethical individual. He got caught up in bad real estate deals and got desperate."

"How bad is it?"

"Is $20 million bad?" one volunteers. "Maybe for the Reich-manns $20 million is nothing. They lost $20 billion. But for us, it's a catastrophe."

"Twenty million?" another interjects. "That's just the tip of the iceberg. I have a friend who Low lent $250,000 to start an elec-tronics business. It too went farblonzhet."

"This is a humpty-dumpty business," says the third, a Gerer Hasid. "It will never get put back together."

"Then what will you do?"

"We will tighten our belts," the young Gerer smiles. "We're right in step with the government." He goes back to his studies.

There is still plenty of money in the community. There are nurs-ing home moguls who have constructed institutions for both Jews and non-Jews. There is Sol Kest, a big giver and local real estate developer, who reportedly offered Low—just before the scandal broke—$60,000 to leave town for ten years and whose wealth is hyperbolically estimated at $800 million by desperate Hasidim looking for a financial savior. And there is the bittersweet aware-ness that in comparison to the adversities suffered by other Jewish communities, this is strictly minor league.

Outside in the parking lot behind the kollel, young boys from the day school next door play a game of basketball. Many of them are blond, and one or two look Eurasian.

"Hey, who are you?" they yell at me in Yiddish, having heard me speak it to the kollel students. "Are you a Jew?"

"Yeah."

"Then why aren't you religious?"

I shrug.

They smile mischievously and resume their game.

For many Jews, Los Angeles is the last way station on the road to total assimilation, a road that started in some dreary Eastern

European *shtetl* and continued on to New York, Chicago, and finally California. Here many, if not most, will shed their identities like molting snakes, fading into the woodwork of distant suburbs and soaring like eagles in their respective professions. But not the Jews of Fairfax. For them, the Low saga, and the anguish it has spawned, is but a fleeting phenomenon, a mere blip in the endless electroencephalogram of Jewish history.

CHAPTER 5

Uman, Uman, Rosh Hashanah

UMAN, UKRAINE

In the middle of the Ukraine, on a road remarkable for its smoothness and lack of potholes, sits a huge boulder requiring special deftness on the part of the driver to circumnavigate. A car must slow down, and as it does, appearing seemingly out of nowhere is a seedy pair conjuring up images of Boris and Natasha from the cartoons. These are local mafiosi, and they demand *protektzia* before a vehicle can proceed. This renegade form of toll operation can be paid off in kind, usually in nylons or a few ballpoint pens, in the local currency, or in dollars. But it must be paid, or the grave of the eighteenth-century visionary Rebbe Nachman of Bratslav cannot be reached.

Rebbe Nachman, who was born in the late eighteenth century in the Ukraine, has over 5,000 hard-core followers throughout the world, mostly in New York and Jerusalem. He was no hippie—his greatest struggle was against sexual immoderation—but much of what he says smacks of the sixties. He is the great grandson of the

Baal Shem Tov, the founder of Hasidism. His charisma was so great, and his utterances so insightful, that his Hasidim have never elected a successor. Consequently, they are the only major Hasidic group without a living rebbe. Hence they are called the Dead Hasidim, because their rebbe is deceased.

Nachman has been called crazy, but he was far from it. His philosophy is best revealed through his many stories and parables, which involve such transcultural archetypes as shipwrecks, madmen, hidden treasures, and lost kings. Nachman was no ascetic, and he celebrated the physical union between husband and wife. He also put tremendous stock in meditation, which he thought was best done outdoors.

Nachman was also a student of Gematria. A form of numerology, Gematria attempts to determine the mystical relationship between words of the same value. For example, Moses was a *tzaddik* who stood between the destruction of the Jews and their elevation to favor in the eyes of God. The Hebrew word for destruction is *shmad,* whose letters consist of *shin, mem,* and *daled,* with a numerical value of 344 (*aleph,* the first Hebrew letter, is assigned a value of one, *bet,* the second, a value of two, and so on). Moses in Hebrew is Moshe, whose letters have a numerical value of 345, and favor is *ratson,* with a value of 346. Therefore Moshe, at 345, stands numerically between destruction and favor.

The appeal of Nachman is transmitted not only through his stories, but in the comprehensive way his sayings have been collected and interpreted by a series of followers beginning with his disciple, Reb Noson, who painstakingly transcribed his utterances.

Nachman, who died in 1811 at the age of forty-one, is buried in Uman, a town of 70,000 in the central part of the Ukraine, about 120 miles from Kiev. Ever since the collapse of Communism, the Ukraine has been mired in an economic and political morass that seems to get worse with each passing month. The Ukrainian currency makes the Russian ruble look like the Swiss franc. In fact, Ukraine bears some antimatter resemblance to Switzerland: Nothing works here. Even the best hotels are frayed at the edges. Decent food is virtually unobtainable. The hyperinflation can give any African or South American economy a run for the money. And the president, Leonid Kravchuk, takes continual heat for concessions he is making to the Russians over nuclear warheads.

All this takes place against a backdrop of rising crime that makes everyday life debilitating. For an unescorted foreigner to walk the streets at dusk would be the height of lunacy. Unscrupulous cab drivers would happily slit their riders' throats for the equivalent of $50–about four times the median monthly salary. Trans-Ukrainian train compartments routinely have their interiors sprayed with sleep-inducing ether, thus rendering the passengers oblivious to the roving gangs of thugs who deftly clean out a wallet in a matter of seconds. Every hard currency restaurant or bar is teaming with hypertrophic heavies dressed like Jethro Clampett on Easter Sunday, who are either protecting the diners or seeking protection money from the boss.

The country is starved for fuel. Any lengthy trip necessitates a search for petrol that has the intensity of a high school scavenger hunt. Once a source is identified, the gasoline is collected in large metal cans and packed into the trunk. Then one crosses one's fingers and prays that there is no rear-end collision, for more than a few infernos have been set off this way.

But all of these risks and inconveniences pale next to the unique experience of visiting the grave of Rebbe Nachman on Rosh Hashanah, when 4,000 Hasidim from around the world arrive in a spiritual fervor in order to fulfill the request of Rebbe Nachman that whoever believes in God should come to visit him on Rosh Hashanah, the Jewish New Year.

The boarding gate for the flight to Kiev from Warsaw has the feel of a war zone. It's virtually empty, with a few Western businessmen and returning Ukrainians, maybe because the *International Herald Tribune* of that day warns of typhus outbreaks near the Bug River and persistent cholera epidemics. A well-dressed Polish matron on the train from Krakow to Warsaw had alerted me to this earlier in the day.

"Kiev? Kiev?" she repeated incredulously, as if someone had just doused her with cold water. "Do you know what's going on there? Typhus, cholera, diphtheria." She read off a litany of diseases like some quack advertising his snake-oil. "It's an epidemic," she concluded. Since she seemed like the type of person who would jump on a stool at the sight of a mouse and scream at the top of her lungs, I ignored her entreaties. "Don't eat anything," she said to me as I was getting off the train. "Don't eat fresh fruit! Wash your hands ten times a day! Are you vaccinated?" I jumped off as fast as I could. In fact, I later found out that the epidemics are confined to certain rather remote areas.

And now here I am on Air Ukraine flight number 124 to Kiev, where the carpet bunches up in the middle of the aisle and the toilet door has a sign that reads "Out of Order" taped to it with what looks like a used Band-Aid. I sit down next to a man who could pass for Wayne Newton and smells like the makeup counter at Bloomingdale's. After hearing my fears, he does his best to soothe me. "Don't worry," he says. He's lived in Kiev on and off for the past few years, setting up a casino in one of the hotels there for a Floridian entrepreneur. His entire career has been in the gambling trade, taking him to casinos in far-flung places such as Addis Ababa and Iraq, where he was a gaming adviser to Saddam Hussein. He tells me to stay at the Dniepro, a hotel in the center of town.

Upon arriving in Kiev, we share a cab to the hotel. The airport itself is stark, somewhat reminiscent of a bureaucratic hell, a

Ukrainian version of the village in *The Prisoner.* Now that the experiment in Communism has failed, one can almost view it in hindsight as a quaint historical anomaly, were it not for the fact that it was accompanied by a quantum of human suffering with the density of a dwarf star.

"How much money do you have?" the customs guard asks. "Twenty-seven hundred dollars," I reply with the forthrightness of an Eagle scout. "Let me count," he says, and begins thumbing through my money with the dexterity of a riverboat croupier. Later on in the cab, I realize that I now only have twenty-six.

As I look out at the almost deserted streets, it becomes clear that the whole country has come to a virtual halt. A deep, grinding depression has set in. People crawl along aimlessly, like a Fritz Lang movie at sixteen RPM. There are endless rows of boarded-up shops. The streets are rutted out and the traffic lights are haywire, following their own logic, blinking to the notes of some inaudible *Internationale.* Cars are parked haphazardly, and it's eerily quiet, as just before some final, snowy apocalypse.

Into the midst of all of this have plunged about twenty Hasidic families from the United States and Israel who have taken it upon themselves to minister to the needs of Kiev's shrinking Jewish community. At the forefront is Rabbi Yaakov Bleich, who arrived in Kiev when the old system was on its last legs and who convinced the government to turn over a synagogue to his organization, Yad Yisrael, which is backed by Agudat Israel, an umbrella group composed of most of the ultra-Orthodox, with the notable exception of Lubavitch and Satmar.

My room at the Dniepro looks as if the Battle of Stalingrad had taken place in an IKEA showroom. It can only be described in anthropomorphic terms. It's sallow, like the face of a Ukrainian coal miner, and the atmosphere is gray. Outside the door sits an enormous *babushka* staring off into space in a flowered robe and slippers. It is apparently her job to keep an eye on things. She gives me a big, toothy smile.

The bar downstairs is full of young Arabs dancing up a storm in a haze of cigarette smoke with local women done up like mannequins for McCrory's. The entire scene is reminiscent of a proletarian Copacabana. The room is huge, and the food, seemingly every bit of it, is covered in dollops of aspic. I strike up a conversation with one of the Arabs, who begins to regale me with tales of foreign businessmen found with their throats slit. This sends me to my room in a paranoid state, and I begin to pile pieces of furniture against the door. At 5:30 A.M. I wake up to what sounds like an air-raid siren, quickly pack my bags, and head downstairs.

Across from the check-out desk, a middle-aged man with a face full of *weltschmerz* and the grizzled lines of Charles Bronson keeps looking around the corner at me as he French-inhales a cigarette. Finally, I ask, "Russkie?" *"Nyet,"* he replies, *"Greco."* I use the one line of Greek I know on him and he stares at me blankly. As I leave the hotel for the synagogue, I see him standing in the doorway, talking urgently into a mobile phone and studying me like an entomologist.

The synagogue is in a residential area surrounded by high-rises with poorly mortared bricks. By the time I reach its gates, I feel like Cardinal Mindszenty seeking refuge at the American Embassy. The gates are locked, and I begin vigorously pounding on the wrought iron fence. Rain is beating down and I am soaked.

Eventually a caretaker appears and he ushers me into his shack. Sitting inside are three old Jews, each with a five o'clock shadow and a cane. *"Fin vu zeit eer?"* Where are you from? I ask them in Yiddish. They look at me like three trained chimps. "Where are you from?" I repeat. Finally, one says, "Gruzin," and that explains it. They are non-Yiddish speaking Sephardim from Georgia. Then they continue their see no evil, hear no evil, speak no evil routine. The caretaker, a healthy young Slav in the full flush of youth, points to an enamel sign with black Cyrillic script. Something on it says 8:30. I assume that's when services begin and I sit down to wait. The old-timers commence a game of backgammon as the caretaker picks up a yellowed copy of the local press and begins thumbing through what looks like the want ads.

About half an hour later, a young Hasid comes barreling through the courtyard with the vigor of a Merkava tank. Robust and barrel-chested, he pulls a set of keys out of a box and opens the synagogue door.

It's your basic run-of-the-mill Eastern European *shul*. Doors are unhinged, half-eaten packages of Joint Distribution Committee–donated matzo clutter a corner, and the entire place has the putrid odor of two-week-old gefilte fish. Hebrew inscriptions cover the arch of the main door, and it's clear that the *balabatim*, the burghers who built this place in Czarist times, had hopes for a better future than actually transpired. The ghost of Stalin looms larger here than any occupying force.

At about 8:00 A.M., the place begins to hop. Western Hasidim trot in with a missionary zeal. They have effected a kind of bloodless putsch here: The old-time regulars from Kiev have basically given up the ghost and let the outsiders take charge. By the time services begin, only a few dozen indigenous old men remain, but the sanctuary is brimming with young Hasidic families from the West and local *ba'alei teshuvah* teenagers, who sway like skyscrapers in an earthquake when they pray.

Each of the Hasidim has an assigned task. Some teach, some are liaisons with the government, others help with emigration. They have branched out to smaller cities and have divided up the territory with the punctiliousness of Mafia dons. Kiev is Karliner-Stoliner country, Berdichev belongs to the Skverers, and

Zhitomir is Lubavitcher turf. Each town has its own *cheder*, where classes are taught in Yiddish and students are segregated by gender. The schools have experienced phenomenal growth as parents rush to get their children out of deteriorating public institutions and into Jewish ones, where the standards are much higher. The Kiev cheder has grown from zero to 560 students in three years.

I take a seat next to a wild-eyed Hasid of local extraction, who gratuitously informs me in Yiddish that there are still between 9 million and 11 million Jews left in the former Soviet Union, and every last one, God willing, will move to Israel. You get an F in demography but an A in excitability is my unspoken response. It seems pointless to add that jamming another 10 million Jews into Israel would make North Dakota look like Hong Kong in terms of population density.

Karliner-Stoliners are known as "the screaming Hasidim" because it is their *minhag*, or custom, to yell when they pray. It is their belief that yelling creates *nusach*, or melodiousness. Their entreaties sound much like a cross between a yodel and a hog-call, and the Torah reader's occasional bellows have the same effect on a dozing supplicant as Haydn's Surprise Symphony is supposed to have on a concertgoer. It startles even the most hidebound daydreamer out of deep reverie.

Stoliners are also known for their ability to make a joke about almost anything. To them, depression is particularly dangerous because it can lead to sin. So the best way to avoid it is through puns, witticisms, and most importantly, *niggunim*, or melodies designed to raise up sagging spirits or reinforce good moods. All Hasidim have niggunim, but the Stoliners are famous for them. Along with the Modziters, they are the most prolific in composing these hummable ditties. There are niggunim to be sung when one is low, when one is happy, when one wants to honor friendship, and for any other number of reasons. Previous rebbes in the Stoliner line were highly musical and composed many such songs.

As I look at the crowd, it is hard to deny that something of a renaissance has taken place here. The Hasidic bureaucracy includes one individual who does nothing but coordinate the logistics of bringing in tons of kosher food from New York and Israel. Children who didn't know the meaning of the words *mazel tov,* congratulations, now babble away with foreigners in Yiddish and *daven* the *shmona esrai,* a ubiquitous prayer, like lifers. And everyone is young: Very few of the Hasidim are over forty. This is a fact throughout the former Soviet Union where the Chief Rabbi of Russia—at least the one recognized by Hasidim—is thirty-four, and the Chief Rabbi of Belarus is a mere thirty.

Toward the end of services, one of the Karliner-Stoliners shakes my hands and asks me what I think of Kiev. Before I can answer, he proclaims that the Midrash, the collection of rabbinical stories and commentaries, says the world is built on three things: *kinneh, teveh,* and *chesed,* or competitiveness, desire, and kindness. "Without kinneh we won't plant crops, without teveh we won't procreate, and without chesed we won't let each other survive. The Ukrainians have no kinneh, no drive," he maintains. "Communism has destroyed it." He walks away, then turns around and winks roguishly. "Teveh they got plenty of. Chesed I couldn't tell you."

Rabbi Bleich, a sardonic twentysomething in charge of operations here, is universally admired for his persistence in dealing with the local authorities. It is he who has forged this core of ultra-Orthodox volunteers. Bleich, a Stoliner from Brooklyn, is in a sense returning to his roots—his great-grandparents left the Ukraine for America nearly a century ago.

Each of the volunteers here has their own project. Velvel Tabak, a twenty-four-year-old from Monsey, flies in a turboprop every

Thursday to Chernovitz near the Romanian border to conduct Sabbath services and teach Sunday school. He is jokingly known as the Chernovitzer Rav, or rabbi. Once a center of Jewish settlement, Chernovitz is now a mere relic, decimated by war and subsequent waves of emigration. Tabak's wife, the daughter of a modern Orthodox scientist from Montreal, runs the girls school there.

Parents of these young idealists have mixed feelings about their mission. They are proud of the objective but dismayed at the living standards. To them, this may as well be Burkina Faso. Dilapidated apartments, a dearth of consumer goods, and unfriendly locals is the norm. Yet their children continue to come, lighting up the dark skies of Soviet Jewry, commuting between *shtetls* on single-engine aircraft and in military vehicles, teaching Hebrew and leading prayers.

There is a Ruvane from Detroit, the son of an agnostic lawyer, crammed with his wife and two children in a ground-floor apartment with little except a picture of their rebbe on the wall. Ruvane, who has the placid gaze of a holy man–his wife counterbalances this with occasional hilarious cracks about life here–teaches at the local school. Many of his students are Jewish only on their mother's side, and consequently blue-eyed and blond-haired. For someone who has never seen it before, there is nothing like looking at a spitting image of Yuri Gagarin with *payess*.

After services, Ruvane invites me to spend the night at his apartment. I willingly accept, feeling that I'm a marked man at the hotel. But first I go to lunch at the home of the Chernovitzer Rav. At one time this would have been a particularly auspicious position, but now, with Chernovitz reduced to 2,000 Jews, it is more modest yet absolutely crucial in the general scheme of things.

Kiev and Chernovitz are not the only Ukrainian communities being brought back to life. Cities steeped in the collective Jewish subconsciousness—Lvov, Kishinev, Zhitomir, Vinnitsa—are all witnessing minor revivals. And in each one, a different Hasidic group, with different customs and different patrons, prevails.

Leaving the cloistered confines of the synagogue and walking outside is something akin to entering an Edward Hopper painting. Everything is austere, stripped down to the bare essentials. Trees lack leaves, windows lack shutters, cars lack doors. We walk past gray tenements, through empty parks in a miasma of poverty and frustration. An occasional non-Jewish acquaintance from the neighborhood will nod at one of the Hasidim, who returns the greeting. Finally, we reach the apartment house of Velvel Tabak, the Chernovitzer Rav. We climb a flight of stairs that would do any Lower East Side tenement proud, past gaping holes covered with thin sheets of plywood, and come to a door with a *mezuzah* attached to it. Inside we are greeted by Aviva Tabak, Velvel's wife, clutching a steaming plate of cholent. A bracing concoction of beef, beans, and potatoes, cholent is the sine qua non of Sabbath afternoon meals, because it cooks all night and doesn't need to be heated up on the day of rest. Its origins are shrouded in mystery; some say it originated among medieval French Jews, others trace it to Spain. Above Aviva's head is a photo of her with her students in Chernovitz.

Soon a man arrives with his five children. He is Elimelech, the logistics expert from Mea Sha'arim, who sees to the importation of kosher food into the Ukraine. He is twenty-eight and speaks only Yiddish. Even though his family has been in Israel for at least eight generations—there had been a trickle of Hasidim emigrating to the Holy Land from the eighteenth century up until World War II, after which it became a torrent—he refuses to use Hebrew because it is the *lashon kodesh,* or holy tongue.

Elimelech is a diminutive sort with a truculent glare and prematurely gray hair. He is an in-your-face antisecularist and looks easily antagonized. Seeing me, though, his blue eyes begin to twinkle. "A *freier yid*," a free, or uninvolved Jew, he exclaims. That's okay, he assures me in Yiddish, as long as I'm not connected with any non-Orthodox organization. If you're not against us, you're with us, he seems to be saying, but if you're Reform or Conservative, you're against us.

Elimelech sits down at the table with his children, who also speak only Yiddish. It seems as though his wife is in Israel for some sort of minor operation and he's here with the children. He's handling it just fine, he assures me. His children learn separately from the local children, due to the tremendous disparity in background. This is true for all the Hasidim here.

He begins to inveigh against the peace settlement. He doesn't like Rabin or Arafat, but he reserves his worst venom for Peres. Peres is giving away the farm. Peres is an *apikoros,* a traitor, a no-goodnik, and Rabin is not much better. You can't trust the Arabs, there will never be peace. But what about the Egyptians, I protest. The Egyptians, he announces as if this is some undeniable fact, are different. They are mild. All the while I am thinking that this man has never served in the military; he doesn't even recognize Israel. Trying to reconcile this paradox is literally giving me a headache.

But he is an Israeli in the same way that a member of the DAR is an American: His family arrived there 250 years ago, with the influx of the kabbalists and mystics who joined Rabbi Isaac Luria in the northern city of Safad. Hence he is as un-European, and consequently as unscathed by the Holocaust, as a born Hasid can get. He has an explanation for this, too. It was the scourge of Zionism that brought destruction on the Jews. Like a fine wine, a state should not be served up before its time; and in the case of Israel, that time is when the Messiah comes. When I am about to say otherwise, his eyes flare, but then he lets me speak. I am, after all, a freier yid, not a threat, not a Conservative or modern Orthodox Zionist. But by now I have nothing to say.

He comes from a family of fourteen children and his cousins
are as many as stars in the sky. It's not good to have one or two or
three children, he tells me. With one or two or three, the parents
tziter, they quake, that something will happen to them. But with a
large family, it's a different story. His brother, a widower with
eight children, just married a widow with six. A Hasidic Brady
Bunch. Before I can ask him how it works, he cuts me off. "They
manage," he says.

His theory that the Holocaust resulted from Zionism is dia-
metrically opposed to that of modern and ultra-Orthodox West
Bank settlers, who maintain that the Holocaust took place because the Jews did *not* leave for Israel. He blames it on Zionism,
they blame it on lack of Zionism. Either way, the victims get
blamed. The perpetrators, somehow, are left out in the cold, mere
instruments of God's wrath.

I spend the night in the ground floor apartment of Ruvane, the
Detroit ba'al teshuvah. His three children are crowded into one
bedroom, and he and his wife in another. I sleep on a couch in the
living room, which also serves as the den and dining area. The
next day I try to arrange a car to Uman to make it to the grave of
Rebbe Nachman well before Rosh Hashanah. This is no mean
feat. There are practically no cars on the road, and this being Sunday, the streets have a post-nuclear conflagration feel. Nothing is
moving. Even if I manage to flag down a driver, they assure me
the petrol situation is impossible.

Finally, a tough-looking local Jew beckons. Built like a line-
backer, in an expensive suede jacket with a thick gold wedding
band, he is leaning up against a Volvo in front of the synagogue,
flanked by two goons.

He seems to be some kind of facilitator, or intermediary, between the local mafiosi and the rabbi. A good man to have on
your side. "You want Uman?" he blurts out with the studied

crudeness of an Israeli colonel. "One hundred fifty dollars," he says. Seeing as how I don't have any choice, I nod affirmatively. "You wait here," he tells me.

About half an hour later, an ancient Lada with a rag stuck in its gas tank chugs up. It has a Ukrainian driver and two Hasidim in the back. One is extremely gaunt and almost otherworldly in appearance. He moves his lips to a book of psalms cradled in his lap. The other is a nonstop talker, a cross between Don Rickles and Joan Rivers. Within five minutes, I've heard his whole life story and gotten his mother's recipe for kugel. Uncommonly cosmopolitan for a Hasid, he has taken several bus tours of the United States and tells me that San Francisco is his favorite city. This is his third trip to Uman.

Yitzy, as he is known, likes to play the prig. At some point he asks me if it's true that *Has V'sholom,* God forbid, modern Orthodox boys and girls "do it" before they're married. When I reply that they probably do, a look of mock terror crosses his face. Later on he tells me that he likes Elvis. In his opinion, Elvis represented the last link to a civilized society. Then the Beatles came and all hell broke loose. It's been downhill ever since. Yet in his own way he is an iconoclast. Traveling around on a bus just to see the sights is not exactly Hasidic standard operating procedure. And San Francisco, while not precisely Sodom, isn't exactly Boro Park either.

We pull over to what can only charitably be described as a rest stop, consisting of an outhouse in the middle of an overgrown lot. Yitzy produces a plastic bag full of Pringles potato chips, and I fall on them ravenously, since it seems as if I've been subsisting on nothing but hard-boiled eggs and cans of sardines ever since I got here.

Nachman's followers have visited his grave almost every Rosh Hashanah from the Napoleonic era to the present. In between, there were some perilous visitations. After 1917, the Bolsheviks made it difficult to get to Uman. Stalin closed the synagogue there in 1937, turning it into a metalworks plant. Then, in 1941, the Nazis deported the entire Jewish population, murdering 17,000. Today there are 2,000 Jews left, after the most recent wave of emigration.

After the war, the Soviets planned a housing bloc over the plot where Nachman is buried, but a convert by the name of Reb Daniel managed to convince the authorities to build alongside the grave rather than over it. The first post-Stalin nonsurreptitious pilgrimage to Nachman's grave took place in 1964, when a group of eleven disciples came from the United States. Up until Gorbachev, visits required reams of documentation and Israelis had to resort to falsified passports. Then Soviet society opened up and the annual gathering began.

The synagogue in Uman is an outdoor pavilion made of corrugated sheet metal and surrounded on most sides by bleak housing projects. Off to one corner, adjacent to a house, is the actual burial site of Rebbe Nachman. It is here that his followers gather to pray and recite the ten psalms—numbers 16, 32, 41, 42, 59, 77, 90, 105, 137, and 150—as a *tikkun,* or remedy, for all sorts of problems. Suspended above the grave is a blue velvet pouch for *kvitl,* notes to God requesting a blessing.

The mode of prayer is unique. After a period of swaying, the devotee will look to heaven with shrugged shoulders and upturned palms, in keeping with Rebbe Nachman's teachings that a supplicant should talk directly—even argue—with God. Then he might do some deep knee bends or jerk his pelvis back and forth with the aplomb of a contortionist. Many other Hasidic groups find the Bratslavers too fringy, particularly their propensity to go out into the woods after dark and loudly proclaim their oneness with God. Generally, however, the teachings of Rebbe Nachman are accorded great respect and his followers are accepted without cynicism.

Upon entering Uman, one is shunted in the direction of a series of multitiered apartment houses with a courtyard in the middle. There housing is informally arranged for the 3,000 or 4,000 Hasidim arriving in buses and taxis from Kiev, but whose flights originated in places that range from Capetown to Melbourne, Benei Berak to Bethesda. Standing in front of me is a lawyer from Vancouver named Sheldon who is making his third trip and a British Hasid who at one time worked for the Chancellory of the Exchequer. But most are Yiddish-speaking born Hasidim, including the twin sons of one of France's preeminent artists, who lives in a tiny Hasidic enclave in the Alps and who became religious years ago. His sons study at a cheder in Antwerp. There is nary a woman in sight, except for the local ones. When I ask why, I am told that Rosh Hashanah is not a family holiday like Purim, and if the men were at home they'd be at the synagogue all day anyway.

One Hasid from Monsey who arrived early with six of his sons rented a number of floors and is charging three dollars a night per bed. The usual residents have cleared out of most of the buildings, moving in with friends and relatives, and have sublet the premises to the visitors. Relations between the two groups is a model of amity. Natives proffer souvenirs and bottles of Pepsi to the dehydrated pilgrims, and Jews from Uman sell handicrafts or just stand around and chat. Most of them speak Yiddish. Unlike much of the Soviet Union, Yiddish flourished during the Stalin era in certain Ukrainian towns that were almost wholly resettled with Jews after the war. These post-Bolshevik shtetls became burgeoning bastions of Yiddish culture, producing actors, singers, and essayists during a time of show trials and purges.

On the elevator to my room, a boy of about three points at me and asks his father, "Who's that *goy?*" in Yiddish. *"Dus iz nicht a goy,"* That is not a gentile, he replies, "That's a Jew." The boy looks nonplussed.

The apartment itself is surprisingly comfortable, with all the basic appurtenances of modern living. Matrushka dolls, pear-shaped statuary with the countenances of beaming peasant women, line the bookshelves, along with various medallions and commemorative bottles of vodka.

Yitzy follows me up on the elevator, plops himself on the bed across from mine, and with the alacrity of a camper unzips his valise. Inside is what appears to be every possible kosher product available. There are beer nuts, borscht, canned fruit, ginger ale, matjas herring, and salami. After the proper blessings, we proceed to gorge ourselves. Sharing the room with us is a ba'al teshuvah from Scotland who looks like he hung out with Eric Clapton in the sixties, and his son, a gangly youth with teeth the color of a manila envelope and wispy payess who speaks English like an eighty-year-old tailor from the Ukraine.

On the floor below us is a sort of combination PX and mess hall, a large apartment occupied by perhaps ten Hasidim who have commandeered the kitchen. The place has the salty ambiance of a crew's galley. Off-color jokes, mild by secular standards, are tossed back and forth. The dining table is presided over by a seventy-year-old from Williamsburg who has a nickname for everyone. He soon starts calling me *"Galiczianer,"* because my accent in Yiddish is inherited from my grandmother who came from Galicia in southern Poland. "Hey, Galiczianer, pass me the salt!" he bellows, and everyone chuckles.

Working feverishly at the stove over a huge pot of soup is a wizened Georgian whose eyes intermittently reflect the innocence of Snow White and the slyness of Wile E. Coyote. *"A bi gezunt,"* You should be healthy, he keeps repeating. *"Bis a hundert und twantzig,"* You should live to a hundred and twenty. He hands me a laminated sheet of paper from the "Cleveland Clinic" announcing in English that his granddaughter is in need of surgery for her epilepsy. I don't know whether to believe him or not. Georgians are long known for pulling off elaborate scams, and few here seem to know who he is, but just to be on the safe side I give him ten bucks. He rushes into the living room to pronounce me a tzaddik.

After dinner, we walk to the synagogue for more prayers at Nachman's grave. By now there are about a thousand tightly packed men, and as far as I can tell I'm the only adult without a beard. There are contingents from France, Italy, Belgium, and Brazil. The anthropological subcurrents would fascinate any social scientist. There are born Hasidim, representing various groups, some solely followers of Rebbe Nachman who study at the Bratslav Yeshiva in Jerusalem or Boro Park. They are dressed in standard Hasidic attire, long *kapoteh,* or overcoat, and wide-brimmed hat. But there is also a large contingent of ba'alei teshuvah of various stripes. They wear baseball caps, cowboy hats, and even headgear made of folded newspaper. This is all acceptable, so long as the skull is covered. Many are Sephardim who speak Yiddish haltingly with Israeli accents, or not at all. A few are Yemenites in exotic headgear and desert-inspired robes. Moving through the crowd like an undertow are local Jews with gold teeth and expectant eyes. Some seem fully convinced that these are the only Jews left in the West.

The overseer at the dinner table comes up and hands me a prayer book. "Hey, Galiczianer, start davening," he orders. I immediately almost instinctively turn to the last page to see how long the service is. "A real Galiczianer," he says to me, wagging his finger impishly. "Always looking for the shortcut."

I turn to the beginning of the book and begin to pray. During a lull, I contemplate the eighteenth-century Haidenack massacre, which resulted in the deaths of 20,000 Jews in the Uman area. Then I think about the Klausenberger Rebbe, still alive in Israel, who lost all eleven of his children in the war, then promptly picked himself up and began leading services in DP camps using the beaver hat of a German soldier as a *shtreimel*. I think about my uncle, a fourteen-year-old boy who was forced to dig his own grave and then shot to death. Then I survey the scene and conclude that if I need proof of a divine presence I need look no further, and if the scene around me is insufficient, then nothing will suffice.

There are many paths to belief. The Lubavitchers will posit to secular Jews that if the sun were a few million more miles away, or if the world didn't rotate on its axis, human life would be all but impossible. Their conclusion is that all of this is a miracle, and the existence of a divine presence therefore undeniable. This argument might give the skeptic a nudge away from agnosticism, but it is the seeming inextinguishability of the Jewish people that gives me a firm shove. I only wish Kierkegaard had provided a parachute.

"This is deep stuff," the only other ponytailed attendee tells me. He is studying at a yeshiva in Safad and looks like he made a killing selling firecrackers in the fourth grade. "Rebbe Nachman's teachings and the *Ein Sof*–the infinite–of the Kabbalah correspond to Buddhism. But we are Jews, in Jewish vessels, not Buddhists. We are here to observe the *mitzvot*. God's hand is in everything . . . " His voice fades away into a trippy silence.

Ukrainian militiamen circulate through the crowd, like half-protective, half-tormenting mythological beasts. Most of them have a preponderance of moles on their faces, and they smoke their cigarettes down to infinitesimal stubs. "From the people that brought you John Demjanjuk," a young American pipes up sarcastically, but no one seems to acknowledge the statement. There are no overt manifestations of hostility on the guards' part, nor do the Hasidim seem to pay them much mind.

The local Ukrainians who have given up their apartments are pretty much oblivious to the goings on. From the president on down, it seems as though the Ukrainian hosts have bent over backwards to accommodate the Hasidim. Still we are cautioned not to go into town unaccompanied because of the threats posed by common criminals.

Every so often after a set of prayers, a young Ukrainian steps forward and offers his services in procuring cars or airplanes to travel around the country in order to visit the graves of noted rabbis. This is *Kayver Tzaddikim,* or making pilgrimages to the burial sites of the righteous, a custom that originated at the grave of Rachel in biblical times. Many Hasidim take him up on the offer and climb onto buses taking them to the local airstrip.

A few teenaged Hasidim gather against a wall to drink Pepsi and tell stories. By now I am pretty much accepted as part of the scene, so they don't engage in any self-censorship. One of them, with the face of Pugsley Addams and a totally shaved head, shrewdly eyes two young women. "I tell you," he announces in Yiddish, "in Israel I heard that if you have a *gummi,* a rubber, you can get a girl here. That's all you need." "Only a gummi?" another asks incredulously. "Nothing else," he reiterates, "just a gummi." This is the first time I have heard a Hasid even discreetly talk about illicit sex. His cohorts murmur vague expressions of interest, but the subject is quickly dropped. The story must be apocryphal, I conclude, because there is less fraternizing between Hasidic men and local women here than between two enemies in a POW camp. There isn't even any ogling.

By evening prayers on the day before the beginning of Rosh Hashanah, we have received hundreds of reinforcements. The overseer at dinner who calls me Galicziander has laid out a blanket displaying religious items for sale. Like a street merchant in front of Bloomingdale's, he holds up his wares: *t'fillin, yarmulkes, tallis* pouches, and pictures of various rebbes. Inside the synagogue a tall redhead with the healthy physique of an Israeli paratrooper and the charisma of a rock star is strumming away on his acoustic guitar. A circle of men dance around him as he sings.

Uman, Uman, Rosh Hashanah,
Ashrenu matov helkenu
Shezaheenu Leheeskarev Lerabenu
Uman, Uman, Rosh Hashanah
(We celebrate our good fortune,
which merited our getting closer to our rebbe.)

The balladeer was at one time a popular singer in Israel. In the early seventies, he turned his back on secular Israeli culture and became a penitent. The circle around him gradually turns into a line that snakes its way through the synagogue as the dancing becomes more and more frenzied. It finally breaks up at 2 A.M. All the while some of Rebbe Nachman's more conservative followers, clearly a minority here, eye the proceedings as Archie Bunker would a love-in.

The next morning I take a tour of the town, accompanied by two local teenagers, one of whom is Jewish on his maternal grandmother's side. The streets are riddled with Olympic-sized mud puddles and the stores are generally devoid of anything except for plastic knickknacks. Food lines are omnipresent, and there are virtually no vehicles on the streets. One of the youths takes me to his parents' apartment, where he shows me the religious books he is studying and a primer for learning Yiddish. His parents seem strangely removed. "My parents suffer some sort of spiritual paralysis," he says professorially. They can't bring themselves to emigrate. But he intends to take his new wife to Israel and is convinced that his parents will accompany them.

On the way back to the gathering, we see a Hasid walking by himself surrounded by a group of rough-looking teenagers. "Aren't you afraid?" one of my hosts asks. The Hasid straightens his back, throws out his chest, and runs a hand down his erect torso. "Here you see a Jew," he says of himself. "A proud Jew." He shambles off like a *yiddishe* Buford Pusser.

Back at the enclave a group of French ba'alei teshuvah have organized a helicopter excursion to the graves of Reb Noson in Bratslav, Rebbe Levi Yitzhok in Berdichev, and the Ba'al Shem Tov in Medzeboz. For $50 I'm in, and soon we are ferried by bus to a nearby military field where a swarthy Central Asian, his shirt halfway open and a plethora of gold chains around his neck, stands in front of a BMW and collects money from the pilgrims. There are four choppers, each holding twenty-two people. I am packed into one that is almost exclusively Sephardic and is piloted by a duo of uniformed veterans of the Afghanistan war. The navigational system consists of a worn road map and the door does not close. Soon we are up in the air above towns, factories, and the much-heralded wheat fields that Khruschev said would bring agricultural plenitude to the Soviet Union. After forty-five minutes, we touch down in a field of clover and are greeted by an elderly woman with a row of gold teeth. She turns out to be Jewish. *"Shalom Aleichem a Yid,"* she gushes. "Hello, fellow Jew."

With the chopper blades still turning, she leads us through tall grass to a nearby cemetery that overlooks a river. There, standing next to the grave of Reb Noson, is a rough-hewn Ukrainian chewing sunflower seeds. He offers me a handful. "Don't take anything from him," she implores. "He killed Jews during the war." The Ukrainian seems to have understood what she said, because he has the smarmy look of a boy caught with his hands in the cookie jar.

The Hasidim distribute themselves around Reb Noson's grave and begin to recite the psalms. An old man from town lets me know that there are fifty-two Jews left in Bratslav, then asks me for some money. The prayers continue for at least another half an hour. Then we board the helicopter and take off to a barren military base for refueling.

When we touch down again it is in a meadow dotted with grazing sheep. As the helicopter lands, a group of schoolchildren run up to greet us. They lead us through the crooked lanes of the village, past bleating goats and meandering pigs, until we come to the grave of the Ba'al Shem Tov, the founder of Hasidism. Again there are recitations of psalms for about forty-five minutes. Barefoot children sell apples, and men provide buckets of water to wash them off in. There are three Jews left in Medzeboz, and none of them is present.

Our final stop is Berdichev, which supports a day school operated by the Skverer Hasidim. The Skverers are a community of about 5,000 in Rockland County, north of New York City, who settled there after the war. They also have branches in Montreal and Israel. All four choppers hit the ground at the same time, and the eighty-some Hasidim proceed to file through a woodsy trail leading to the grave of Levi Yitzhok, a rabbinic scholar known for his emphasis on tolerance and ethical behavior.

After another set of prayers and a helicopter ride, we arrive back in Uman, spent with exhaustion. It is a few hours before the Jewish New Year. At the airfield, we board a bus to take us to the synagogue but the driver refuses to move unless we each give him two dollars. A rapid-fire argument ensues, with the Hasidim shouting boisterously at each other and the driver. Eventually, everyone pays up, but not before some ruffians threaten to let all the air out of the tires. This kind of behavior would not be tolerated by the authorities in the vicinity of the synagogue, but here we are on our own. One hooligan who enthusiastically collects the money strenuously makes a point of saying that he is not anti-Semitic. "Business is business," he repeats again and again.

Conversation on the bus soon turns to the peace talks, and Peres is treated as if he were the author of the Protocols of the Elders of Zion. Finally, a prison guard from Bat Yam pipes up. *"Rabotai,"* he says, using the Hebrew word for gentlemen, "I don't know anything about this. I have no television, no radio, no newspaper. Amalek [the primordial enemy of the Jews] was here yesterday, and tomorrow perhaps it will be someone else. Perhaps not. In the meantime, let us hope for peace." He begins to sing and everyone soon joins in.

As I descend from the bus in front of the synagogue an old man grabs me by the arm. "Where are you from?" he asks.

"America."

"Du bist gemallet?"

I look at him quizzically. He's asking me if I am something, and I'm not familiar with the term.

"Du veisst, gemallet." "You know, circumcised," he says, pointing to his crotch and making a cutting motion with his fingers.

"Oh, sure, yeah, I'm gemallet," I reply.

"What about him?" he inquires, pointing to a local Jew who came with us on the excursion. "Is he gemallet?"

"Oh, I'm sure he is."

"I bet he's not. Ask him."

Before I get a chance to formulate a question, the old man interrupts. "I'll ask him," he says, adding with a sly expression that he knows how to inquire.

They commence a conversation in Russian. "He's circumcised," the old man concludes, letting me know that the Ukrainian's father is Jewish, but his mother is not.

"So where does that leave him?" I ask.

"He's genuinely interested. He has to convert."

"The Germans would have considered him a Jew," I speculate, alluding to a number of Ukrainians of mixed parentage put to death.

"To the Germans, he's a Jew. To the Reform, he's a Jew. To me, he's not a Jew," he snaps. He gives my hair a friendly yank. *"Lo yeheyeh kli gever al eesha,* a man's implements shall not be as a woman's," he says, quoting the Bible. "When you are ready, cut your hair." He mutters something and walks away.

By now everyone is preparing for the New Year. People are in their best clothes, strolling around the pavilion. A boy sits down next to me and extends his hand. "You know," he says, "my grandfather was like you. Modern. He came over to the States an anarchist from Russia. But for some reason he sent my father to a yeshiva. Please, don't tell anyone this. If it were known that there was a break in my family's religiousness, it would hurt my chances for a good match. Anyway, what I wanted to tell you is that there are things in the Torah that prove it was not written by a human hand. For example, in the book of Genesis, the word Torah is repeated every fifty characters and the word for God every twenty-six. It's *moyredik*–scary!" He lectures me like a rabbinical Doogie Howser.

Behind us, the buses that brought the Hasidim are lined up like a wagon train. Thousands are pressed together as the prayers begin. The Talmud says that the body of a tzaddik does not disintegrate. Whether or not Rebbe Nachman's body lies intact a few feet from where I'm sitting, I do not know. But if his spirit is sentient, he is no doubt impressed with the size and spirit of the crowd this year. For after two centuries of the bitter triumvirate of Hitler, Stalin, and the Czars, the Hasidim are back in force. And they're here to stay.

CHAPTER 6

The Last of the Just

DOMBROVA, POLAND

There used to be 3 million Jews in Poland, now there are 6,000. Everyone knows that. There used to be 2.7 million religious Jews in Poland, now there are three. Actually there are six, but that includes three professionals brought in from abroad to help the community in a sort of managed demise. The three indigenous ones include a Mr. Shapiro, who walks around Warsaw with a beard and *yarmulke,* and who trains the occasional young person who pops up in Hebrew and text. That's the only one in Poland proper, called Congress Poland before the war. Then there are two in Galicia.

Two religious Jews left in Galicia. The headlines should proclaim it like the discovery of a Japanese soldier still hiding out on Borneo. And they haven't even been to Warsaw. Nor have they been outside Poland. They just did their two-year stint in Auschwitz and returned to their home town, never to leave, surviving postwar pogroms and Communist purges, ignoring entreaties to emigrate to the West, uninterested in travel even to neighboring Czechoslovakia. They are a brother and his sister-in-law, who live together in a small apartment in the little burg of Dombrova about twenty kilometers outside of Tarnow, which used to have a Jewish population of 25,000 and now has officially zero, although there are a few nonreligious Jews scattered here and there like caraway seeds in a well-baked bread.

But I am getting ahead of myself. Krakow is home to eighty official Jews and perhaps a couple hundred assimilationists. Of the eighty, about twenty are regulars at the Remu *shul* on Szeroka in the old Jewish quarter of Kaszimierz. They are not shy about asking for donations. But the head of the community, Czestaw Jakubovitz, is above that. He is a *shtilleh chuchem*, a quiet sage, who carries the names of deceased Krakow families around in his head like a Cray computer. Survivors come from all over the world to visit, and Jakubovitz is more often than not able to identify at least one member of their extended family. Jakubovitz's aunt—who, with her ice blue eyes and fair complexion got through the war on fake papers—is even better at it.

Then there are the gaggle of Jews who work the shul in tag teams, greeting visitors from all lands who have come to see the neighborhood, declared by UNESCO as a world-class cultural entity. There is Yeckel, a burly *shtarker,* or strong man, with thick mutton-chop sideburns, who looks as if he should have a monkey wrench in one hand and a staff in the other. He is the official driver, taking groups out to Auschwitz in his van, and is relatively young, perhaps in his early fifties. "I am Dr. Yeckel and Mr. Hyde," he says. That is the only English he knows. Then there is Tadeusz, who was liberated from Auschwitz when he was six and rejoined with his parents, only to see his mother shot as a suspected Communist by partisans after the war. He has a smile permanently frozen on his face. There is Landauer, who looks like he belongs

on a chaise lounge in Miami Beach, the proprietor of a shirt factory that exports to the Third World, a self-admitted blowhard
who likes nothing more than to sit you down and tell you about
his life. His two boys had the Sony distributorship for a while.

Almost all of them, virtually without exception, are married to
non-Jews. They are all die-hard secularists, who greet visiting Hasidim making *Kayver Tzaddikim,* or visits to the graves of holy
men, with a mixture of brotherly warmth and barely concealed
amusement. But they have the same reaction to all Jews from the
West, who remind them of spoiled children basking in their own
naïveté. They have seen it all and they have no answers, but their
humor is Herculean and their sense of irony is given off like a
force field.

The youngest is Henrik, who is the embodiment of the Eastern
European intellectual in the Trotskyist mold—at least sartorially,
with his oval wire-rimmed glasses and worker's cap. But that's the
only resemblance between him and Trotsky, for he spends his
time leading groups and translating the works of Abraham Joshua
Heschel into Polish, for which there is apparently an audience. He
is the president and one of the few surviving members of the Jewish club located in the old city a few blocks from Kaszimierz, a
roomy space donated by the local government, festooned with
the Israeli and Polish flags and scattered with a few tables and
chairs for lectures. It is here that Landauer gave his lectures in
Yiddish, which deteriorated into repetitive anecdotes of his life. It
is here where wary Jews gathered during the Stalin years and during the equally abysmal period under Gomulka in the late sixties,
when the nation's Jews were asked to kindly vacate the premises.
There is a secretary, who no doubt has the best-filed nails in the
country, and a Jewish woman who hangs around to gossip with
the secretary. Henrik opens the mail and says, "Look at this," in
perfect English, showing me a letter from a woman in Perth who

is seeking information on a long-lost cousin, or something of the sort. He is an endangered species, an independent intellectual, and charmingly aware of it.

Henrik tried Israel for a few years in the seventies, but it just wasn't his cup of tea. The West intimidates him, and he has no desire even to visit America. It's too busy, he says. As for the rest of Europe, he was in Vienna once and that was enough. Yet he is more conversant in Western idiosyncrasies than the most seasoned observer at a university. His mother, who lived with him, died a few months ago, and he is mourning her. He is trying to lose himself by ferrying visiting dignitaries and artists to, among other places, the home of Shmuel Roth and his sister Etka, the last religious Jews in Galicia.

"Have you heard of Roth?" he asks. "You know in Warsaw even the rabbi, Joskovitz, does not know who he is." Joskovitz was sent by Israel a few years ago to preside over the community. When his contract was up he was asked to return home but he stayed, helping with the production and distribution of kosher vodka. There is a challenger to the throne, in Lodz, named Moreino, who returned there some years ago from the West and who steadfastly maintains that it is he, and not Joskovitz, who is the true chief rabbi of Poland. Their feud is all too famous.

"Roth rarely surfaces. Only once a year he comes to Krakow for the *yahrzeit,* or anniversary of the death, of the great rabbi Remu. Other than that he stays in his village. He is like a turtle. Yet he is meticulously observant. Would you like to see him? I took the novelist Aharon Appelfeld out there last week. He loves visitors."

"Sure."

"Then we must hire a car."

Later that afternoon there is a funeral. It is for one of the official members of the community, so everyone would be expected to show up. He was well-liked, a genial old man in his late eighties. But his daughter has gotten into a screaming match with community chief Jakubovitz and has for some reason threatened to kill him. Why on earth she would do that nobody can understand, because Jakubovitz is the embodiment of mellowness. But the net result is that everyone avoids the funeral like the plague and the burial consists of me, Henrik, six Polish pallbearers in navy suits, and a Jew visiting from Australia. There is also the daughter who is muttering under her breath like Muttley, the dog in the cartoons. As she leaves she yells at the cemetery custodian, a world-class lush much loved by the community, with veins crossing his nose like a rural map of Poland. She is all alone in the world and trudges off from the graveyard down a side street. A few weeks later, I find out she has been institutionalized. One has to conclude that there is nothing sadder than a Jewish funeral in Poland, with the possible exception of a mental hospital there.

Henrik pulls on his chin beard. "Let's see, it will cost $100 to have a cab take us to Dombrova. He can wait and bring us back." We go to the center of the town. A cabbie with a cigarette dangling from his lower lip jumps at the chance to drive us there. On the way out we stop in Tarnow, a typically gray Polish city with a huge monument to the Jews and the only Gypsy restaurant in Poland. The monument consists of a soaring segment of the prewar synagogue, the part that housed the ark. It is brick and seems about three stories high. It was preserved by the Lauder foundation and sits in the courtyard of a housing project. Across the street is the Gypsy restaurant. Inside a group of Gypsies sit at a table and welcome us warmly. Their style of dress is dapper and they have a surfeit of gold teeth. It is the off-hours. Yes, they say, they were butchered like the Jews. Yes, they were killed by trigger-happy Romanians. Yes, they were hounded by the Communists. They feel a certain affinity with the Jews, and understandably so.

Our cabbie is getting an education. He has the earnest look of a Horatio Alger protagonist. Had he grown up in the States, I could easily see him as a boy hawking *Boy's Life* on his ten-speed. We continue on to Dombrova down country lanes and rutted roads, past cottages with well-tended gardens and rusty road signs, and into a town consisting of a few buildings and a square with paths crisscrossing it. Our driver asks a local cabbie asleep at the wheel where the Jew Roth lives. The cabbie points to a stucco structure a few blocks away near a grocery store. We drive over there and ring the bell. There is no answer. We ring it again and wait. Finally, a pedestrian asks us who we are looking for. He is a gaunt man in his late middle age and obviously drunk.

"Roth? You're looking for Roth? My favorite Jew? I love Samek [apparently his Polish name]. Hey," he begins to pound on a ground floor window, "Samek, open up! Don't be afraid." Soon a bulky figure in a gray cap and pitch-black sunglasses appears. He has a shuffling gait. It's the shuffle of someone who gleefully goes to work in the morning, a survivor, a stoic. With his dark glasses and cane, he looks like a drawing of a mole in a children's book.

Our Polish interlocutor lunges at him and plants a kiss firmly on his cheek. Roth slaps him on the back and smiles. He is a glad-hander. Suddenly, I realize that this must be the secret to his survival. His sister-in-law, Etka, appears at the door. She looks like a handmaiden to Emma Goldman: strong, self-reliant, with wire rims planted firmly half way down her beak.

"*Vus iz?* What's going on?" she asks in Yiddish. She is curious but not alarmed. The drunk gives a courtly bow. "Paneey Roth," Madame Roth, he says in Polish and utters some formal compliment that Henrik halfway translates as comparing her to some sort of flower. She lets loose with air like a deflating tire and waves her hand semi-disgustedly.

Roth lifts up his glasses and squints. It's Henrik, he realizes, and ushers us in. The apartment is like an exhibit at the Smithsonian: an absolutely pristine relic of a bygone era, right down to the huge radio set with place names such as Herzegovina on it. The stove is for coal, and next to it sits a bucket with black chunks in it. The door has more locks on it than the typical New York apartment. There are chains, keyholes, and a metal rod bolstering the door from the floor. "The *ganverai,* the theft here is terrible," she says by introduction. "Hooligans." She mutters, showing off a new chain lock just added to the collection today. "And it's only been since the Communists fell." She is the archetypical *yideneh,* an iron-willed Jewess, the kind who drained the swamps in Galilee or led a group of young Socialists to settle in the Negev, but she is rigidly Orthodox. Her head is covered with a scarf, and what's underneath may not be her hair at all. Her arms are covered to the wrist.

The first thing Roth does is offer our cabbie a drink. He puts his hand on his shoulder and says something to him in Polish with the bluster of Tip O'Neill. A good bloke, Roth seems to be saying. Roth dutifully translates everything for him. Then he turns to us. "Henrik, who did you bring today? A *yid?* A *goy?* A man?" He looks at my hair. "A woman?"

It takes me a while to remember that this is the deepest Galicia, once so thick with Jews they covered the land like locusts. If Poland were Africa, this would have been the Congo. And here they sit, the only Jews in a fifty-mile radius. Actually, there is another one in town, I learn, a lawyer who is assimilated and has absolutely nothing to do with them.

"What do you want?" Etka asks in a hospitable tone.

"I wanted to meet the only two religious Jews in Galicia."

Shmuel licks his lips in anticipation. Well, you've come to the right place, he seems to be saying. I can see he is about to make a presentation. "Religious we certainly are." He begins to enumerate. "We are *shomer Shabbos*–we keep the Sabbath. We eat only kosher food. *Glatt* kosher. We eat only *Cholov Yisroel* [dairy products milked and processed solely under the supervision of an Orthodox Jew]. I never take off my cap.

"The food we get from Reichberg and the Hasidim who visit with him. You know Reichberg." Mendel Reichberg operates a large travel agency on 13th Avenue in Boro Park that specializes in taking Orthodox Jews to burial sites of *tzaddikim*. It is a no-frills operation with rumpled carpets and metal desks and Hasidic travel agents yelling into the phone. Reichberg often stops in Dombrova when he is in Poland and brings Roth an ample supply of meat.

For years the Roths' sole contact with the outside world were the occasional visits of Hasidim tracking down the graves of ancestors or great rebbes. Now, as they are more able to afford such luxury, they come with increasing frequency, spending the Sabbath with the Roths, singing *zmiros* and eating cholent, visiting the cemetery while the locals, particularly those too young to remember, look upon them as anthropological aberrations.

Aside from the radio and stove, the apartment holds a few stained *teppelach*, pans, a couple of well-thumbed prayer books, and a bed with a gray comforter. There is a second bedroom and a small guest room. Most of the bare-bones furniture is covered by strategically placed lace doilies.

"Well, how do you like my *shtieb*, my pad?" Shmuel asks. By now our cab driver, grimy John Deere cap tilted to the back of his head like some farmer figuring the price of a bushel of wheat, has either lapsed into psychosis or is ready to convert. He looks thoroughly disoriented. "Give him another schnapps," Roth says to his sister-in-law. It is a *mitzvah* for a man to marry his brother's widow, but I am not quite sure if they are married.

"Sure I keep the Sabbath," he repeats. "We've had the same Shabbos goy for twenty years." A Shabbos goy does all the chores for a Jew that are forbidden on the Sabbath.

"Eat some *chaskes*," his sister-in-law says, laying down a plate of delightfully light egg-white cookies on the table. She proceeds to tell me the ingredients.

"What's your name?" Roth asks.

"Chaim," I say, giving him my Hebrew name.

"Oy Chaimel, Chaimel," he says affectionately, taking my face in both hands. "You tell the people in America that the Roths are doing just fine, that it's possible to be *frum*–religious–anywhere."

I ask him how often he leaves the town. Just as I expected, he says once a year, to go to the *yahrzeit* of the Remu in Krakow. "Where do you stay there?" I ask. He doesn't stay anywhere, he replies, he just hires a car, drives into town, goes to the shul, prays, and goes back home. "Hey, you want to see the shul in my home?" he asks. He looks over at the cab driver, who now resembles an exhibit at Madame Tussaud's. He is almost totally catatonic. Occasionally a stunned expression crosses his face, as if he is going through a particularly hair-raising turn on the Matterhorn.

"A *voiler yat*, a good boy," Roth pronounces, as Etka plies the youth with more cookies.

Roth leads me into the sanctuary adjacent to their apartment. It was constructed by his brother over twenty years ago. On the wall is a *trompe l'oeil* mural that resembles an unfurled banner with the words *Boe'ey v'shalom ateret ba'alah, gam besimcho....* This is the last line of Lecha Dodi, the hymn welcoming the Sabbath, when congregants turn to the door to greet its arrival.

Inside the ark is a *sefer Torah*, a Torah scroll salvaged after the war. Roth's personal *minhag*, or custom, is to light thirteen candles at the advent of Sabbath. Why, he doesn't know; it was started by his brother. "Shabbos is coming in a few hours. Why didn't you come earlier so we could talk more? Soon you'll have to leave so you'll be in Krakow by sunset." If I am willing to go the distance, he adds, he'll let me stay here. I am more than willing, but Henrik is starting to look restless. I picture them on a rainy Shabbos afternoon staring out the window. The net effect of this is either the straitjacket or samadhi, depending on the individual. For me it would be Chinese water torture. Even your average Hasid would go bonkers here after two weeks. But Roth is reassuringly normal.

"Look, before you go I want to take you to the cemetery." He throws on a coat. A bitter winter rain is beginning to fall. "I'll show you the monument, then *fuhr gezunteheit*, get out of here." He straightens his *tzitzis*. "Come next time in the middle of the week. We have beds for you." We walk outside. "Listen, you're not going to make fun of me?" he says. *"Hoizek machers* are *ba'alei koyzeh—*fun-pokers are masters of deceit."

He gladhands his way through the town. Pan Roth, how are you today, the townsfolk mutter with an obsequious tilt of the head. He smiles back like a South Side alderman. We pass the main synagogue, a large, hulking structure that held services until the last Jews in the area left twenty years ago. The cabdriver trudges dutifully along behind us, with Henrik holding up the middle. We come to the graveyard at the windswept edge of town. Shrubs grow between the stones. At the center is a monument, also constructed by the Lauder foundation, to the several hundred Jews taken there in the middle of the night and shot point-blank by the Germans. They were put in hammerlocks and yanked out of bed, Roth explains, then dragged down to the local cemetery for a mass execution. It was gruesomely efficient. The monument is made from gravel derived from ground-up stone of old grave markers that were destroyed during the war. Some of the bigger ones were salvaged from a wall in front of a local school when a Polish teacher noticed Hebrew lettering on them. They dot the graveyard like ancient Greek ruins. Roth stands there like a fireplug amidst all this jetsam of a previous era, unconcerned about the weather. He has done this so many times he can do it in his sleep.

Suddenly, a question erupts out of me like a geyser. It is the most obvious of questions, the most stupid of questions, and yet the most unavoidable of questions. "Why did it happen?" I ask. I expect a feral response or none at all.

"Look," he says, "I am a *pusheter yid,* a simple Jew, an *am ha'aretz,* uneducated. How can I answer such a question?" Then he jabs me in the sternum like a Hollywood agent. "It's because the Jews drove on Shabbos, because they didn't keep the *mitzvot.* That's the reason." He backs off. "But don't ask me such questions. Ask me something simple, like what's for dinner."

Back at his home, Roth elaborates. He rolls up his sleeve to show me his tattoo. One reason he believes in God is because a guard at Auschwitz let him meet with his brother, whom he hadn't seen for four years. For this transgression he could have been shot. Instead they both got out alive.

"And I believe because a Polish woman took me in and fed me for twenty-eight months," Etka adds. Suddenly I am overcome by a strange melange of weakness and guilt. Superimposed on this like a thin film on the surface of cholent is a gnawing sense of self-pity. This soon passes. To paraphrase Mick Jagger, living in this town you must be tough tough tough tough tough. The Roths are more than tough. They are the human embodiments of beef jerky.

In the cab I realize that the ostensibly simpleminded cabdriver has had virtually the same thoughts as I.

That night, in a dismal neighborhood a few kilometers from the old city, there is a poetry reading in the building that once housed the pharmacy in the Krakow ghetto. Its proprietor committed numerous heroic acts. The building has been converted to a museum. Sitting next to me is a stocky geologist whose Polish Catholic father was incarcerated in Auschwitz for reasons he's unaware of. Across the aisle, smiling and chatting amiably with an older woman, is Mr. Reiner, who passed me earlier in the day and told me to get a haircut. Reiner was shot in the head at Plaszow, the camp made famous by *Schindler's List*, and nursed himself back to health in the barracks. His wife is a Schindler *jüde*, and his son a professional violinist and Jehovah's Witness. Inside display cases are pictures of the Plaszow concentration camp and its director, Amon Goeth. One shows him just before he is about to be executed, after being found guilty by a postwar tribunal. His face is locked in an expression of unexpurgated terror.

Henrik does not like to plumb the depths. There is too much depth to be plumbed. But he momentarily waxes philosophical. A curious case, Roth, he says. A total mystery. And the mysteriousness is in his simplicity, not his complexity. Staying in Poland is difficult enough. Staying religious in a small town in Poland is a singular achievement. And faith by definition is simple, he adds. One either has it or one doesn't.

Or one is torn between the two positions, like a rider trying to straddle two horses and barely hanging on to either one of them.

CHAPTER 7

Deadheads and Diamond Cutters

ANTWERP, BELGIUM

Strolling across the platform at the train station in Copenhagen is a family of impeccably dressed Hasidim on their way to Antwerp, my destination as well. Seeing them, I feel like I've come across Bigfoot because finding a Hasidic family in Denmark is about as easy as finding a group of Tutsi in Manhattan. There are perhaps twenty Hasidic families in the entire country.

The father of the family could pass as an English banker, with his blue Borsalino perched precariously on his head, and a well-groomed goatee that puts him sartorially to the left of most Hasidim but to the right of the average clean-shaven modern Orthodox. His wife is done up like a fin-de-siècle noblewoman, and the children are dressed like John John and Caroline in the Rose Garden.

I trail them onto the train like a secret service agent and take the compartment adjacent to theirs. Within minutes, I am exchanging *bon mots* with the children in Yiddish.

As we converse, the father looks nonchalantly over his shoulders while he arranges his bags on the overhead rack, and asks if he can share my compartment with me. It seems as though a strange woman has reserved a space in his, he explains. Even though his wife and children are in there, he is forbidden by *yichud,* the rules of modesty, to be in close proximity to a stranger of the opposite sex for any lengthy period of time. I gladly offer him the vacant bunk across from mine. Soon the train is rolling into the night and we are engaged in vigorous conversation.

His name is Chaim, and he is a spry man in his late twenties with a penchant for the Queen's English and a hearty laugh. He was born and raised in Sweden by a nonreligious family, he tells me. His father, who was born in Poland, escaped occupied Norway during the war and made his way through the forests to Sweden, where he later met and married Chaim's mother, a native Swede.

The story of his father's surreptitious entry into Sweden prompts him into telling the story of the Jews of Norway, about half of whom survived by hiding, while the other half were tricked into attending a meeting organized by the Gestapo that culminated in their being rounded up and put on a transport to Auschwitz. These Jews were not religious, but were highly assimilated into Norwegian culture. In effect, one day they were sitting in their homes eating the smelly delicacy lutefisk, and the next day they found themselves in a concentration camp.

Of the 750 sent to the camp, twelve survived. Of the twelve, two are still alive. Chaim knows both of them. One refuses to relate his experiences, and the other wrote a book. Chaim maintains that it is the hand of God that saved these two. Upon hearing this, I cannot resist asking him if God sent the 750 there and saved the twelve, or if the Germans sent them there and God saved the twelve. I picture a huge celestial hand scooping up the twelve he knows like a clump of sod, while the other 738 are left languishing in their barracks. His answer to my question is succinct: Who knows why any were sent and any were saved, he says. *"A mensch tracht und Gott lacht.* Man tries to fathom the unfathomable and God has a good laugh." No use trying to figure it out. It was *beshert,* fate.

He makes his living in a most unusual manner. He just completed a book on rural eccentrics living in western Sweden who refuse to accept the appurtenances of modern life. It is a big coffee-table book, which he laid out on his Macintosh in Antwerp and sells to bookstores throughout Sweden. This takes him to remote areas. One time a big fat accordion player waddled up to him at a rural social hall and announced that his mother was Jewish. She had settled there after the war. On another occasion he came across an Israeli-owned pizza parlor at an obscure junction. When he walked in, he says, the owner almost fell in his sauce. Generally, though, the Swedes don't give him a second glance.

His book on eccentrics is just one of a series of folkloric tomes he has written, including a collection of Icelandic legends of Swedish settlers several hundred years ago. The latest book sells for $66. Perhaps this explains his prosperous appearance.

After studying at a *yeshiva* in Jerusalem, he concluded that if he wanted to live in Europe, Antwerp was the only place to be. Today his children attend the Vishnitzer day school in Antwerp, and he is a member of the Vishnitzer congregation there.

We both fall asleep. At about six o'clock in the morning, he wakes up with a start. "My wallet is missing," he says. Methodically, he begins to search through his pockets. I feel under his bunk and discover his wallet, which he opens to find all his money gone. "How much was stolen?" I ask. "Three or four thousand kroner," he replies with relative equanimity, "about $400 or $500."

I can't help myself. "If you didn't practice yichud," I say, "you wouldn't be here and your money wouldn't have gotten stolen."

He dismisses my assertion with a wave of the hand. It was beshert, he says.

As we get off the train in Antwerp, Chaim and I exchange addresses. We plan to meet again.

Antwerp, situated in the most industrialized area of Europe, is home to its largest Hasidic community. About 20,000 Jews live here, the majority of them Orthodox. Before the war, there were 50,000 Jews. About half of them survived by fleeing to France or Switzerland; the others retreated to a section of Belgium that the Germans were unable to capture in World War I because of its iciness. The Germans succeeded on the second go-round. After the war, Antwerp was a way station for displaced Jews on their way to America. Many of the Hasidim who were versed in the diamond trade stayed. They were from Hungary, Poland, Romania, and other countries.

Jewish diamond merchants have been in Antwerp and other Flemish regions since they brought their skills with them from Spain and Portugal after the Inquisition. Today the cutting trade in Antwerp is in decline—it's being done much more cheaply in India or other parts of the world—but buying and selling is still huge.

Hasidim dominate the diamond business in Antwerp, with Belzers, Vishnitzers, and Satmar ascendant. There is also a smattering of Lubavitchers as well as other groups. Everyone gets along, and the little tension that exists is not between the Satmar and Lubavitchers, but between the Satmar and Belzers, who don't see eye to eye on the issue of Israel. There are three community centers: Shomrei Hadass, Machzikei Hadass, and the Portuguese synagogue for the Sephardim. All three are religious.

On a corner across the street from the train station, I collar a beefy modern Orthodox businessman and ask him directions to Reb Yankel's. Reb Yankel is famous throughout the Hasidic world as a *tzaddik*. He arrived in Antwerp after the war and is the only

Hasidic rebbe in the city. His followers have no name and he attracts Hasidim from various groups. People come from all over to get his blessing—it is not uncommon for an infertile couple to fly in from New York for the weekend. At his *beit midrash,* a sort of cross between a study hall, synagogue, and crash pad, visitors are constantly stopping in to see him and have a quick read in a liturgical text.

The streets of the Jewish quarter in downtown Antwerp are cobblestoned and dotted with gold and diamond shops. This is the Hasidic last stand on the continent, a circling of the wagons after the rout. Jews rush up and down the street with bulging briefcases, some chained to their wrists. About three-quarters are bearded Hasidim, the remainder clean-shaven modern Orthodox with caps on their heads. Yiddish is absolutely, unequivocally, the dominant language. A few words of English—"but," "okay," and the like—are occasionally heard, but the indigenous Flemish is virtually nonexistent. Israeli Sephardim speak to each other in Hebrew, but even they seem to know at least some Yiddish. Not knowing Yiddish here is like being a surfer and not knowing the meaning of "tubular." In business one might survive without it; but in the communal life, it is a severe, debilitating handicap.

I enter Reb Yankel's and am greeted with the usual *ballagan,* something less than squalor but something more than a mess. Coats are piled haphazardly in a corner, and several women methodically stir soup in chipped enamel pots, while others seem to be preparing kishka, the skin of cow gut stuffed with flour and spices. Inside the main study hall, a group of men are arrayed around a table like Dutch Masters on a cigar box. One of them is enormously fat, with straight gray *payess,* pale blue eyes, and a mellow expression on his face.

"Is this Reb Yankel's beit midrash?" I ask, knowing full well that it is. The fat one extends his hands. "You've come to the right place." He introduces himself as Moyshe Aaron Reich, son-in-law of the venerable Reb Yankel, who has been feeling very weak of late. Reb Yankel is holed up in his apartment next door, and only a select few have seen him the past few weeks.

Moyshe Aaron invites me to have a look around. I climb the stairs and enter his apartment. The doors are open. Fish languidly swim around in a huge aquarium tank, and a variety of food is laid out on the kitchen counter. The two people there seem oblivious to my presence. "Help yourself to the food," one of them finally says. It does not take long to realize that there is not a scintilla of paranoia here. Here I am, a total stranger wandering around Moyshe Aaron's private digs, and no one gives me so much as a glance. The level of trust is Olympian.

I wander back downstairs to the book-lined prayer room. Moyshe Aaron is talking on a cellular phone, and a New Yorker on a European business foray, with symmetrically dangling red payess and a chastened expression on his face, introduces himself. Before long he launches into his tale of woe. He had a net worth of $12 million, with $60 million in real estate assets, when a business associate accused him of fraud and launched massive litigation against him, forcing him into insolvency. Bankruptcy is no alternative, because the creditor claims fraud and that would not be excused in a bankruptcy court. The creditor is an Orthodox Jew—a bloodsucker, he adds.

After concluding his story, he looks at me with the lugubriousness of a bloodhound. Flats in Tribeca he'd owned, even apartment buildings in the Bronx. "You know how I'd keep the drug pushers out? When I'd go to collect rent, I'd buy a few joints and pass them out to the guys in the street. I'd even pretend to smoke one myself." He sucks on an invisible cigarette. "I'd pin my payess up under my hat and buy the guys a few beers. Once I caught them dealing drugs on the roof of one of my buildings. I asked them to leave, to take it somewhere else. Simple, nothing emotional, and they did."

Listening to all of this is a tall, thin Hasid with longish red hair who turns out to be a *ba'al teshuvah* originally from Vancouver. He went through the Chicago Democratic Convention riots and was a voting rights organizer in the South, as well as a VISTA worker in fulfillment of his conscientious objector status. Moyshe Aaron seems to sense that we're kindred spirits. "Yossele," he instructs him, using the Yiddish diminutive of Joseph, "take care of him. See to it that he doesn't stay in a hotel. Feed him." Yossele, or Yossi, as he calls himself, seems only too happy to oblige, and instantly launches into a Neal Cassidy–like rap. He knew Abbie Hoffman, he knew Jerry Rubin, he got hurt at the Democratic Convention, he tells me, twisting his payess.

"This place," he says, referring to Reb Yankel's, "is like you took two hits of the sweetest acid and came on in the middle of a Grateful Dead concert. It's like Woodstock in the sixties, but without the sixties and without Woodstock. If you'd walk in here tripping, you'd appreciate the altered state of reality. Listen, let's say you swallowed two drops of liquid acid, dozed off, and woke up. Then you'd find yourself here like two hundred years ago.

"This is a socialistic Utopia," he continues. "Sure we're all capitalists, but I mean the social security network—it's in the blood. You can eat here, you can sleep here, you can hang out here, and not pay a penny. When I hurt my knee last year, I didn't have a minute to myself for two weeks. I was laid up and people came to visit day and night. They brought food, they brought money. I'm talking complete strangers. It's mystical. God forbid a guy falls down and slips on a puddle of grease—it's all over the place, man. You better not be Leticia Baldridge to hang out here. Have you ever seen Hasidim eat, at least in this place? One guy asked for a fork, we didn't have any. Anyway, God forbid someone slips on a puddle of grease. So he slips and breaks a leg, and he's not Belgian. I mean, he's not covered by social security. Everyone pitches in, man. It's totally spontaneous.

"The proportion of good people here is enormous." Yossi continues without stopping for air. "There are bad people but not nearly as many. And I mean *good.* It's developed over generations. A child is brought up to see things in a certain way. It's like the Bolsheviks wanted a Hasidic society without the ritualistic parts. Most of them were Jews, you know. But you can't have one without the other.

"You know, there was a macrobiotic group here, but it sort of folded. Anyway, you have to be careful what you eat and drink. This is the mouth of the Schelde. All the *schmutz* [dirt] of Europe flows here."

He lets me know in no uncertain terms that he hasn't smoked pot in ten years, but he's searching for a theological justification for it, and if he ever finds one he'll go back to it. Until then, "*Has V'sholom,* God forbid, I should so much as even look at a reefer!

"Have you ever gotten high? Had an altered state of consciousness? Read *The Lord of the Rings?* Then you'd appreciate it here. Once I wandered up to Moyshe Aaron's and there was a little old lady on the couch. From America. She wasn't even religious, man. She got tired of her hotel and someone sent her here. She spontaneously was invited to sleep on the couch.

"Just go back up there and open Moyshe Aaron's fridge. Packages of smoked salmon fall out. Don't eat salt or meat cooked on aluminum. It leads to Alzheimer's. I heard it on the BBC.

"Questions people ask–like does God exist and if so, so what–make no difference here. I mean these are perfectly normal, modern questions. Only a Jew can understand that God's will and our free will work hand in hand. It would drive other people crazy. It's like a Möbius strip, it's in and out, up and down, together. It's yin-yang, but more than that. Everything in Judaism is expressed in a paradoxical form, two contradictory elements both presented as being true. Judaism presents free will, that a person controls how he or she acts–not dominated by chromosomes or experiences. It influences you but you can overcome it. But simultaneously

Judaism teaches you that not a leaf falls without God's control. How can we understand this? We can't. Because we're inside the creation. Like a Möbius strip, it's both inside and outside–they're one and the same. This confounds the Western Aristotelian mind.

"It's like physics has proven: Light is both a wave and a particle. How can it be both? Before you didn't know this. In Judaism it's the same contradiction and we live with it.

"My hair was as long as yours. Longer. I cut it. I was at a Grateful Dead concert in Switzerland twenty years ago. I got separated from my group and lost my passport. I had to go to Berne to get a new one." Yossi's narrative becomes somewhat murky at this point, but somewhere along the way, he ended up in Antwerp.

"One day, two or three years ago, I came here to the beit midrash and a guy was cussing out Moyshe Aaron in Hebrew, an Israeli. I asked him, 'Why are you screaming at Moyshe Aaron? He is generous, he gives everything out to everyone; people work, they say prayers, have lots of kids, pay *schnorrers*.' There's a big panhandling scene here, man. I once found a schnorrer banging on a window at 1:00 A.M. They come at all hours. It's famous here, the generosity. So why is the guy screaming at Moyshe Aaron in Hebrew? And Moyshe Aaron does everything. He cleans up, picks up for people."

"So why was he screaming at him?" I ask.

"I don't know. We just took him outside. No yelling, no screaming, no nothing. And he left."

A burly mountain of a man marches up to us and begins to listen intently. "This is Shimon Meyer Goldschmidt," Yossele informs me. "He's in Neturei Karta. Do you know what Neturei Karta is?" I nod my head affirmatively. Neturei Karta is the most extreme anti-Zionist wing of the Satmar Hasidim, none of whom are exactly Golda Meir.

"World Jewry would be much safer without Israel," Shimon Meyer says in his deep English accent, sounding a lot like Alfred

Hitchcock introducing a commercial. A greengrocer who owns a shop adjacent to the beit midrash, he makes no attempt to hide his views, even to those much less so predisposed. He rails against Israel. "The State should be dismantled and the Jews there would be much better off under U.N. protection. Lousy Israel," he intones, seemingly for my benefit, but Yossele assures me that he is not putting on an act.

"If I ever set foot in Israel, my father, Leibl, would drop. He is more of a fanatic than I. When I was a mere seven, our neighbor in London, Yisroel Goldstein, came by collecting for the Jewish National Fund to plant trees in Israel. I gave him a farthing. Do you know how little a farthing is?" He draws the word farthing out like taffy. "You know what my father did? He asked who came to the door and I told him what I did. He said, 'You get that money back—I don't care how little it is—or you don't come back in the house!' I went running to my uncle, who pleaded with my father. My father refused to listen. So I went to Yisroel Goldstein and got the farthing back from him. The next day all London is saying Leibl Goldschmidt is a fanatic."

Like a veteran of civil rights marches, Shimon Meyer recalls the anti-Israel demonstrations he participated in. The biggest was the 30,000 at the United Nations protesting the beating of the Toldos Aharon Yeshiva students by the Israeli police. Toldos Aharon is part of Neturei Karta. "What did they beat them for?" I ask.

"They burned pornographic bus stops that showed scantily clad women in advertisements. They gave the police plenty of warning to take them down."

"Shimon Meyer doesn't sell fruits or vegetables from Israel," Yossele informs me. "No produce from Israel," Shimon Meyer concurs. "I do not support Israel and do not want Israel to exist." He proclaims this in the statesman-like cadence of Abba Eban. "But 99 percent of the Hasidim here are really pro-Zionist. Closet Zionists. I get into arguments with them all the time."

"What about allegations that Neturei Karta advised the Palestinians at the peace talks?" I ask.

"Lies. Perfidy. By the way, have you read *Perfidy,* by Ben Hecht? Come to my shop and I'll give it to you. No, we did not advise anyone. Do you know the word *shadchen?*"

"Yes, it's a matchmaker," I answer.

"Well, you know shadchen is spelled *shin, daled, kof,* and *nun.* Shin is for *sheker,* or lies, which matchmakers tell. Daled is for *davar,* or talk, which they have plenty of. Kof is for *kesef,* or money, and nun is for *noitl,* or to take. Shadchen are liars. A girl is beautiful, they say, but she is actually ugly. A guy is handsome but really, he has a *hoiker,* a hunchback. Those allegations are pure propaganda, shadchen. I," he concludes, "am the only proud anti-Zionist in all of Antwerp. The other two or three are in the closet. One time a woman came into my shop who spoke only Hebrew. I told her to never come back again." Shimon Meyer gives me a broad smile and wanders off.

Yossi turns to me. "Man, you've got to live here for three months, not as an observer but as a participant. Chairman Mao said to taste an apple you have to bite into it. You don't even have to learn, just hang out here, drink coffee, eat rolls, you'll change. You'll put on *t'fillin.* It unites you with the collective and makes you a part of history. Put them on every day for years and then you'll have something to say."

He produces a pair of phylacteries.

"By the way," I ask him, "can women wear these?"

"They can," he assures me. "Rashi's daughter put on t'fillin. But it's discouraged."

"How come?"

"How come?" A slightly abashed smile crosses his face. "I'll tell you how come. For one thing, everyone knows a woman can't control her bodily functions as well as men—especially if she's pregnant. Now, you should beg pardon, but you are supposed to take t'fillin off if you pass gas. A pregnant woman would be constantly taking them off and putting them back on. It would take her forever to get through the prayers."

He slips the pair of t'fillin around my arm and across my forehead. I recite the prayer accompanying the laying of t'fillin, which includes a line that those going to funerals will earn a place in the world to come. "By the way, man, that reminds me. An eighty-year-old man dropped dead this morning and there's a funeral for him this afternoon. You should go to it with me." I readily agree.

After finishing the prayers, he has me take off the t'fillin. As I unwind the leather strap wrapped elaborately around my arm, he continues his soliloquy.

"There is no single group, no single social organization, with our continuity. The same laws apply today as 2,000 years ago, the same holidays, the same customs. No other system has succeeded like this one—not Marx, not Freud, no one."

"What about the Amish?"

"Everything they have is based on our Old Testament. Where would the New Testament be without the Old? It would be like a man walking on sticks instead of legs. And we are the most socially just system."

"How about the Confucians, or the Buddhists?"

"Confucianism is about being socially correct, not just. Buddhism is about compassion. That's great, but it's hardly practical. Does Buddhism go into detail about what happens if a wall shared by two neighbors falls on the property of one of them? Judaism does."

At about two o'clock in the afternoon, we go to the funeral. A white Volvo with the words *"Hevrah Kaddisha,"* or holy fellowship, on the windshield slowly carries the casket up a side street, while several hundred men accompany it on foot. At the end of the block, the procession breaks up and the participants each go their own way. But before they do, they take turns washing their hands in pails of water provided by nearby merchants.

"You see that?" Yossi asks. "*This* is community. Where else would a merchant hearing that there is a funeral provide something for the procession?"

The body is to be taken to Israel for burial and will be accompanied by Moyshe Aaron, who intends to make a twenty-four-hour round trip to Jerusalem and return in time for Sabbath. It is preferable for a body to be buried in Israel because at the time of the resurrection, all bodies will have to be buried in Israel in order to be revived. Otherwise, as Yossi puts it, "they will have to *schlepp* to Israel under the ground and a burial in Israel avoids the *schleppernish.*"

Yossi turns to greet someone in Yiddish on the street corner, and they engage in a five-minute conversation. Afterward, he looks at me. "You know when I became religious? It started when I was in Chicago doing my VISTA thing. I discovered Polish sausage. One day I went to get a nice big Chicago Polish sausage and a voice said, 'You're Jewish.' I turned around and no one was there. So I skipped the sausage. Then many years later, I was at Shakespeare & Company in Paris with a friend—I had been living in Brittany in this village—and out of the blue my friend turns to me and says, 'You're Jewish, why don't you act like one?' I went back to Brittany and thought about it for a while. Everyone in the village liked me and I loved everyone. The Bretagnes are not like the French, they're a totally different race. So after thinking about it, I went to Israel. I spent three years there, and when I came back I was religious.

"My first day back in Brittany I was invited to a barbecue. I brought my own kosher chicken and the barbecue was set up in the garage of the house. We were all in the backyard while the food was cooking when I accidentally leaned against a knife that had *foie gras* on it. I went to wash my hands in the kitchen and saw the barbecue on fire with the flames shooting to the ceiling, which was covered with highly flammable insulation. I yelled for help and the group put it out. Two minutes later the whole house would have burned down. When my friend's father, the owner of the house, tried to thank me, I explained to him that it was because I touched the knife that wasn't kosher and went into the kitchen to wash my hands that I saved the house. It took me five times to get it across to him. After that, I realized that following the *mitzvah* of washing after touching unclean food made me save the house. That sealed it. I've been religious ever since."

The next day, Yossi invites me to his home for Sabbath. We meet at Reb Yankel's in the late afternoon and proceed to his flat. It is a comfortable apartment in an old building, and serves as a storage depot for cosmetics he and his wife import from Paris to sell in the community. They have been married for six years and have no children. His wife, Shani, has a degree in history from a French university. She is part Bulgarian and part French and was raised in a nonreligious home.

Tonight is the third night of Hanukkah, so the menorah must be lit. This is no simple procedure. First, Yossi goes to the sink in the kitchen and takes a double-handled cup and pours water over each hand–first the right and then the left–three times. He dries his hands with the meticulousness of a surgeon, wiping each finger thoroughly. Then he returns to the living room and fills the menorah up with oil, after carefully attaching wicks to small metal contraptions that float in the menorah. After this he strikes a match, says a blessing, and lights each wick. He opens a hymnal to the song *Ma'oz Tsur,* which expresses Israel's hope for the reestablishment of the Temple and calls for swift redemption from oppression. It has about twelve verses and he sings each of them slowly, repeating the first one. Then he begins to recite the psalms, including the one for Hanukkah, *Mizmor Shir Hanukkah Habayit.* All this takes about half an hour, after which Shani appears with the food. But instead of eating, it's back to the sink for another ritual wash, to be followed by the lighting of the Sabbath candles and the recitation of the entire evening service. This is followed by the blessing over the wine, a return to the sink, and the blessing over the bread. After this we eat.

Following the meal, my expatriate host breaks into *zmiros,* Sabbath songs, after which he opens a book of Hasidic sayings by Aryeh Kaplan and begins to quote the Seer of Lublin. " 'It is written,' " he reads, " 'behold, let all who are thirsting go to water. The Torah is likened to water. It is also written, is not my work like fire? The Torah is also likened to fire. Likewise, there are two evil inclinations, one heats a person to sin.' It is carnal. 'The other cools him off, making him too lazy to keep the Commandments. Our sages teach us that God said, I have created the Evil Urge, and I have created the Torah as its remedy. Therefore, regarding the Evil Urge that heats a person up, it is written, go to water. Regarding the urge that cools one down, it is written, my word is like fire.' "

We talk for a while longer, and I go into the next room to go to sleep. As I am dozing off, I hear Yossi and Shani laughing gleefully into the night.

The next morning we go to Sabbath services at the beit midrash, where the ailing Reb Yankel is brought in on a wheelchair to say a blessing over the Torah. His congregants eagerly crowd around him, elbowing their way to the front of the sanctuary. *"Mir shtippen zoch,* we're pushing ourselves," someone says. It's a black wave squeezed tighter than the front row at a Guns N Roses concert, swaying in whichever direction the rebbe turns, always seemingly on the verge of falling over like a row of dominoes. When the rebbe leaves, everyone sits down.

Following services, Shimon Meyer takes a seat next to me. "Once I asked the rebbe for a blessing on a trip to London. I went to the airport and realized I had forgotten my passport. The plane was leaving in ten minutes and the airport was exactly a ten-minute trip from my house. I raced home and my wife told me I had put my passport in my *tallis* pouch, which I had with me all along. I raced back and the plane was beginning to go down the runway. But since the rebbe blessed me, I knew I'd get on that plane. I told the attendant I had to get on and she ordered the plane back. This never happens. But because the rebbe blessed me for this particular trip, this is what happened. And when I got on the plane, there was only one seat left. Another time, the rebbe came to the hospital and blessed my wife when she went into labor. He said '*Mazel tov, mazel tov.*' She had twins."

Sitting across from us is a Satmar Hasid who converted to Judaism ten years ago. He has a degree in Romance languages from Budapest University and operates a grocery store in the neighborhood. "Why Satmar?" I ask. "I'm an extreme person," he replies. "It's black or white, all or nothing for me."

Later that evening there is a small feast called *shalosh seudah* in the beit midrash. Situated comfortably in the center of the room is Moyshe Aaron, picking away at a plate full of fish heads with his fingers, as is the custom when eating fish. Yossi hovers over him like a solicitous butler. Suddenly Moyshe Aaron plunges his hand into a fish head and gives a scoop to his disciple, who promptly stuffs it into a baggy with a piece of Moyshe Aaron's challah. A disembodied fish eye is visible through the plastic.

"I take by Moyshe Aaron," Yossi explains. "I hold him in great respect." It is customary for followers to take *sherayim,* or leftovers, from a rebbe's plate.

A man walks by, collecting money for a wedding. He has a small pile of bills. Another man, an Iranian Jew who is visiting from Jerusalem, is collecting for his son, who is recovering from meningitis. He is thirty-five and has nine children. "*Baruch Hashem,* bless the Lord, my son recovered. Now I need $5,000 to pay the doctor."

"Israeli socialized medicine didn't take care of it?"

"It always helps to pay extra," he says, making a gesture of money passing under the table.

Yossi announces that it's time to go home to light the menorah. We make our way to his apartment, and upon arrival he goes to wash his hands. This is not the first time today. He has washed when he woke up, after going to the bathroom, and before and after every meal. In none of these ritual ablutions does he use any soap. He is especially careful when he wakes up to wash each fingertip, which is the repository of bad energy given off by the soul during sleep.

"What does your family think of this?" I ask him. Both of his parents are dead.

"Well, my cousins think it's okay. But my aunt thinks I'm a pain in the ass."

After the meal, Yossi methodically sweeps the table for bread crumbs and carefully deposits them in a Tupperware container. When I ask him the reason for this, he wordlessly pulls out a copy of the *Shulchan Arukh,* which deals with the laws of daily conduct, and opens it to Section 180, the law regarding bread crumbs. It says that it is not permitted to destroy pieces of bread bigger than an olive, because it leads to poverty; but more stringent authorities say it is forbidden to destroy any crumb if all the crumbs on the table are collectively as big as an olive. Obviously, he is erring on the side of stringency.

Not every ritual is law. Some of it is custom. In order to ensure prosperity he rapidly daubs drops of wine on his eyelids, in his pants pockets, and at the nape of his neck. The entire procedure is accomplished with such finesse that his hands seem to be several places at once like a minstrel doing a frenetic spoon dance.

Shani announces that she forgot to *bentsch,* or say grace after the meal. Yossi interrogates her like a district attorney. "Did you eat anything after dessert? Are you hungry?" No on both counts. "Then you bentsch," he says with the authority of Dr. Kildare ordering an autopsy. "You bentsch."

Yossi rises to go to the bathroom. He refuses to talk while he's in there. It's a *makom tumeh,* or impure place, and it's best not to be verbal. However, he has developed a highly variegated system of grunts to get his point across. Some are staccato and some are drawn out; the meaning is in the inflection. This mode of communication extends itself to the period between washing hands and saying the blessing over the bread, when there is supposed to be no speaking. But gesticulations and animal-like noises are not included in this injunction.

Upon Yossi's return, Shani announces that they are expecting a visitor, a friend from Jerusalem who is visiting Antwerp, where he lived for a couple of years. Not long after this, a huge American in a baseball cap with an ample belly and a five-day growth of beard appears in the doorway. He is about twenty-five.

"Stuart, how are you?" Yossi exclaims. Before the visitor can answer, Yossi announces that he'll be with us in a few moments, after he recites the *Tillim,* or psalms.

"Your Tillim bores the hell out of me, and you know it," Stuart snorts. He has the look of a suburban miscreant, the kind who swallows a handful of downers and walks through a plate glass window at McDonald's. As Yossi chants silently, Stuart explains that he ended up in Antwerp after following the Grateful Dead around for a few years and somehow found his way to Reb Yankel's. After studying here, he moved to Israel. Now he lives in the Jewish section of the Old City and has joined Kach, the organization of the late Meir Kahane. At this point, Yossi stops *davening* and looks at Stuart incredulously. Stuart stares back at him like the cat that swallowed the canary.

"It's true, man," he says. We sit in uncomfortable silence. Kahane is hardly a hero with the largely—at least professedly—anti-Zionist Hasidim, although there are supporters here and there.

"There's no such thing as the Palestinians," he announces abruptly. "There are only Arabs." He waits for my reaction. "You know," he says, thrusting his chest out like a rancher surveying his spread, "you look at Jerusalem at sunset, at the panorama, and you know none of it will ever go back to the Arabs."

I have an appointment with Chaim, the Swedish ba'al teshuvah I met on the train, so I excuse myself. Stuart offers to walk me there. A block away we pass his place and he invites me up. We climb a steep set of stairs, at the top of which is a padlocked door. He unlocks it and we enter a room crammed from floor to ceiling with furniture of every description. In the middle is a small mattress wedged between two armoires. Taped to the wall is a picture of the Lubavitcher Rebbe. Stuart lights up a pipe and slips a Frank Zappa tape into his boom box. Soon he is spouting Kahanaisms while we are listening to the Mothers of Invention.

"I've got to get back to Israel, man. This place is bumming me out." Suddenly, he picks up the phone and tells the operator he wants to call Israel. Within seconds he is having a conversation with his roommate. "Listen, man, I want to tell whoever is crashed in my bed to get out by tomorrow night 'cause I'll be there. Yeah, yeah, I know. Hey, what's going on over there? Animal House? What's all the noise? Okay, I'll see you tomorrow, bro. Take care."

He hangs up the phone. "The guys I live with, I turned them all on to Kach and now they're more into it than I am. I come from a liberal background, you know. My parents were both in Mississippi. Yossi doesn't have a monopoly on being a civil rights volunteer." He takes a toke. After a few more minutes listening to the music, I say I have to get going. He gives me a big bear hug.

I walk over to Chaim's flat at the edge of the Jewish section. By now it is pitch black and it has begun to drizzle. Every other car seems to be a late-model Mercedes with a Hasid at the wheel. Chaim greets me in the doorway wearing a *shtreimel*. "Every Hasid wears Shabbos garb after Shabbos until going to sleep," he explains.

In the kitchen, his wife serves me tea while he produces one of his books, his latest about the rural eccentrics. It's in Swedish. "Look at this picture." He opens the book. "This fellow practices folk medicine on the people's backs. He's apparently quite good. But he didn't want his picture taken because he was afraid the hospital would feel he's a competitor and would mistreat him if he ever went there." The picture depicts a Swedish peasant with his backside resolutely turned to the camera. Chaim doubles over with laughter.

"And look at this one. This man's shack had so many holes in the floor he covered it with sand and old newspapers. They all refuse social security, you know." He turns the page. "This woman has lived in the same house since 1903, with the same maid since 1924. They fight constantly. And this fellow with the ancient Volvo only uses it to drive in the field to milk the cows. So it has only 4,000 kilometers on it."

Chaim is a Vishnitzer Hasid. The Vishnitzers originated in Romania and have two rebbes, brothers, one in Israel and one in New York. Most of the Vishnitzers in Antwerp pay allegiance to the one in Israel. The Israeli rebbe's daughters married incredibly well. One is married to the grandson of the Satmar Rebbe, one to the son of the Skverer Rebbe, whose Hasidim occupy the town of

New Square to the north of New York, and one to the son of the Belzer Rebbe. It's the matrimonial equivalent of winning the Publisher's Clearinghouse Sweepstakes. This is all the more remarkable in that the Belzer and Satmar Rebbes don't get along at all.

The Vishnitzer Hasidim have a disproportionate number of players in the diamond business. One of them, Yitzhak Kaszirer, if not the wealthiest Jew in Antwerp, is certainly the most benevolent. He has singlehandedly underwritten the cost of the Vishnitzers' beit midrash in Benei Berak, a structure so opulent that even the rebbe had reservations about it. Kaszirer has also donated money for the construction of the Chabad House in Antwerp and other major projects.

Chaim announces that he is leaving tomorrow for London with an Antwerp contingent to visit the Vishnitzer Rebbe, who will be there for a few days. He recommends that I go to the Vishnitzer beit midrash on Monday morning if I want to meet Kaszirer.

The next day I am at Shimon Meyer's market picking up a copy of *Perfidy*, by Ben Hecht. It's a no-holds-barred criticism of the modern Jewish state by a nonreligious Jew. "Please," Shimon Meyer admonishes, "don't call it the Jewish state, call it the Zionist state." He offers up anti-Zionist nostrums while customers come in and out. Then he suddenly remembers that Reb Yankel has announced that he will take visitors today.

"Hurry down the block to the rebbe's house. Ring the doorbell. He's seeing people right now. Give him your Hebrew name and your mother's Hebrew name, not your father's." Although a Jew is announced by his father's name when he is called to the Torah, it is his mother's name that he is identified by on more intimate occasions.

I cross the front of the beit midrash to the rebbe's house. A boy rushes up the steps in front of me and rings the bell. We are let in but suddenly passed up by a flood of jostling young men. There is a line in front of the rebbe's study and we wait patiently. Then we are let in one by one, in assembly-line fashion. At the center of the room is Reb Yankel, slouched in his wheelchair, like Jean Paul Getty after a stroke. I am led to his table.

"*Vuz iz dein nummeh?* What's your name?" the rebbe's assistant, or *gabbai,* asks.

"Chaim Meyer ben Beileh."

"Chaim Meyer ben Beileh," he repeats in the rebbe's ear. The rebbe shows no sign of cognizance.

"Live and be well," the assistant tells me, and hands me a dozen or so garlic cloves. Outside the room everyone is standing around with garlic cupped in their hands. I eye my treasure trove and wonder what to do with it. "You should eat the garlic," someone tells me, "because the garlic is sharp when it goes in your mouth, but sweet when it enters the bloodstream. It is a *segulah,* a treasure that brings prosperity."

A bookstore owner invites me over for lunch. His wife has had fifteen children and looks amazingly svelte. A young son about age six stands on a chair and delivers the weekly Torah portion in Yiddish. "Joseph dreamed there were seven fat cows and seven skinny cows. The seven skinny cows ate the seven fat cows but they didn't become fat." He rocks back and forth on his heel like a child evangelist. The performance is mesmerizing.

That evening at the beit midrash there is the menorah lighting ceremony. As the menorah is filled with oil, about a hundred boys gather to watch. A young man of about twenty is invited to light it. Immediately afterward, he is pelted with dozens of towels. The boys flay him exuberantly, striking him repeatedly in the face. He cowers in mock terror and rushes quickly to his seat.

"This is done so he will find a bride this year. We bring up a different eligible young bachelor every night of Hanukkah," someone explains.

Early Monday morning I set out for the beit midrash of the Vishnitzers. Situated on a small side street, it has also been built with Kaszirer's money and is probably the best-appointed prayer hall in Antwerp.

"Is Mr. Kaszirer around?" I ask someone. He points to the podium, where a ruddy-faced man who looks as if he just stepped out of a sauna is putting away his t'fillin. He is impeccably dressed and carries himself regally. I walk up to him and introduce myself, but his wife has just passed away a few weeks ago and he is in no mood to talk. He shuffles me off to his secretary, Fishel Dick, who is standing in the corner. Fishel Dick has the ingratiating face of William Frawley trying to convince Ricky to let him do a vaudeville act at the Copa. "What do you want to know about Kaszirer?" he asks politely. Before I can answer, he says, "Whatever you want to know, I can tell you." He leads me into the breakfast room behind the beit midrash, where a group of men are having coffee, rolls, and cake, compliments of Kaszirer. They are almost without exception all in the diamond trade. They sit around a few long tables, tell jokes, and exchange light gossip while gearing up for a day of work. The atmosphere is very relaxed.

One non–diamond merchant is a young man who spent two years studying in the huge Lakewood Yeshiva in New Jersey. He has just returned from a few weeks in Miami with two of his children. "I was staying in the Fontainebleu, and these American Jews, you can't tell them from *goyim*. I was on the elevator with a group from B'nai Brith with name tags. One was a couple named McCarthy. 'You let goyim on the tour?' I asked someone. 'Sure,' they said. I couldn't believe it." He shakes his head back and forth in apparent amazement.

Another member of the breakfast club is a retiree eager to tell his war story. He is ninety-three. During the war he was sent from Auschwitz to clean up the Warsaw ghetto after the uprising. His best friend was non-Jewish, a Polish professor and an ardent anti-Semite, who said the only good thing the Germans accomplished was to make Poland *Judenrein*–free of the Jews. Anyway, they were friends. The Pole used to needle him: "Where is your God?" he'd ask. "I don't see any God." One day the Pole got the idea to smuggle some contraband out of the ghetto. They almost got caught. The next day the Pole wanted to try it again. My narrator refused but the Pole went ahead anyway. He was caught and shot on the spot. As he lay dying my narrator went up to him and said, "I just saw my God."

Kaszirer started out with nothing, Dick tells me. He became one of the biggest diamond middlemen in the world, buying from the CSO, the London-based marketing arm of DeBeers, and selling to jewelers. A while back he was suspended from the CSO for doing an end run around it by dealing directly with the Russians, so he set up his own diamond-cutting plant in Moscow.

Fishel Dick invites me to the Diamond Exchange. There are four, actually: One sells polished goods, one rough goods, and two are a mixture of both. The exchange I am taken to is called the Diamondkring, a multistoried office building with a restaurant and club and Hasidim rushing in and out. The club is a series of long tables with some merchants eying stones under magnifying lamps while others gather to kibitz in front of chess games or backgammon. There are video terminals giving up-to-date prices of gold, silver, and the currencies. Groups of Orthodox Jews stand around the screens and discuss the markets in Yiddish.

To hear Yiddish spoken in this environment is like seeing a

ghost resurrected. It is at once eerie and heartening, the same feeling I had when a non-Jewish Flemish-speaking waiter took my order in Yiddish earlier in the day. If not for the war, this would no doubt be a scene repeated throughout the continent.

Yiddish and computers are a heady mixture, like some atavistic relic joined to the space age. There was a time, twenty or thirty years ago, when secular Yiddishists were convinced the language was going the way of Welsh or Cornish. They discussed the possibility of setting up an island somewhere as a Yiddish colony, a sort of wildlife preserve for an endangered tongue. That won't be necessary now.

"Five or ten million is not much in this community," Fishel Dick tells me. "Five million is comfortable, ten million is wealthy. But there are many with much more money. Applebaum, Loeb, Glass, Brachfeldt, Plucznik, Wechsler, Spitz, Spiro, Steinmetz." He begins to tick them off. "These are the big names along with Kaszirer. Forty-five years ago they were hungry. Now they have their own jets. They vacation in St. Moritz at the Edelweiss Hotel, where they try to find *shiduchs* for their children."

Although there are ten struggling *melameds,* or schoolteachers, for every affluent diamond merchant, nowhere, he assures me, is there such an immense agglomeration of wealth in such a small community.

My last night in Antwerp is spent in Yossi and Shani's apartment, where a friend comes to visit. She is a gawky divorcee in a knitted scarf, with a head that bobs up and down like Big Bird's and a voice cracking like a pubescent youth's. Fluent in five languages, she grew up in Paris and has been divorced twice, once from a Satmar and once from a Lubavitcher.

"The *get* in Antwerp will cost me 20,000 Belgian francs," she complains. A get is a divorce certificate.

"Why did you get divorced?"

"From my second husband? He was seen running around London in blue jeans, T-shirts, and without a head cover. He could only be doing one thing in that state, and you know what that is." She looks at me with mock severity.

"We're trying to make him into a Hasid." Yossi nods in my direction and winks.

"A person shouldn't be what he doesn't want to be," she retorts. "Either way, he's still a Jew."

"But what kind of Jew? His soul is enshrouded in darkness. He is like a car without an engine. For him, it's all culture. Yiddish—I have no need for Yiddish, for Zionism, for courses in Jewish history. He needs the fear of God!" Yossi rants like an elfin Jimmy Swaggart.

"Forget it. I know the type," she says, appraising me like a sociologist. "He's not there yet, and he may never be. In the meantime, let him enjoy life."

The next day I leave Antwerp, realizing that it is the closest thing in existence to a prewar urbane Jewish community. It is ardently European and takes great pains to set itself apart from its Israeli or American counterparts. Its quintessentially European combination of *panache* and *gemütlichkeit* is unduplicated anywhere else in the Hasidic world. Antwerp summons forth visions of Berlin or Vienna in their Jewish heyday. In this sense it is a unique vestige of a time long since past, something that was fading well before the deluge; but at the same time, it may serve as a blueprint for the Hasidic future, a potentially golden age of harmony and plenitude.

CHAPTER 8

Lake Oybegone

POSTVILLE, IOWA

O odem Horishon hut nicht du gepisht. Adam didn't take a leak here. This is how my grandmother described a place so far off the beaten path that it's practically extraterrestrial. Indeed, if the Diaspora were the solar system, Postville would be Pluto. Yet this town of 1,400 nestled in the rolling hills of northeastern Iowa is teeming with Hasidim who traverse the streets like extras in a *Fiddler on the Roof* production. What brings them here? Money. Lots of it.

In three short years, Lubavitcher entrepreneur Aaron Rubashkin and two of his sons have tapped into the glittering motherlode of the *glatt* kosher market, an industry that is expanding almost exponentially as its traditional customer base continues its demographic explosion and more and more members of the general public become disenchanted with conventional food inspection. This expansion is especially notable given the fact that a pound of glatt kosher ground beef sells for around $4, or twice as much as the nonkosher variety.

Glatt means smooth, which refers to the lungs of the carcass. In order to be glatt, the respiratory organs must be unblemished by any scars or adhesions. It can, however, have these flaws and still remain kosher, so long as they have not produced holes allowing air to pass through. This is determined by a *bodek*, or inspector, who inflates lungs like a bicycle tire and puts water around the scars after peeling off the scabs. If there is any bubbling, the cow is not kosher. If there is no bubbling, the cow is kosher but not glatt. Glatt developed in the last century at the behest of Satmar Hasidim who wanted a higher standard of purity. Glatt is mentioned in the Talmud, but it is considered a sort of ideal rather than the prerequisite that the Hasidim have made it into.

Downtown Postville reflects the ethos of Iowa, a state known for its liberalism on social issues and its succession of Democrats in the Capitol. This is no gun-rack-and-pickup type place like small-town Nebraska or Wyoming to the west; it is under the genteel influence of Wisconsin, just across the Mississippi. At the entrance to Postville stands a billboard proclaiming it to be the boyhood home of Dr. John R. Mott, winner of the 1946 Nobel Peace Prize. The citizenry is mild without being bland, and the main drag unblemished by boarded-up shops or any Wal-Marts lurking in the distance.

Postville is tolerant, but until the Hasidim arrived its tolerance had been largely untested. There are no blacks here, and the Hispanic population is small and largely invisible. As for Jews, open a dictionary to the word *Judenrein* and a picture of this area might as well appear. Even Prairie du Chien, Wisconsin, one of the few regional towns of any size, lists not a single Cohen, Levine, Shapiro, or Kaplan in its phone book. But it is here in tiny Postville that boys with the truncated *payess* of the Lubavitcher movement—

Lubavitcher men generally don't have payess longer than an inch–play tag outdoors, and vigorous arguments in Yiddish can be heard in front of Fat Freddie's Charcoal Grill.

Inside the general store, a young mother helps her son pick out makeup for the upcoming Purim festivities. She is Leah Rubashkin, wife of one of Aaron's sons, Sholom, who came here five years ago from the Lubavitcher stronghold in Crown Heights to revive a shutdown meat-packing plant purchased from the Hygrade Corporation. Sholom and his brother turned it into the single largest glatt operation in America, supplying one-third of the market with beef, chicken, lamb, and veal. Today the Rubashkin company, Agriprocessors, does between $70 million and $80 million a year in sales at a profit margin variously estimated to be between 2 percent and 10 percent.

All this transpired because paterfamilias Aaron saw an inefficiency in the market and exploited it. Until the Rubashkins came along, no glatt operation of any size slaughtered cattle in the farm belt. Moving the live cows to Jewish population centers cost an extra five cents a pound. But by *schechting* here, the Rubashkins are able to pass on the savings to wholesalers. Nor do they pay princely sums to their nonunionized labor force, some of whom have been brought over from Poland and Czechoslovakia. But their presence in Postville is nonetheless appreciated: Before the shutdown the plant employed 70 people, and now it has over 200.

Aaron Rubashkin started out with nothing when he arrived in the United States in 1952, having spent the war years in Uzbekistan, but he wasted no time in building up a major beef and chicken distributorship in New York. Now he is a *geveer*, a pillar of the Lubavitch community and its Chabad outreach organization, occupying a rarefied space alongside such luminaries as David

Mintz, inventor of Tofutti, Yosef Deitsch, a plastics manufacturer, and the Australian mining magnate Joseph Gutnick, who received a blessing for *parnassah,* or livelihood, from the Lubavitcher Rebbe, which was widely interpreted as a buy signal for the stock of his company, Great Central Mines. (This drove the price up threefold in a month and led to calls for an SEC investigation.) Chabad is also supported by such non-Hasidim as Ronald O. Perelman, the head of Revlon, and Edmond Safra, honorary chairman of the Republic Bank. The Rubashkins also own a textile business called Cherry Hill, which has been used as a conduit for political contributions, including a $20,000 donation to a right-to-life candidate in a 1990 New Hampshire congressional campaign.

Aaron is a sturdily built sixty-six-year-old with a perpetually bemused expression on his face. His English is excellent. With his steady gaze and bushy beard, he resembles an Old Testament prophet wandering the streets of Iowa. His home is in Boro Park, but he is visiting Postville for the Purim holiday. He is accompanied by his wife, a tough-talking attractive woman in an elegantly coiffed *sheitl,* or wig, and his grandson, a native Israeli who grew up in Safad, where one of Aaron's sons is the Chabad rabbi. Despite his origins, the grandson is an all-American-looking kid of seventeen with a propensity for consuming inordinate amounts of vodka, a socially sanctioned act this time of year because it is Purim and there is a rabbinic injunction to celebrate *ad lo yada,* or until one does not know the difference between Mordechai, one of the protagonists of the Purim story, and Haman, the villain.

Aaron's two sons, Heshy and Sholom, run the daily affairs of the business. While Aaron appears to be laid-back and contemplative, the sons rush through town like chickens with their heads cut off. This is somewhat appropriate, since the plant decapitates between 12,000 and 15,000 birds a day.

This passion for business has its limits, however. Around the family table or during the Sabbath, shop talk is taboo. Even outside these parameters, it would be unfair to characterize Heshy and his brother as business drones. Like many Lubavitchers, they are the closest thing to being the regular guys of the Hasidic world. They go to G- or PG-rated movies–Heshy in particular does a passable imitation of Steve Martin–although television is still off limits. In a sort of minor milestone in small-town history, Heshy accepted hog farmer Kendrick Groth's invitation to go water-skiing on the Mississippi. Snowmobiles intrigue him. But at the plant's executive offices during the work week, the scene is intense. As guys in red windbreakers with names like Virge and Dale stand around and talk cattle, one brother strong-arms the other into his office and slams the door shut. This is a futile gesture because their ear-piercing arguments can be heard through the paper-thin walls. "I know broilers like the back of my hand," one of them will say. "Well, I know chicken prices like I know the Humash," the other will retort, referring to the Pentateuch, or Five Books of Moses, "and chicken prices are not going anywhere."

All this is conducted in the rapid-fire combination of Yiddish and English that is the hallmark of *yeshiva* studies, except in the yeshiva Hebrew is substituted for English. It is very garbled and purposefully cryptic. Unlike many other Hasidic groups, Lubavitchers will use Hebrew in normal conversation despite the fact that it is the holy tongue. They note that Hebrew was the vernacular of the Jews in ancient times, and claim that Satmar and other Hasidic groups' reluctance to use Hebrew stems from their anti-Zionism and has nothing to do with religion.

In the Postville Citizen's Community Center, whose austere architectural style and Spartan interior reflect the modest civic virtues of sons and daughters of the town's original Northern European immigrants, Leah Rubashkin, dressed as a clown for Purim, lays out plastic forks and knives along with paper plates on long institutional tables. While Hasidim might give an approving nod in the direction of Thanksgiving with a well-prepared turkey, or even blow off a few firecrackers on the Fourth of July, Halloween is strictly *goyim naches,* a diversion for the gentiles. So it is Purim that fulfills the seemingly universal urge to dress up in costume. Although Jewish tradition bans masquerades because they often involve men getting dressed up as women and this violates biblical law, on Purim the breach is allowed.

In the community center kitchen, Rubashkin family factotum Cletus, a non-Jew, koshers the oven with a torch and lays aluminum foil over nonkosher surfaces. Cletus, a ruddy-faced local with an eager-to-please attitude, seems to be everywhere at once. One minute he is in the kitchen, supervising the koshering operation, the next minute he is at the plant, maniacally working the sausage-stuffing machine.

Hasidim shuffle in. There are two brothers of unusually sweet demeanor from Israel, here for a two- or three-month stint to earn some extra money. One tilts his head when spoken to like the dog on the RCA label. Trailing them is a Moroccan Jew, also an Israeli, who has moved here with his wife and children to work for the Rubashkins. He is in black hat and Lubavitcher garb, a mode of dress totally at odds with his Middle Eastern heritage. Aaron Rubashkin arrives with his wife and grandson, and then the Rubashkin brothers appear, talking and gesticulating rapidly to each other. In all, about seventy or eighty Hasidim are present for the festivities.

In a classically Hasidic division of labor, the men sit and chat on one side of the room while the women lay out trays of cold cuts, along with salad and kugel, on the other. The salad consists of cucumber and tomatoes. Hasidim rarely eat leafy greens because they require a painstaking search for nonkosher bugs on each leaf. The cold cuts are everywhere, with oversized trays in evidence at morning services and even in the plant offices. One row of pastrami, one row of corned beef, and one row of smoked turkey: the penultimate Hasidic perk.

Most of the children are clowns, but some are creatively done up as artists or pirates. One toddler is dressed as a ballerina, down to tutu and ballet slippers. His long hair contributes to the image. He will not receive his first haircut until his third birthday. Then, in a ceremony known as the *upsherinish,* he has his locks shorn by relatives and friends as he recites the first three letters of the Hebrew alphabet. Each time he says a letter he is invited to dip the letter, in cookie form, into a bowl of honey and eat it. The initial haircut is not until age three because the Torah says that after a tree is planted, three years must go by before its fruit is picked.

Children dressed as animals are conspicuously absent. Dressing as or wearing the image of a dog, cat, or pig is strictly forbidden. These animals are *tumeh,* or impure. Some years back, the Lubavitcher Rebbe issued an edict that no toys in the image of impure animals may be kept in the house. That goes for stuffed animals, as well. Pets are permitted, but only if they serve a purpose, like catching mice. Otherwise, if they can't be eaten, they shouldn't be touched.

One of the Israeli brothers takes a sheepskin scroll out of a silver container, unrolls it, and begins to chant: "*Vayehee bemay Ahashveros,* and it was in the days of Ahashveros." This is the *Megillah,* or Book of Esther, commemorating the rescue of the Jews from almost certain annihilation in ancient Persia. He chants slowly and methodically. Finally, he recites the name of Haman, the enemy of the Jews, and all hell breaks loose. Children vigorously shake boxes of juju fruit, men pound the table, and boys pop balloons. Poor Haman, I think, just another schnook in a long line of bad guys who wanted to exterminate the Jews. Little did he know that his name would be blotted out at a Megillah reading 2,500 years later in Postville, Iowa. It's like the Germans—they thought they'd have a thousand-year Reich, but instead they have a thousand-year stain on their collective conscience. And the stain—like an absorbent paper towel placed on top of a spill—just keeps on expanding.

I take a place next to Aaron, who is situated between a few workers, far from the head of the table. Not all the Hasidim are trained as *schochets* or *mashgiachs*. Many just work on the line. And as in most Hasidic communities, there is a curious form of egalitarianism at work here. Although the Rubashkins make seven figures a year, the Hasidim all eat together, pray together, and study together. They drive the same kinds of cars, and the owners' homes are not much different from those of their employees. The Hasidim see each other in the morning for prayers, all day on the line, and once again at evening services. On the Sabbath they are together for long stretches, breaking into spontaneous Busby Berkeley–like precision dance steps on the prayer floor, and eating at each other's houses, where the communal singing, or *zmiros,* goes on for hours. It is community in its truest sense, and an absolute abnegation of the anomie and atomization so pervasive in the contemporary world. Even by the standards of other Hasidic communities, it is all very cozy, for there is nowhere to go—no shopping center, no kosher grocery store, no commute to the city. Yet there is no discernible disharmony, and they approach everything with the enthusiasm of a group of people spearheading a reconnaissance mission to the most distant outpost of the Diaspora to establish a Hasidic colony there.

A Hasid dressed as Snidely Whiplash animatedly delivers the sermon. Set against the backdrop of the Postville Citizens Community Center, the scene is mildly Felliniesque. A few men in drag nod approvingly at the speaker as the little boy in the tutu circumambulates the table. The sermon, or *drash,* is spewed out in the characteristically truculent Hebrew-Yiddish mix of the yeshiva. The Moroccan sitting across from me translates it into a pellucid Yiddish. Although Arabic is his native tongue, he has been around Ashkenazic Hasidim all his life and his Yiddish is virtually flawless.

Large bottles of Smirnoff's are passed around, and everyone pours themselves an inch or so. For most, this will be all they have; but for a few of the more intrepid this is just the beginning of a lost weekend. The Israelis seem more intent on following tradition. Aaron Rubashkin's grandson downs a shot and breaks into a medley of old Hasidic favorites. A blond *sabra* who looks as if he would have been a horsewhipper in the old country attempts a handstand. He falls to the ground with a thud.

I ask Aaron how he got into this business, and he tells me that he saw an ad in a trade journal for a shut-down plant. He decided to investigate, and arrived in Postville with a small platoon of mechanics. The plant was dusty but not decrepit. Moreover, "It had a *hecksher,* a seal of approval, from the EPA."

The profit margin is thin, he claims. When I ask him how thin, he points to the tray of cold cuts. "The meat is the revenue, the profit is the parsley," he says, rolling a sprig of the garnish between his thumb and forefinger. "How thin?" I persist. "About 10 percent." Later, when I mention this to Heshy, he says this is gross and a more accurate figure is 2 percent.

Since Purim is not a biblical holiday, it is permitted to discuss business matters. Aaron asks the men around him for stock tips, then begins to explain his options strategy on a piece of paper. "Salomon Brothers I bought for fifty, calls I sold for two and a half. So if the stock goes down, I . . . " his voice trails off.

Everyone in the room is waiting for a few transcendental meditation practitioners who are supposed to arrive from Maharishi International University in Fairfield, Iowa. They called to ask if they could spend Purim with the Hasidim in Postville. But the weather is bad, and they never materialize.

The next morning, the TM students show up at Leah Rubashkin's. There are only two of them, both Jews, a veterinarian and a chiropractor. Three thousand of the 10,000 residents of Fairfield, Iowa, are affiliated with the university, and a sizable proportion of them are Jewish.

That afternoon, prior to the onset of the Sabbath, there is a Purim *seudah,* or festival, with celebrants going from house to house like slightly inebriated carolers. By the end of the process, a few are thoroughly drunk. The blond sabra gives the resident Israeli accountant, the only secular Jew in the bunch, a generous slap on the back of the neck that sends him reeling and leaves him unable to recite the Mourner's Kaddish, or prayer for the dead, over his father that night. He stumbles through it like a neophyte. Another Hasid twirls around like a hippo hit with a stun gun and smacks into a podium constructed out of two-by-fours.

The party ends with everyone congregating for evening prayers at the rabbi's house, a slightly Gothic structure situated across the street from the town's only cemetery. Astroturf covers the porch and the overall appearance is of a backdrop for an *Addam's Family* set. But although the exterior is spooky, the interior is homey. The living room has been converted into a sanctuary, with rows of benches facing the ark. Upstairs is a series of dorm-like bedrooms. Everyone in Postville knows about it. "Where ya goin'?" a solicitous local will pull up to a bewildered visitor and ask. "The rabbi's house? Hop on in." Before you know it, you've learned more about the Iowa State High School Wrestling Championship than you ever thought possible.

The general reaction of the townsfolk to the Hasidim seems to be one of relieved bemusement—relief at the economic viability they are bringing to Postville, and bemusement at their idiosyncratic behavior patterns. But there is a vague undertone of fear that perhaps the Hasidim are planning to "take over" the town. "I noticed in the *Herald-Leader* that last month they owned eight homes. This week it says they own twelve," someone at the local newspaper tells me. I try to mitigate this sense of foreboding by explaining that the glatt kosher market is a limited one, and the room for expansion is not all that great. But my listener isn't buying it, and I'm not sure I am either. For someone like Aaron Rubashkin, the sky's the limit.

One minor contretemps was an imbroglio involving two young Hasidim who came up with the idea of robbing a convenience store. On September 27, 1991, Pinchas Stillman, the Colombian-born adopted son of an Orthodox Jewish couple in Queens who was raised in the Lubavitcher community of Crown Heights, and Pinchas Lew, son of a Brooklyn rabbi, went on a hold-up spree. Both were working in Postville. With Lew behind the wheel, the unlikely pair of bandits took a lopsided vehicle with a temporary spare and no license plates to the town of Ossian, where Stillman flashed his .357 Magnum in the face of an elderly popcorn vendor and made off with $70. Then he shot a grandmotherly clerk at a convenience store in nearby Decorah after she rang a silent alarm.

Like characters out of Woody Allen's *Take the Money and Run,* the two Hasidic *pistolleros* were easily spotted in the lopsided, licenseless car. As the main instigator and gunman, Stillman got a fifty-five year sentence, which he is sitting out in the Iowa Men's Reformatory in Animosa. Lew got sent to a halfway house in New Jersey. Since the two were only recent arrivals in Postville, they were not known to the community and very little was said about it in town.

Stillman receives letters from Lubavitchers around the world. There was some hope that he might get out early for good behavior, but those hopes were dashed when he attempted a breakout and had another five years slapped on to his sentence. Meanwhile, the bullet is still lodged in his victim.

After evening services, everyone takes a seat or stands around a large table. The place of honor is occupied by Manis Friedman, Chabad rabbi and author of a well-known book, *Doesn't Anyone Blush Anymore?* a sort of marital guide to the perplexed. He is a popular speaker, and not just with Jewish groups. Rabbi Friedman is acknowledged to be one of the best speakers in the Hasidic world, and Lubavitchers are generally known to have great English speakers. Friedman has driven down from St. Paul with two of his fifteen children to spend the Sabbath with his fellow Lubavitchers in Postville. Sitting on either side of him are the two emissaries from Fairfield, and seated across from them is the Reverend Roger Katz, parish priest for the town of Postville. This juxtaposition proves fortuitous for a good theological discussion.

Katz, whose great-grandfather was a Jewish immigrant from Bavaria, is a regular at Sabbath morning services and has compiled an enviable collection of Judaic tomes. From his *siddur,* or prayer book, Katz produces a crinkled photograph of his great-grandfather and grandfather, cardboard suitcases in hand, upon arrival from Germany before the turn of the century. His grandfather proceeded to marry a local farm girl, and the net result is that all of his cousins are Christian. "But we have a very strong innate affinity with the Jews," Katz insists. "All of us have close Jewish friends." His knowledge of Jewish matters outside the biblical is limited, having lived in Iowa all his life. "Are you a Hasidic?" he asks, sizing me up earnestly. He is a fixture here, and all the Hasidim call him rabbi.

Rabbi Friedman begins to talk about how wisdom is accompanied by pain. This sets the lanky vegan veterinarian from Fairfield squirming in his chair like a precocious schoolchild trying to make a point. "The whole purpose of wisdom is to transcend pain," he finally blurts out.

The topic of conversation shifts to desire. The veterinarian says that to overcome suffering, one must overcome desire. Overcoming desire is laudable, but not enough, Rabbi Friedman retorts. Abraham got to that level of purity, but then God called on him to perform the *mitzvot,* or commandments, embodied in the Torah.

"But once you get to a certain level of purity, *everything* you do is mitzvot," the veterinarian asserts, adding that simply doing commandments without any feeling or meaning attached to them is pointless.

Friedman replies that *doing* the commandments is in fact the whole point. Then with a flourish he proclaims that the God of Eastern religions is a God that doesn't demand anything.

The veterinarian begins to discuss the Kabbalistic notion of *devikut,* or cleaving to God in prayer, which is said to lead to equanimity, a state of being oblivious to praise or insult, which in turn leads to illumination and oneness with God. Then he brings up *Atziluth, Beriah, Yetsirah,* and *Assiyah*–the four levels of spiritual hierarchy–and the infinite transcendent Godhead, *Ein Sof.* It is as if he is trying to bring Alan Watts and the Lubavitcher Rebbe together into one grand synthesis.

Friedman listens calmly. Then Reverend Katz has his say. "Devikut, or clinging, is not the only form of worship," he maintains. "There is also adoration, contrition, supplication, and so on." The Hasidim listen in almost reverent silence.

The discussion moves on to Heshy's house, where his wife, Basia, the daughter of a Yale-educated doctor who became religious twenty years ago, has prepared the Sabbath evening meal. On the way there, walking through the quiet residential streets, the veterinarian tells me that he studied Kabbalah, Jewish mysticism, under an ordained rabbi who has written several books on the subject and lives in Chicago.

Heshy interrupts the soliloquy with the abrupt observation that real estate is very expensive in Postville. "Really?" I reply, taking the bait. "Yes. You know there are many old people here and they don't want to move out, so you have to offer a *farmaygen,* a fortune, for one of their houses. Why, you can't get a decent home here for less than forty, fifty thousand."

Heshy's house is the nicest on the block, and seemingly the only one without a pickup parked in front of it. The inside has been totally gutted, with walls knocked out and the floor covered with parquet tiles. Hasidim seem to be enamored of these tiles, and for good reason: Carpeting would be a bother for families with frequent guests and large numbers of children; and they can never be completely sure if all the *chametz,* such as bread crumbs and other forbidden products, is out of the pile when cleaning for Passover.

The women have prepared a vegetarian feast for the two devotees of the Maharishi. It is chock full of various Middle Eastern delicacies, such as hummus, eggplant salad, and tahini. For the regulars, who include a number of men living here without their families, there is the standard Eastern European fare: roast chicken, boiled potatoes, and lightly poached whitefish.

The room is adorned with three pictures of the Lubavitcher Rebbe, each in a different medium. There is a photograph, a watercolor, and a drawing of him in front of the Western Wall, a place he's never actually visited. It shows him looking inspirationally off into the distance while clutching a *lulav* and *etrog,* the set of branches and citrus fruit that are waved in all directions on the holiday Sukkot, symbolizing that God is everywhere.

At some point, with the exuberance of a beer hall tenor, a boy breaks into a spontaneous rendition of "I believe with all my heart that the rebbe is the Messiah the King." The other children join in but the parents seem reticent. At the conclusion of the meal, we say the *Birkat,* the grace after meals, and break into more song. Then everyone retires to their guest room.

The next morning a local whose acquaintance I made earlier informs me that a settler in Hebron let loose with a volley of bullets on a group of praying Arabs and at least forty are dead. Next he turned the gun on himself. This proved later to be incorrect. I arrive for morning services at the rabbi's house and announce it to the crowd. The reaction is mute. Then, after a few moments, one of the Israeli brothers with the sweet demeanor pipes up. "After doing such a thing he killed himself?" There is a Borscht-Belt–like pause. "He should have danced!" Another takes me by the arm and confides to me in a stage whisper, "He didn't have to kill forty innocent people. He only had to kill one." "Who?" I ask, playing a reluctant straight man. "Rabin," he deadpans. All this is said with more than a hint of irony. There are comments that this is a terrible act. But the undertone is clear. No tears are shed over the Arabs.

The Lubavitchers are among the most militant of all Jewish groups in their desire to retain the territories. The ultra-Orthodox response to this issue is confusing and contradictory. Where some Hasidic groups, Satmar in particular, would like to see the State of Israel dismantled and the Jews allowed to live peacefully under United Nations or even Palestinian governance, there are others, such as Lubavitchers, who while not willing to call themselves Zionists, behave like them in the extreme. While they take pains to reject Israel as the resurrection of the Davidic kingdom that existed before the destruction of the Temple, they see the establishment of the state as a sign that the age of redemption is near.

There is yet another camp, that of out-and-out ultra-Orthodox doves, most notably the followers of Rabbi Eliezer Schach. Rabbi Schach is the Walter Brennan of Israeli politics. The feisty ninety-eight-year-old at one time controlled pivotal seats in the Israeli parliament through his party, Shas; and although Schach and Shas are now on the outs, he is still scrapping for a fight. He has recently called for the rescission of Coca Cola's kosher certification for running immodest ads, and much to the consternation of

the Israeli right, does not hesitate to proclaim the territories nego-
tiable. Schach's rationale for this is *pikuach nefesh,* the doctrine that
the preservation of life supersedes almost everything, including
land. He is not a Hasid, but a Mitnagged, and the head of the
Ponovezh Yeshiva in Benei Berak. But lest anyone think his liberalism with regard to the territories extends itself to ecumenicalism,
it should be noted that Schach, unlike most Hasidic rebbes, is
openly contemptuous of nonobservant Jews. He reserves his
greatest animosity, however, for the Lubavitcher Rebbe, whom he
regards as a hoax.

Finally, there are the ultra-Orthodox sympathizers of the Gush
Emunim, the bearded settlers who are even more nationalistic
than the Lubavitchers and who advocate widespread settlement
of the territories, particularly the West Bank. The most extreme elements are followers of the late Rabbi Meir Kahane, who called
for the expulsion of all Arabs from Israel and the territories. The
spiritual forefather of Gush Emunim was Rabbi Abraham Isaac
Kook, who settled in Israel in 1904. Kook had no qualms with calling himself a Zionist, and saw the return of the Jews to Palestine as
marking the beginning of divine redemption. His son, Zvi Yehuda
Kook, head of the influential Mercaz Harav Yeshiva, carried this
one step further by proclaiming that the establishment of the State
of Israel was an event heralding the onset of the Messianic era.

So on the issue of the territories, there are roughly four camps
at odds with each other in the ultra-Orthodox world: The nationalistic followers of Rabbi Kook, who proclaim themselves religious
Zionists and reject the notion of waiting for the Messiah to establish a Jewish state; the more mildly nationalistic Lubavitchers, who
are Zionists in all but name and whose views on the territories
probably represent the plurality in the Hasidic world; the Satmar
and their allies, who see the establishment of the State of Israel as a
sacrilege; and the dovish followers of Rabbi Schach. But ultimately,

regardless of differences on territorial concessions, unity far out-weighs strife among the Haredim, or ultra-Orthodox. The differences between ultra-Orthodox groups are mere rivulets compared to the sea between themselves and the rest of the world.

"Let the Arabs have Uganda," a Hasid standing next to me in the rabbi's house sanctuary concludes, alluding to the proposal of the British earlier in the century to put a Jewish national home-land there. "How do you know where to put the ark?" I ask him, changing the subject. The ark must be against the eastern wall be-cause supplicants face Jerusalem when praying. He lifts up his sleeve and displays a miniature compass attached to his watch-band. "Never leave home without it," he says with a smile.

After services I am led to the Moroccan's house across the street from Heshy's. His Iraqi-born wife, her head covered with a scarf, serves up classically Ashkenazic food—cholent and boiled beef—and laments her distance from her family in Israel. Three children play on the floor of the rented house, and my host feels compelled to vent his opinion on the Hebron massacre. I can't help but re-flect on how traditions are overlapping. The Rubashkins, with roots in Russia, hosted a largely Middle Eastern dinner the night before, while these Middle Eastern Jews dine on cholent and the husband explains his political position in Yiddish.

"If they don't like the situation, *bevakasha*, please, this way to the Allenby Bridge," he says of the Arabs, making a sweeping mo-tion with his hands. "For the troublemakers, it's *Aravim bahutz*—Arabs out. You can't reason with a donkey. Most of them are like donkeys." I shift in my chair uncomfortably. "You beat a donkey." Any objections on my part are met with a stone-like oblivious-ness. Rabbi Yissacher Dov Rokeach, the Belzer Rebbe, who says a country of 4 million cannot dominate a nation of 2 million, would have a lot to say about this viewpoint.

That evening, after the Havdalah ceremony closing out the Sabbath, I grab a ride with a local. "What are you doing tonight?" he asks curiously, looking at me as if I am some hybrid sort of fish or a latter-day Minotaur, half-Midwestern and half-Jew. "Me? I don't know." "I'm holing up with a six-pack and watching the basketball game," he offers. I decline his unspoken invitation, and ask him to drop me off at Heshy's.

Aaron Rubashkin is standing in front, hands in pocket. When he sees me, he puts his arm around my shoulder and looks out at the horizon like a visionary. "One day, you know," he says, "we will have a real community. When I first came here, the hospital had just closed. They couldn't find a doctor. If only I had gotten here in time, I would have found them a *Hasidische* one. One day there will be a Hasidic pharmacist here, and Hasidic businesspeople." I have no doubt he's right. As the Hasidic enclaves of Brooklyn bubble over, Hasidim will stake new roots, not just in Iowa but all over the country. This is just the start of a benign outgrowth.

Postville is only the beginning. But as for this town, not only should the Hasidic presence bring continued prosperity, but a sort of fame in this state that is now reserved for the Amish settlements around Oelwein, the Amana colonies close to Cedar Rapids, and the transcendental meditation university in Fairfield. Who knows, perhaps some day the town elders will erect a sign at the entrance to the city next to the John R. Mott billboard. It could read "Welcome to Hasidtown, USA," and a local *badkhn*, or comedian who shows up at Jewish weddings, could have a whole shtick about the place. He could call it Lake Oybegone.

CHAPTER 9

Haredi Harvard

LAKEWOOD, NEW JERSEY

The owner of the motel I'm staying at in Freehold, New Jersey, has a Yiddish accent. Upon registering, I casually look up from the clipboard and ask her where she's from. Poland, she replies. Ah, Poland, I rhapsodize in Yiddish, as if it were the garden spot of Eastern Europe. "Hey, Morris," she calls out over her shoulder to her husband in the next room, "a customer speaks Yiddish. So what are you doing here?" she asks. I tell her I've come to see the largest *yeshiva* and *kollel* in the world, the Beit Midrash Gevoha of Lakewood, known as the "Haredi Harvard" because of its strict entrance requirements. "Yeh?" she grunts somewhat noncommittally. She doesn't seem overly enthusiastic.

"What do you think of them?"

"Who?"

"The Hasidim."

She pauses a moment. Then, with the same bile that fueled Jackie Mason's assault on Ed Sullivan, she lets loose with a barrage.

"To tell you the truth, we have nothing in common with them. We went through the war—what do they know?"

When I remind her that most of the older generation of Hasidim were also in the war, she shakes her head.

"Them? Survivors? Practically none. My Morris was in Auschwitz. Ask him what he thinks of the Hasidim. Morris, come here," she orders. He shuffles in like Foghorn Leghorn auditioning for a part, cigar clenched firmly between his teeth. "What do you think of Hasidim?"

Without missing a beat he begins to intone,

Huset Ganef
Geh Ka' Chrzanow
Koif a fayert
Lieg in drayert.
Hasid, you crook
Travel to Chrzanow, for a look
Buy a horse
Then drop dead, of course.

It's a child's nursery rhyme my grandmother used to chant on those rare occasions when she saw a Hasid in Nebraska.

Upon concluding this acerbic little limerick, Morris peels the stogie off of his lower lip, clutches the gooey end between thumb and forefinger, and takes a deep bow. Then he exits without a word.

"I spent the war in Salzburg with four sisters under false papers. We worked in a factory. We were constantly worried that the Poles we worked with would finger us. Sixty members of my extended family were killed. Both my parents. Brothers. Phooey, the Hasidim. What do they know? There's blood on their hands. They told us not to join Zionist youth. To stay in Europe, not to go to Palestine. To wait for the Messiah. Instead of the Messiah, we got Hitler.

"They have their customs. Meat over here. Milk over there," she says, verily spitting this out. "Going around in *payess*. No cutting on Shabbos. No combing your hair on Shabbos." She mimics them with the vehemence of a four-year-old ridiculing her baby brother. Then she straightens up. "Medieval. That's what they are. Medieval people.

"Listen, I know they come here to visit the yeshiva. They stay by me. Good customers they are, but I want nothing to do with them. Tell me, after 1 million children were thrown in the ovens, how can I believe in any of their nonsense?"

I take my key and proceed to my room. Then I remember that I neglected to bring a *yarmulke*, which I'll need when I visit the yeshiva. So I go back to the front desk and mention this to her.

"Morris, give him a *kappeleh*, a little hat," she demands. He soon produces one from a back room. It is a yarmulke of the ersatz taffeta variety, the kind you find at a Conservative synagogue in a box next to the front door. To the Orthodox, it has neophyte written all over it. To make it worse, along its rim are inscribed the golden words, "Bar Mitzvah of Ronny Frank, Temple Beth El, March 6, 1993." I make a mental note to find out who that is when I give it back.

The Yeshiva Beit Midrash Gevoha is technically not Hasidic. It is Litvish, or based on the Lithuanian mode of pedagogy perfected in the eighteenth century that emphasizes hair-splitting analysis of the law and commentary. The more mystical, or openly emotive, aspects of Hasidism are downplayed, although the study of the Kabbalah, which preceded the Hasidic movement, is part of the curriculum.

In a way, comparing Litvisher Orthodoxy to the Hasidic version is like comparing mainstream Presbyterianism with the Southern Baptists. If old-style religion is Hasidic, then the Litvisher approach is pure Robert Schuller. But after the deluge of World

War II and the resulting decimation of both groups, most of the differences between the Hasidim and Litvishers have disappeared. Those that remain extant are generally rooted in personality rather than doctrine.

One remaining characteristic that distinguishes a Litvisher yeshiva like Beit Midrash Gevoha from a Hasidic one is its almost monomaniacal approach to study. This does not imply that young Hasidim are slouches. Far from it. But students at Hasidic yeshivot do tend to spend a bit more time hanging out, talking about their rebbe, and perhaps studying at a slightly slower pace.

The Litvishers, or Mitnaggedim, jelled as a movement in response to the rise of Hasidism. Mitnaggedim literally means opponents, and they opposed Hasidim passionately. They greeted Hasidic rebbes, often considered charismatic miracle-workers by their followers, with profound cynicism. Although many adherents were attracted to Mitnaggedism outside the borders of Lithuania, it was there that bitter strife between the two groups routinely unfolded.

One noticeable difference between the two groups in the late 1700s was a deep schism over how to sharpen knives used to kill cows. The Hasidim insisted on finely polishing the knife so that any imperfections could easily be discovered. That way one could be certain there weren't any nicks that could render the animal nonkosher. The Mitnaggedim disregarded this practice, claiming that an overly sharp blade itself leads to nicks because it is so easily dented. The nicks cause flesh to tear during the *schechting* process, which is also nonkosher.

The battle heated up to the point that the Mitnaggedim threatened excommunication to anyone who ate the product of Hasidic *schochets*. They asserted in a public proclamation that the Hasidic knives were blemished with the taint of heresy. This attitude spread from Lithuania to parts of Poland, where those employing highly polished knives in the schechting process were not allowed to be counted as part of a quorum in synagogue worship and were barred from marrying into Mitnagdic families.

The Hasidic response to this was a generalized disdain for Mitnaggedim as being all too often aware of the letter of the law while ignoring its spirit. An old Hasidic joke about two wealthy Mitnaggedim sitting in an empty sanctuary after services has one trying to outdo the other in modesty. The Torah teaches humility, and one of them, as if to show adherence to this commandment, proclaims himself to be nothing. "I am nothing in the eyes of God," he cries.

"You are nothing?" his friend, another successful merchant, responds. "*I* am nothing."

Soon a lowly *shammes,* or synagogue sexton, who shuffles around the room passing out books and picking up stray prayer shawls, passes the two burghers, and upon hearing their exchange, he too pronounces himself to be nothing. The first wealthy businessman, upon hearing this, eyes his colleague and explodes, "Look who's calling himself nothing?"

The Mitnaggedim, like the Hasidim, have their own stellar line-up of leading intellectual lights. One early figure was Elijah Ben Solomon Zalman, more popularly known as the Gaon, or Genius, of Vilna, who was said to have spent virtually every waking moment engrossed in the holy texts. When that was impossible, such as during a sojourn in the bathroom, he did equations in his head.

Toward the end of the eighteenth century, the Gaon of Vilna issued an edict demanding that the testament of the Hasidic founder Ba'al Shem Tov be incinerated. He blatantly compared Hasidism to a sore on the body of Israel. Despite Hasidic attempts at reconciliation, the Vilna Gaon refused to meet with the other side. Yet other Mitnaggedim were even more virulent. The Rabbi of Pinsk, Avigdor Ben Yosef Hayim, for example, told the Russian government that the Lubavitcher Rebbe of the time was guilty of treason for raising funds for Jewish settlements in a Palestine that was then controlled by the Turks. The Russians arrested the rebbe, Shneur Zalman of Lyadi, but he was eventually acquitted.

One hundred fifty years after the Gaon of Vilna's death, relations between the two groups are a model of peaceful coexistence. The Gaon's postwar equivalent, Rabbi Moshe Feinstein, got on well with many rebbes. Feinstein, the personification of the towering intellect, authored the *Iggeret Moshe,* a monumental collection of responsa, or answers to questions on a wide variety of subjects.

Like the Gaon of Vilna, Rabbi Feinstein also had his nose stuck perpetually in the holy books, and was known for being engrossed even while waiting for the elevator. It is said, somewhat improbably, that he went through the entire cycle of the Talmud 400 times. This would be the Talmudic equivalent of the three-minute mile. A mere ten times in one lifetime would be considered a great achievement. When Feinstein died in 1986 at the age of ninety-one, 75,000 people attended his funeral in New York and 250,000 in Jerusalem. He was eulogized as the world's leading authority on rabbinic law, as well as a righteous and considerate person.

Other giants of the Litvisher world in recent years have included Rabbi Eliezer Schach, powerful head of the huge Ponovezh Yeshiva in Benei Berak, Israel, and Rabbi Aharon Kotler, founder of the Yeshiva Beit Midrash Gevoha in Lakewood.

The 1,800 students at Kotler's Lakewood Yeshiva are well aware of the standards set by their predecessors. The school itself is a sprawling campus of architecturally eclectic buildings—ranging from the drab to the ornate—set on thirteen acres of highly desirable suburban real estate.

Lakewood and a few other *yeshivot* make this town a center of Jewish learning. Indeed, the Orthodox quarter takes up an entire section of the city, which is located in south central New Jersey and has a population of 45,000. While there is a relatively large number of liberal nonreligious Jews, it is the Orthodox who exercise a disproportionate amount of clout at the polls. They vote in block and they vote Republican, at least in local elections.

To call Lakewood purely Mitnagdic is something of a misnomer, because at least a quarter of its student body comes from Hasidic backgrounds. In any case, today the differences are barely discernible. What representatives of both groups have in common, though, is an uncommon appetite for learning.

While there is no Barron's guide to yeshivot, or strict hierarchy in terms of prestige or quality, it is generally conceded that Lakewood is second to none. And while judging a yeshiva may be a highly subjective and inscrutably arcane affair, in one clearly quantifiable area Lakewood is without equal. Its library has a world-class collection of books, most of them rare.

Many of the students here possess a panoply of unexploited talents. Most are mathematically adept. Some are computer jocks. But the gifts remain latent because secular subjects are off-limits, not by virtue of Jewish law, but because of their tendency to lead a mind down the wrong path. Yet when it comes to Talmud, all the students have an inordinate amount of *sitzfleisch*, or ability to spend long hours parked on a bench, studying.

The typical twenty-year-old seeking admission has to pass a battery of tests and undergo a fine-toothed inquiry into his academic and personal background. The tests themselves are oral and conducted somewhat informally, but they are painstakingly thorough. As might be expected, most of the students receive financial aid—tuition, room, and board runs $6,000 a year. To supplement tuition, the school is supported by a Who's Who of Orthodox heavy hitters, including Yitzhak Kaszirer of Antwerp and the Reichmanns of Canada.

In terms of undiluted devotion to matters academic, Lakewood blows away even the most esteemed of American universities. Developing a well-rounded personality is not, to put it mildly, a conscious objective. Intramural sports, theater, swimming pools, and socials are all outside the realm of acceptability. The closest thing to a weekend kegger would be a slug of après-prayer schnapps on Saturday morning, and the roughest equivalent to a fraternity initiation rite would be a memorized recitation of prodigious chunks of the Talmud in front of an admiring audience. While an occasional game of tennis in a public park or catching snippets of a Yankee doubleheader on the radio is not completely unheard of, energy is overwhelmingly devoted to study. Most anything else is stripped away in the acid bath of talmudic inquiry. Indeed, a description of the school bandied about to outsiders is "No Knicks Here," as if even one of the most compelling aspects of secular life is unworthy of scholarly attention.

This is true not only for professional sports. The sixties, Vietnam, civil rights, Watergate, and the Iraqi invasion all passed by in a blur. Even matters close to the Jewish heart, such as the establishment of the State of Israel, Knesset politics, the doings of the Anti-Defamation League, and the latest utterances of Louis B. Farrakhan, scarcely make for small talk. The collective eye is always on the big picture, and the big picture is the Torah and its attendant commentaries.

I enter the campus on an idyllic summer afternoon and stroll to the main dorm, past a stream of students leaving afternoon prayer services. In no time, I am accosted by a group of yeshiva *boochers* who want to know why I'm here. After an initial moment of hesitation, their suspicion recedes into a mild curiosity. They are a mixed lot. Short, tall, some in jackets, others merely in shirts, some with a proliferation of peach fuzz on their faces, others in beards, all with payess of one length or another. As I lean against a rail, they proceed to pepper me with questions. After their interest is satiated, I ask them to give me a tour.

They lead me to the director's office. Everywhere I look, people are standing around, talking in groups. Actually, there are four directors, all related in one way or another to Aharon Kotler, the Lithuanian rabbi who founded the yeshiva when he escaped from Europe in 1941.

The director I am introduced to is Malkiel Kotler, his grandson. Between answering phone calls and talking to aides, Malkiel tells me in his own laid-back fashion that his grandfather founded the school as a reaction to the more worldly curriculum of Yeshiva University, the educational arm of American modern Orthodoxy. Yeshiva University puts secular studies, particularly the sciences, more or less on a par with Judaic ones, although its interpretation of Jewish law is unswervingly literal.

Aharon Kotler had no use for this unholy oeuvre, and he was equally disinterested in what some Mitnaggedim considered the spiritual grandstanding of Hasidic rebbes. So he turned his back on both worlds and established his own institution, based on the blueprints of Mitnagdic centers of learning in the old country.

Now his grandson leans across his desk and looks me in the eye, asking me why I am not more religious. I rub my chin and pull on the waistband of my pants, finally volunteering that I'm more religious than my parents. That's not enough, he says. I consider other plausible responses in my mind. I wasn't raised religious. My grandmother dined on Jimmy Dean's pork sausage. I love rock and roll. None completely satisfactory. I want to tell him that I'm alive because of two people, Raoul Wallenberg and Josef Mengele. Wallenberg, because he gave my aunt a protective pass to a Swedish house in Budapest and she managed to find a safe place for my father. Mengele, because he stood at the gates of hell and after considering my mother's appendix scar for a moment sent her to the barracks. Wallenberg died, ostensibly at an early age, in some godforsaken *gulag*. Mengele frolicked on a South American beach well into his sixties. If I could even remotely explain it, I'd sprout payess tomorrow.

Finally, I manage to steer the conversation to another subject, but not before Rabbi Kotler lets me know that the *ba'al teshuvah* is held in greater esteem than even a righteous *tzaddik*, because he or she has tasted forbidden fruits yet managed to reject them. I in turn tell him that I see the outline of a divine hand in the revival of Hasidism after the war. That's the best I can do. Stymied over my equivocations about my personal beliefs, he finally holds the door open and invites me to wander the campus freely.

I am taken by several students into the main dormitory, which consists of endless rows of rooms with three or four beds in each of them. The monotony of the empty wall space between the *mezuzah*-laden doorways is relieved by an occasional cork-covered bulletin board, posting such services as offers of rides to Boro Park and alerts on nonkosher products. One rather dramatic announcement warns that certain items of clothing may be *shatnes,* or a forbidden mixture of wool and linen. "The following garments were recently found with shatnes," the leaflet proclaims. "A Sara Roberts jacket, purchased in Loehmanns, style #5441, Lot #3152. The fabric, a black and white plaid, is listed on the label as 50% rayon. The collar and cuffs are a black linen-look fabric containing polyester and LINEN." Also, a "Jones New York yellow and black plaid jacket, style #131846. The content label lists 59% wool, 34% cotton, 5% rayon, and 2% other fibers. Some of the pinstripes in the fabric contain a LINEN and silk blend. Any garments with a linen look must be tested even if no wool or linen is listed on the label." It is signed "the National Committee of Shatnes Testers and Recorders, 402 Yeshiva Plaza, Lakewood, New Jersey."

They maneuver me into a cinderblock-walled dorm room. I see three dressers, each with imposing cans of Right Guard and jumbo-sized bottles of Listerine. There are also scratched-up wardrobes and bookshelves lined with impressively earnest titles. Almost all the books are scripture-related, but there is the occasional novel, typically depicting a miracle-working rabbi. One corner of the room, however, is festooned with newspaper headlines and clippings of magazines, mostly consisting of phrases like "Big Shot," "A Real American," and "Winner." Crepe paper is twisted around light fixtures over the bed.

"What's this?" I ask.

"Oh, one of our friends is getting married. This is how we celebrate the engagement," the son of a New Jersey construction company executive tells me. He takes it upon himself to expound upon the differences between Hasidic and Mitnagdic engagements.

Unlike young Hasidic couples, whose initial encounters might consist of a brief stroll in the park or a visit to each other's parents, the Litvishers go all out in the entertainment department. A trip to Manhattan is practically *de rigueur,* climaxed by a visit to a glitzy lounge at a luxury hotel. The Plaza and the Hyatt are perennial favorites. If the initial flicker of interest intensifies, the next step is a thorough investigation into each of the party's reputations. Scores of people are interviewed, with a thoroughness that would be the envy of a CIA recruitment officer. This includes chats with elementary and high school teachers, and checking out parents, grandparents, aunts, and uncles for any black sheep. A black sheep generally means anyone who has let their religious commitment lapse. Perhaps the term *albino gorilla* would be more appropriate than black sheep, because it is so rare a phenomenon.

Although shedding the trappings of religion was a common phenomenon earlier in the century, today the movement is almost entirely in the opposite direction. Most Hasidim, upon inquiry, will relate that they know of not a single individual who has left the fold, or perhaps they may have vaguely heard of one or two who shed the trappings of Hasidism but still remained Orthodox. Going any further than that would leave even the most independently minded Hasid hopelessly unmoored in an alien society.

Assuming that the investigatory hurdle in the search for a spouse is negotiated, then other dates are arranged, including an excursion to Hacker's Hitters and Hoops, a Manhattan billiard and ping-pong emporium that has become the Pop's Malt Shop of the Mitnagdic dating scene. A stroll through Battery Park City is also not out of the question, nor is a boat ride in Central Park. The point is that the couple gets to know each other in different settings. If all goes well, an engagement takes place. All of this is an expensive proposition, so an anonymous fund has been set up at the yeshiva to provide a $50 stipend for each date. A student need only go in and take it.

The engagement itself is a modest ceremony involving an exchange of gifts. A contract, called *t'nayim,* is signed, prescribing the place and date of the proposed marriage. Then a plate is broken. There is no penalty for breaking the engagement contract unless otherwise stipulated.

A ring is given only at the wedding. This wedding ring has to be wholly owned by the groom and cannot have been given to him on the condition that he use it to get married. If he has received it from someone else, then it must be a gift with no strings attached; otherwise, it is not truly his.

As the window air-conditioner whirs and sunlight comes through the blinds, my guides seat me on a tired mattress and begin to enumerate their schedules. After a 7:00 A.M. wake-up call, they rise for *Schachris,* or morning prayers. Then they go to the mess hall, where breakfast is served in rotating fashion, since the room is not big enough to accommodate all the students.

From 8:30 to 9:30 there is study of Halakha, or law, based on the 613 commandments of the Torah. The 613 commandments, according to the construction executive's son, are "like the constitution. They are the basis for all the other rules."

A typical halakhic issue, albeit a rudimentary one, is the question of what is to be done when a Jew is on the verge of starvation but is unable to obtain kosher food. Other halakhic matters include how to pray, when to speak during prayer and when it is forbidden to speak during prayer, and which way to put on a jacket (right hand first).

Essentially, there are two categories of law. One category is rooted in common sense, or natural law, such as honor your father and mother, do not kill, and so on. The other is an injunction whose purpose is not fully understood but is nevertheless obeyed because it is God's commandment. Not eating pork is an example of this, although less religious scholars often give the reason as the avoidance of trichinosis.

Some of the commandments are relatively easy to perform. I am told by the students that God made it this way in order to facilitate the earning of merits, enough of which lead to the reward of *Gan Eden,* or paradise. The sages describe Gan Eden as a place where one can study all day because it is this activity that is the ultimate in pleasure. Gan Eden is life without a body, where God's divine presence shines on everyone. According to the Kabbalah, it is not a realm of perfection, but merely of overwhelming good, and there is yet a higher realm, *Atziluth,* that is even purer.

The Book of Genesis identifies paradise as being surrounded by four rivers, the Pisher, Gishon, Tigris, and Euphrates. This sounds like modern-day Iraq, hardly a celestial Utopia. But this is Gan Eden on earth, the material realm of Adam and Eve before they got their eviction notice. The ethereal equivalent, where souls go, is correspondingly surrounded by the same four rivers, but in a metaphysical form.

Gan Eden is not to be confused with *HaOlam HaBah*, or the world to come. The Talmud says that the present world, *HaOlam Hazeh*, lasts 6,000 years. After HaOlam Hazeh, the world enters a period of confusion, but at this point the picture becomes murky. Some say this period of confusion lasts 1,000 years. In any event, at some point, HaOlam HaBah arrives. HaOlam HaBah, like the interim period, is also a nebulous concept, but it is generally identified with the return of souls after the Messiah comes. Rabbis argued whether or not the returning souls would be accompanied by their bodies. Maimonides, the famous Jewish philosopher, said the resurrection would only involve the soul, but Lubavitchers, for example, adamantly insist the resurrection involves both body and soul.

If not enough merits are earned or a certain number of sins are committed, then one must make *teshuvah*, repentance, or one does not enter the gates of heaven. Breaking a negative commandment, like driving on the Sabbath, is a sin, but not doing a positive one, such as neglecting to say a blessing over a meal, is simply an omission, with the result being that no merit is earned.

A nonrepentant sinner goes to hell. Usually this involves fire, although there is also a hell of snow for someone who neglects to study and instead whiles away his time with idle activities. The notion of hell comes mostly from the *Zohar*, the best-known kabbalistic work, although hell is also referred to in the scriptures. Malachi speaks of it as the day when all evildoers will be burnt like stubble.

There are various types of hell. The hell for speaking idle words is having one's soul placed in a sling and shot from one corner of the universe to another. As the soul is careening through the cosmos, the letters from the idle words that cover the soul fall off. Finally, it is pure. There is also a hell for gluttony, for lust, and for passion. Some rabbis insist that Jesus was boiled in a molten vat of semen for being a philanderer (kids, don't try this at home) but this is far from universally accepted.

Where one goes after death is determined when the soul departs the body. Righteous people, the male tzaddik or the female tzaddiket, go straight to Gan Eden, as do righteous gentiles and minor sinners, but others have to face a scale of justice. "Everything is taken into account," a student says. "If someone is born a Jew but raised a gentile and doesn't know any better, then that is considered, too." Most authorities see hell as a temporary phenomenon, lasting until the soul is purified. Twelve months with time off for Shabbat is usually given as the time period; but for those who rebel against God, hell lasts forever.

I use this discussion as an opportunity to slake my curiosity about another subject.

"Do you believe in reincarnation?" I ask.

"Sure," the youngest of the bunch tells me. He spent his childhood in Lakewood because his father has himself been a student here for over thirty years. "You can even come back as a soda can," he says, pointing to a crumpled Pepsi container. "No, no," he swiftly recants. "It has to have a soul."

"You can come back as a blade of grass," someone else interjects. "That is, your soul comes back in that blade of grass. Or you can come back as a fish. Suppose you didn't concentrate on making your blessing over a meal, you may come back as a fish, and someone will make a blessing over you."

As we walk out into the sun, they tell me that reincarnation is actually discussed at length in the Zohar. No wonder they tell you not to study Kabbalah in earnest until you reach forty or you might risk insanity. It's the literary equivalent of a loaded gun, a never-ending maze with halls of mirrors, trap doors, and stairs leading nowhere. M. C. Escher in print. And it is accepted in toto by both Mitnaggedim and Hasidim. In fact, *gilgul*, or reincarnation, is not even alluded to in the Talmud. As a concept it is intriguingly reminiscent of karma, because the Jewish mystics say that the soul goes through different reincarnations in order to overcome inherent flaws.

"I want to ask you a question," someone says to me. "If the Messiah comes and afterward there is the resurrection, in which of its many incarnations does a soul return?"

"I don't know. Which one?" I assume it's the most recent.

"The answer is all of them. Because each incarnation represents a different character flaw and a different opportunity to redo the *mitzvot* that were missed in a previous life."

The intensity of this conversation and the allusions to esoteric liturgical texts leave no doubt in my mind that this is the place for totally committed scholars. Voices take on an excited cadence when they discuss the material with me. There is no "Generation X" phenomenon here. One set of contemporaries follows the next in lock-step, with few discernible differences. The young crowd has its own singers–Mordechai Ben David and Avraham Fried, to name two–and a healthy propensity to patronize *glatt* kosher restaurants and pizza parlors. These are still largely *terra incognita* for the older set, who remain firmly wedded to schmaltz-laden meals at home and who turn up their noses at meatless cholent and other such nouveau concoctions. Moreover, younger Hasidim and Mitnaggedim tend to vote Republican, unlike their traditionally Democratic seniors, and can occasionally be seen tooling around in sporty imports, something totally foreign to their station-wagon-loving predecessors. But aside from these superficial differences, there is no such thing as a generation gap. The continuum of study proceeds on its own rigorous path.

Beyond the typically brilliant Lakewood Yeshiva student, there are those who are even more brilliant. They are the *illuyim*, or prodigies. They wear no signs around their necks, yet everyone knows who they are. There are two types of illuyim, the *boki* and the *lamden*. The lamden is analytically deep, possessed with gifts of insight, while the boki has knowledge in astonishing breadth. The boki is likened to Mt. Sinai, where the Torah was given in its entirety. The lamden, on the other hand, in a continuation of the mountain metaphor, is said to be *oker harim,* able to rip peaks out of the ground with his analytical skills and his capacity to reconcile seemingly irreconcilable shreds of thought. The *pilpul,* or talmudic brain-teaser, is the lamden's game.

After a morning session of Halakha, the day begins in earnest. The first session of Talmud lasts from 9:30 to 1:45. The second starts at 3:30 and goes to 7:15. The Talmud, some 5,000 pages long (or 9 megabytes in the CD-ROM version), is a vocation in and of itself. It is often likened to a sea. An English version that is being prepared by Israeli scholar Adin Steinsaltz looks as if it may number in the hundreds of volumes before it is finished.

At present, most of the yeshiva is studying marriage contracts. Different age groups study it at different levels of complexity. As a legal instrument, the marriage contract, or *ketuba,* is rich in interesting provisions. For example, it is standard that the husband is obliged to provide perfume, jewelry, and clothes to his wife. The reason for this is to save his wife from embarrassment in front of her friends. The wife, in turn, presents a dowry to her husband, which can be itemized in exhaustive detail.

We walk across a courtyard to one of the larger study halls. It is jammed with perhaps 300 students, each of whom has his own *shtender,* or lectern, used for leaning on while arguing with or gesturing to one's partner. All around me young men pull on their beards, twirl their payess, pound their lecterns, or jump up and down to make a point. To the uninitiated it looks like mass hysteria, or at the very least a particularly intense charades tournament. Four or five instructors circulate the room to answer questions or to check on their students' progress.

While this is going on, their female counterparts are in their own seminaries, studying Halakha, learning elementary school teaching skills, and getting a taste of the Talmud. This is the case only until marriage, and applies only to Mitnagdic women and some of the more worldly Hasidic sects, like Lubavitch and Gerer. Among Satmar, women marry at an early age, usually seventeen or eighteen, and their already attenuated religious studies come to an abrupt end.

The analysis of marital contracts at the yeshiva ties in with the notion of contracts in general, a venerable and well-trodden realm with an immense number of facets. Questions of what makes a contract legal, how signatures are verified, who is qualified to serve as a witness—gamblers, thieves, and chronic liars, among others, are not—take up huge reservoirs of mental energy. The students eat, sleep, and breathe their subjects. There are no digressions. This may be the closest thing in the modern world to the Greek ideal of the academy. Admittedly, the curriculum is narrow. But other than that it is an atmosphere of unconstrained and uninterrupted intellectuality.

As we stand in the back of the room, one of my guides takes pains to point out that all these legalisms have an ethical component. For example, if an individual owns a farm and wants to sell it, he or she is obligated to offer it to the farm's neighbors before putting it up for sale to the public. If someone discovers a hole on public property, it is his or her responsibility to cover it.

This emphasis on ethics makes me think of the proverbial ethical train wreck. "How do you feel about Ivan Boesky?" I ask.

"Ivan who?"

I pause momentarily. Boesky donated a tidy sum to the Jewish Theological Seminary. Even though it is a non-Orthodox institution, Hasidim often use its library as a place to study or do research. Their lack of awareness leads me to embark on a quiz.

"Do you know when Israel was established?"

One of the students pushes his spectacles up on his nose and takes a stab. "Nineteen fifty?" he practically whispers.

"What came first, the French Revolution or the Russian one?" Now they look at me as if I am nuts. "We don't study history," one finally replies. End of quiz.

Another student launches into a fascinating disquisition on *mamzerut,* or illegitimacy. A *mamzer* is not, as commonly supposed, the product of a coupling outside the bounds of matrimony, but rather the offspring of a woman who cannot marry the child's father. This usually means a woman who is already married, but it could be the outcome of an incestuous relationship.

Mamzerut is a sort of caste or class. A mamzer cannot marry anyone except another mamzer. The same goes for their children and children's children, ad infinitum. Yet while a mamzer cannot join a congregation, the Talmud says a learned mamzer deserves more respect than an ignorant Kohan, or priest. The mamzer's untouchability, as it were, is confined to a very limited area. "I met a mamzer once," someone says. "It was in Brooklyn. He was unmarried and I asked him why. He said he was a mamzer."

At this point, we are shushed by someone in the back row and move out into the hall. "JC was a mamzer, do you know that?" the illegitimacy expert proclaims, alluding to Christ. "He is mentioned three times in the Talmud. The rabbis considered him a sort of magician who led people on the wrong path." Later on, when I call up the name Jesus on a CD-ROM version of the Talmud, I find that this is indeed true. Instead of heaping scorn and degradation on Jesus, the Talmud hardly mentions him at all. When he is alluded to, it is almost with an air of resignation. For someone who diverted a large chunk of the Jewish people from their religion, this seems somewhat surprising.

The final word on Jesus comes from a Satmar student, one of the few here. "The idea of immaculate conception makes no sense at all," he postulates, "because if God was going to make a person only from the woman, why not go all the way and make him from thin air?"

Just before the nightly meal, there is a forty-five-minute *Mussar* session. Mussar is a Mitnagdic concept originating in the nineteenth century that was devised to promote moral and ethical development. Rooms in synagogues were set up for people to gather together for moral reflection and meditation while ethical passages from the Talmud and Torah were recited. Today Mussar sessions are typically held in the evenings, when the subdued light reinforces the reflective mood. The texts are chosen for their ability to inculcate students with good character traits, such as honesty in business dealings, modesty, and thrift, and to discourage bad ones, like excessive materialism. In the Lithuanian yeshivot, some of the more zealous Mussar instructors had their students go out and mingle with elegantly attired shoppers while they themselves were dressed in rags or they were told to wander around penniless in order to get a perspective on the teachings. This is no longer the case, but Mussar remains a largely Mitnagdic phenomenon.

The Mussar movement, and ethicality in general, is most often identified with a drive earlier this century to eliminate gossip. It was led by the Chofetz Chaim, a seminal figure in Lithuanian Jewry, who wrote several books on the subject and even composed a morning prayer asking for protection against the sins of slander. The Chofetz Chaim was a widely respected figure and well-known for his almost compulsive ethical behavior. Stories about him are legion.

On one occasion, one of the non-Jewish customers in the Chofetz Chaim's general store left behind a herring, and the Chofetz Chaim didn't remember which customer it was. The next day he gave each of his non-Jewish customers a free herring, just to make sure he wasn't cheating anyone. He would check the weights of the scales in his shop every day. He would avoid passing the homes of his accounts receivables because the Torah says not to be a demanding creditor. Once a Rothschild sent him money for one of his books, overpaying by a few francs. The Chofetz Chaim promptly returned the excess.

The Mussar movement also strives to eliminate such traits as procrastination and to cultivate a sense of alacrity. It is believed that *zrisos,* or dispatch, leads to a kind of spiritual cleanliness.

A typical day at Yeshiva Beit Midrash Gevoha ends with a solitary review of the subjects studied that day. This often stretches late into the night. Some of the most zealous students, the *masmidim,* can be found in the study hall at three in the morning.

My final stop at the yeshiva is a visit to the library. On the way there we pass a collection of lockers, one of which has a combination lock whose code is known to everyone. It contains a veritable pharmacopoeia of medications, to which anyone can help themselves when they feel the need.

The library itself is an appropriately somber chamber. Books are uniformly bound in black, as if any nod in the direction of aesthetics is a supplication before a false god. Here, as everywhere else, style, at least in its conventional sense, is deeply subservient to substance. The card catalogue system in the library is a no-nonsense set of drawers holding thousands of smudged three-by-five cards. Books are checked out by signing one's name to a piece of legal-sized notebook paper taped to the wall. It's all charmingly antiquated, but the books get read.

"Look, look over there!" one of my guides excitedly exclaims, pointing his finger to a lone figure deep in thought. "He was the *haus yingl* for Moshe Feinstein." A haus yingl is a sort of hybrid between an errand boy and a valet for a rebbe, a great honor for a young man, although Feinstein, being Mitnagdic, was not a rebbe but rather a revered rabbi, or rav.

"He was with the rabbi during his later years on the Lower East Side. Come over here, I'll show you some of Rabbi Feinstein's works." He takes me over to a shelf holding the collection of responsa written by the late genius. I randomly open a book to a page concerned with the question of what sort of *tzitzis* to wear on a hot day. "Dear Rabbi," it reads, quoting a letter from an Isaac Tsin in the late sixties, "is one prohibited from wearing a woolen set of tzitzis on a hot day because he may be tempted to take it off due to the oppressive heat?" No, the rabbi replies, since removing a *talit katan,* or tzitzis, would violate a mitzvah, it is certainly not prohibited to wear it, even one of the woolen variety, on a hot day.

What one ultimately does with this enormous corpus of knowledge depends on the individual. Some, by dint of generous parents, in-laws, or a knack for garnering stipends spend their entire lives at the yeshiva. Once he gets married, the yeshiva student technically becomes a kollel student, but the program doesn't change dramatically. Others go into business. One student spends his day on the phone in the morning trading S&P futures with a floor broker in Chicago and studying in the afternoon. But whatever they end up doing, there is a widespread sense of gratitude at being here. The learning is exhilarating and the environment a sliver of suburban utopia a short ride away from the teeming streets of Brooklyn.

My guides walk me to my car. On my way out of town, I ask a bearded talmudist who is engaged in a Manichean battle with his lawn mower how to get to the nearest kosher restaurant. As he begins to answer, two of his daughters race across the plush turf and ask in Yiddish who I am. They are a pair of blond-haired, green-eyed preschoolers who in their effervescence could easily be mistaken as the offspring of a Midwestern wheat farmer and his wife.

"You speak Yiddish at home?" I ask the father. I am somewhat surprised, because many of the Mitnagdic men are more likely to use English, particularly with females. "Sure," he replies, "my children talk to me only in Yiddish." Suddenly, a vintage Cadillac Eldorado cruises by. It has the dimensions of a tugboat, and its top is down. "Hey, Moishy," my direction-giver yells in the driver's direction, "where did you get that one?"

"North Carolina," the neighbor bellows back as he pulls into his driveway and deposits six children on the doorstep of his classically suburban split-level. The scene is pure Norman Rockwell, a ranch house facing a split-level with immaculate lawns and animated children, except there are tzitzis, payess, and the children's squeals of joy are in Yiddish.

"Oh, the restaurant," the father of the two daughters turns back to me. "You make a right and drive until you see the supermarket. In it is a restaurant with its own entrance and *kolleh gedilleh*–all kinds of goodies."

I find the supermarket instantly and settle into a formica booth near the cash register. People come and go with the requisite zrisos, or dispatch, ordering sandwiches and sifting through the buffet, which prominently displays perspiring slices of gefilte fish and cubes of rock hard kugel. Families are squeezed around small tables, energetically passing shakers of salt to one another. Babies spit up and men jabber into cellular phones with their hands covering the mouthpiece, as women orchestrate the details with the virtuosity of Leonard Bernstein.

After a hearty meal I drag myself back into the parking lot and overhear two black women talking to one another. Both wear disgusted expressions on their faces. "I can't stand them," one of them says, clearly alluding to the Hasidim. "They think they own everything." "Mmm-hmm," the other replies. By the time I get to the car, I see in the twilight's silhouette some sort of confrontation taking place between them and the Hasidim parked in an adjacent car. It's hard to discern the details but it seems almost forced, like a preordained choreography that neither party has any control over.

By the time I get to the motel, it is dark. I quietly pass the innkeeper's desk but she pops her head out. "Well, how was it?" she asks. "What, the yeshiva?" "Yeh. Did they try to *schnorr* money off of you? Did they run you off the campus?" I decide there is no point in trying to change her mind. I mumble something noncommittal and tell her that I will be checking out the next day. Then I hand her back the yarmulke.

"By the way," I ask politely, alluding to the words inscribed on its rim, "who is Ronny Frank?"

"That's my grandson," she proudly proclaims. "A fine boy. Oh, I forgot to tell you. When he finishes high school, you know where he wants to go? The yeshiva." She shakes her head, brimming with pride.

CHAPTER 10

Bungalow Summer

THE CATSKILLS, NEW YORK

In 1969, I was sent to camp a few miles from the Pennsylvania–New York border. A couple of camp maintenance men, who spent their mornings picking up garbage and heaving it onto a truck while chanting "Ho, Ho, Ho Chi Minh, NLF is gonna win," asked me if they could borrow my sleeping bag to take to a rock concert. When I finally saw them a week later, I asked for it back. "Oh, man, we lost it in the mud," was their terse reply. The mud was Woodstock, and this summer, as every summer in the Catskills north of New York City, the hills are alive with the sound of Yiddish. Only this time the Hasidim are looking for solace amidst the ubiquitous signs of Woodstock II.

"Official Woodstock Guide Pick-up Site" announce placards above the cash registers at food and fuel outlets on the New York State Thruway. The guide itself is instructive. "What is love?" an attached coupon asks. "Do you love your music? Do you love playing in the mud with 250,000 strangers? Do you love pizza? Do you love your life? Woodstock '94 and Pizza Hut."

Are the furrow-browed rapacious businessmen who are putting on this brouhaha merely incarnations of the smooth-browed young men they once were, or have they metamorphosed into something new and more ominous? One thing's for sure: The lanky young Hasid, his index finger absentmindedly scratching the base of his beard while he strolls across the lot of a McDonald's at a roadside oasis, could care less. Nor could the two Hasidim in the back of a taxi ferrying them from South Fallsburg, epicenter of the Catskills summer bungalow colony scene, back to Boro Park–a trip that, the cab driver tells me while filling up his vehicle, runs them a tidy $175 each way.

"They're in the diamond trade, you know," the cab driver confides. "Most of them are, anyway. Diamonds may be a girl's best friend, but they are also a cab driver's."

For those with more limited resources, there are bus services such as Emunah, which generally charges $110 per van load, each way, and provides a curtained aisle to separate men and women during prayer services. This can cause problems, and in recent months a Russian émigre by the name of Sima Rabinowicz refused to relinquish her seat on the men's side of the aisle so that they could commence their supplications. She took her case to the New York Civil Liberties Union, which is representing her in court. In the meantime, men who share the bus with Sima have it stop and wait while they debark and *daven.*

At this time of the year, the permanent Hasidic population north of New York City swells from around 20,000 to well over 50,000, as eager refugees from the urban battlefield take up residence in bungalow colonies and retreats, which are often little more than clusters of shacks centered around threadbare quads sprinkled throughout the several-thousand-square-mile area that constitutes the Catskill region. For a family from Williamsburg or Crown Heights, these meager resorts tucked away in mountain hollows amid thick growths of deciduous trees are often the closest thing they will get to a vacation.

Encroaching on the bungalow colonies are a burgeoning number of camps for children and more conventional hotels. Most are modest, but some resorts approach a level of luxury that would meet the standards of even the most jaded traveler. But whatever the mode of accommodation, a certain cadence of daily activity that cuts across all socioeconomic boundaries unites everyone. Most of the day is taken up with study, preparing and eating meals, a bit of idle socializing, with a minimum of organized physical activity, and none of the planned diversions that would be offered at other resorts.

The Catskills and points south, nearer the city, are not only known for the Hasidic influx, but also for the proliferation of New Age retreats. South Fallsburg alone boasts two ashrams, one of which is run by a Jewish swami, and there is the Foundation for the Course in Miracles, a Christian organization with a former Jew at its helm. There is also a retreat center run by a reconstituted group of Jews that sees itself as the next big leap forward in the evolution of Judaism and proudly wears the label of "neo-Hasidic." It is Elat Chayyim, the Woodstock Center for Healing and Renewal, an outgrowth of Rabbi Zalman Schachter-Shalomi's Philadelphia-based P'nai Or, and it holds seminars on such subjects as "Jewish Liberation Theology" and "Exploring Jewish Prayer" against a picture-postcard backdrop of farmhouses and mountain trails.

Part of an even larger movement called Jewish Renewal, the Woodstock Center and the ideas from which it is spawned have attracted thousands of adherents in recent years. Rabbi Schachter, its central figure, is the Polish-born son of a Belzer Hasid; he grew up in Vienna, where he attended both a traditional *yeshiva* and a left-wing Zionist high school. This eclectic mix produced a singularly iconoclastic and controversial thinker.

Schachter received his *smicha,* or ordination certificate, from the Lubavitch yeshiva in Brooklyn in 1947, having fled Europe via Morocco some years earlier. Afterward he took on a number of assignments, including a pulpit in Winnipeg, and finally ended up in Philadelphia, where he developed nothing less than his own offshoot of Judaism, a new strand of thought whose central objective revolves around making prayer, rituals, and commandments more meaningful to the contemporary spirit.

The father of ten children, Rabbi Schachter—or Zalman, as he is more commonly referred to—has lectured and studied with native American elders, Buddhist lamas, Catholic theologians, and guru Baba Ram Dass. He has been called everything from a charlatan to a saint. As for his being neo-Hasidic, that is something open to debate. "Neo" as a prefix is pregnant with possibilities, and it may or may not apply to the teachings of Zalman. Just as Herbert Marcuse was a neo-Marxist, Irving Kristol a neo-Conservative, and members of Nirvana were neo-hippies, the philosophy espoused by Schachter may be arguably neo-Hasidic. But as far as any strict resemblance to conventional Hasidism goes, Zalman Schachter is to the Lubavitcher Rebbe what the Beastie Boys are to Steve and Edie.

The charismatic troika that runs the Elat Chayyim retreat consists of Zalman, Arthur Waskow, a rabbi out of the Reconstructionist mold from Philadelphia, and a younger disciple of Zalman's, Rabbi Jeff Roth. This is not to suggest that the set-up is in the least bit patriarchal. Most of the remaining positions of responsibility seem to be occupied by women, and the rabbis often defer to them during services.

Elat Chayyim operates out of a rented lodge, Su Casa, situated in the hilly vicinity of Woodstock. The main dining room serves up three sumptuous vegetarian meals a day, which are accompanied by lively discussion and debate. Upon walking into the unadorned mess hall, one is confronted with the sight of perhaps 150 people, most of them Jews in their forties, at least 80 percent of whom are female. At first glance, I feel like I've stumbled onto the food concessions pavilion at a Holly Near festival. Many of the guests, savoring a typical meal of spanikopita, pesto, eggplant parmigiana, and brown rice, seem to be products of the antiwar movement.

The couple I sit next to have between them made it to Woodstock, the Mobilization Against the War demonstration in Washington, and the militant May Day protests. A man across the table from me, who hails from Berkeley, strenuously attempts to convey the Hasidic nature of the movement. Jewish Renewal is true Hasidism, he asserts. It is the New American Hasidism because it incorporates the concepts of pluralism, egalitarianism, and feminism, as well as respect for Native American culture and sympathy for the Palestinians. The latter have suffered more than the Jews, he argues somewhat incredibly.

Most of the women I talk to were present at the beginnings of the feminist movement, and seem in one way or another to have been connected to Betty Friedan or NOW or Kate Millett. They were the shock troops for the SDS, licking envelopes and boiling water, mimeographing leaflets and serving as intellectual punching bags. Now they've come full circle, poring over kabbalistic texts like dedicated Semitic scholars, taking courses with titles such as "Davenen with Your Life: Exploring Jewish Prayer Forms," and "Devikut and Vipassana: An Exploration of Buddhist and Jewish Methods for Transforming Consciousness."

"Lenny Bruce said, If it's bent, it's okay. If it's broken, it's not," a man in the dessert line tells me. "We bend the tradition, but we don't break it." It has to be bent, he argues, or people won't get it. And if they don't get it, he concludes, "We will disappear."

For many, if not most Jews, prayer seems to be an empty, time-consuming experience that leads to random acts of absurdity like hiding Mickey Spillane novels in High Holiday prayer books, or engaging in prolonged and lovingly detailed mental overviews of one's personal financial statement during a sermon. To a sizable plurality of Jews in this country, the Judaism conveyed to them by mainstream institutions is emotionally sterile if not utterly bankrupt. It is an organizational Arnold Schwartzenegger but a spiritual Don Knotts. People are looking for something with emotional resonance, and for many, Jewish Renewal fits the bill. It links prayer to the heart. Ritualistically, though, it is the virtual antithesis of Hasidism. The image of a woman clad in a tie-dyed *tallis,* holding up the Torah with an adulation reserved for a newborn baby, would be greeted by most Hasidim with the same sort of enthusiasm that would be accorded Carry Nation if she walked into PJ Clark's during happy hour.

But this is but a minor ritualistic faux pas in a long litany of contretemps that would send most Hasidic rebbes into apoplexy. So it is not surprising that Elat Chayyim claims to be only emotionally Hasidic, not halakhically so. "We are not a halakhic [legalistically based] Jewish movement," the blissful executive director of Elat Chayyim, Jeff Roth, tells me. Roth, who also holds a master's degree in social work, has a healthy predilection for giving out spontaneous hugs the way John D. Rockefeller handed out dimes.

Roth and I are walking past an imposing set of slogans written in block letters with a black magic marker on a huge drawing pad. It says, "It Is Perfect. You Are Loved. All Is Clear. I Am Holy." This quartet of maxims is a chant of Zalman's, and each phrase corresponds to a different kabbalistic realm.

With an infinite amount of patience, Roth takes it upon himself to give me a crash introduction to Kabbalah. After a few moments, he stops and invites me to a lecture he's giving in the lodge this afternoon. When I arrive, he is passing around a *Shviti,* a framed diagram spiraling in an arabesque fashion around the Hebrew letters יהוה, or yud-hay-vov-hay. This is the tetragrammaton, the ineffable name of God, a name so holy that only the high priest could pronounce it on Yom Kippur, also referred to as Yahweh, or Yehovah.

The Shviti is hung on the eastern wall of a house in order to designate the direction to face during prayer. The term comes from the phrase "*Shviti Hashem L'negdee Tamid,* I place God before me at all times."

Roth tells us to focus on the name for God in the Shviti's center, which bears an intriguing sort of cross-cultural resemblance to a mandala. Jews today, he says, don't even know how to pronounce the name of God, since we don't know the vowel structure of the four letters. Most Jews refer to God as Adonai, which means Lord or Master, but Jewish Renewal sees this as hierarchical. God, Roth emphasizes, is immanent and inherent rather than transcendent. This is in the tradition of the Ba'al Shem Tov, who saw God everywhere.

At Elat Chayyim, God is referred to in prayers simply as "Ya," intriguingly close to the Rastafarian Ja. So old familiar prayers with the name Adonai are replaced by the term Ya, and most everything referring to God is gender neutralized.

When Roth discusses the pronunciation of God's name, I am reminded of yoga breathing. He intones the letters of God's name, YHWH, without any vowels. The first syllable, yeh, is an inhalation, the second, wah, an exhalation. "One hay is an inbreath, one hay an outbreath," Roth tells me. "The yud, the initial letter, is the empty lungs at the beginning of the process, the vov, in the middle, the straightest letter in the Hebrew alphabet, is like a full balloon, or the lung when it is full. God is a process. Zalman calls it Empty-In-Full-Out. In-Out is the flow; Empty-Full is the form. Breathing in and out is a reciprocal process. We breathe out carbon dioxide, the trees breathe it in. God breathes out into the dust of the earth. We breathe it in."

He points once more to the Shviti, and quotes once again the passage Shviti Hashem L'negdee Tamid. "Shviti's root, grammatically, means to equate, and l'negdee means to negate. God is me and also the inverse of me.

"Another way to look at it," he explains, "is through the yin-yang." You wouldn't hear Manis Friedman talking this way, I think to myself. "The two hays are like the yin and the yang. The yud represents the dots in the yin-yang, and the vov is the line connecting the two. Vov, which means 'and' in Hebrew, links the lower realm of the hay, the physical world—the world of I-it, as Buber called it—to the higher realm of the yud, the world without form, beyond space and time. 'I Am Holy.' That's the yud, Atziluth, the spiritual world, the first letter. 'All Is Clear.' That's the hay, the intellect, when your mind understands the big picture of how God works. 'You Are Loved.' This is the emotional world. The vov links people to one another. It is the Great And. I-it becomes I-Thou, or I-You. Buber called God 'the Great And.' 'It Is Perfect.' This is the second hay, the physical world. So there are four letters and four realms, one for each."

Roth concludes his lecture by repeating his assertion that God is everywhere, and reminding his listeners that this emphasis on the immanence of God puts Jewish Renewal squarely in the lineage of the Baal Shem Tov, who saw the divine in everything. "And like the Baal Shem Tov, our mission is to serve God with joy."

As I look out the huge picture windows at the majestic scenery, my attention is drawn from the realms of God to the pool below. There, a group of mostly nude women, partly obscured by shrubbery, hold hands and dance 'round and 'round while singing *Hinay Matov Umanayin,* an old Sunday school favorite. This is their ritual immersion in preparation for the Sabbath.

Later on it's the men's turn. This time it's the hot tub, where the group of men strip down to immerse themselves. We are told to close our eyes and breathe rhythmically, and to concentrate in sequential order on our head, our arms, our legs, and our genitals, the latter of which "bring us joy and which bring us trouble, which bring us hope, for a continuation of ourselves into the future." Then once again we immerse ourselves, individually and in unison. Our speaker is Arthur Waskow, who ends the session with the song *Mayim, Mayim, Mayim,* an invocation for rain from Israel's prestate days, usually accompanied by a dance, and a staple of the Jewish summer camp circuit.

That night and the next morning, Sabbath prayer services become impromptu jam sessions, with congregants breaking out instruments and the resident tennis instructor, a former captain of the Stanford team, tooting on his horn as Rabbi Roth strums his guitar. A woman who donated a Torah her family inherited from a Brooklyn synagogue when it closed passes it around lovingly. Another woman announces to the group that her parents gave her an English name when she was born on a refugee boat leaving Genoa for the United States in 1950, and she wants to change it to Haviva, Hebrew for "precious." After a plethora of hugs and a blessing for good fortune and peace from the Berkeleyite, she sits down and the service resumes.

About three to four of the prayers are familiar, the rest being either improvisational renderings or totally original. Even the familiar ones are performed with a creative flair. The *Shema* is repeated four times, once in each direction. Every time that it is said, the participants make two triangles out of their bodies: one below with legs apart and the other above with arms raised up and stretched out. Then they bring their arms down to the ground to scoop up imaginary water and sprinkle it over themselves and each other. A few lines of the weekly Torah portion are read, some in Hebrew but mostly in English, with a fair amount of liberty taken in the translation.

Late in the evening, after Sabbath has ended, I hop in my car to make a run over to the Nevele, a nearby resort where Mal Z. Lawrence, the last of the great Catskill *tummlers,* or comedians, is performing. The Nevele is one of the few resorts left that still regularly features performers who cater to fans of a certain age, Frankie Valli and Tony Martin being representative of headliners. Tony Martin, who until recently I had thought of as some unsavory hybrid of Dean Martin and Tony Bennett, turns out to have sung with Sinatra in the forties.

The Nevele is a fading complex just outside Ellenville, a few miles from the Jewish Renewal retreat. It could easily serve as the backdrop for an Efferdent commercial. Everyone here looks in some way related to Albert Shanker. Gaggles of Italians who are dressed like extras for the *Goodfellas* nightclub scene and Jews who know every self-deprecating phrase in Yiddish and flaunt it with abandon circulate throughout the lobby.

The building itself is reminiscent of an Intourist hotel somewhere deep in the interior of the Soviet Union. Watermarks discolor the chipped marble foyer, and the furniture is straight out of the fifties, conjuring up images of Meyer Lansky's Havana Riviera congealed in time for eternity by Castro's benign neglect, its doorknobs and towel racks capable of sending any Melrose Avenue retro furniture dealer into an acquisitory frenzy. The carpet is a kaleidoscopic undergrowth of nausea-inducing swirls, and a big brass plaque affixed to the wall reads "President and Mrs. Lyndon B. Johnson slept here, August 19, 1966."

I step into the ballroom and take a seat. A waitress abruptly orders me to move my chair and walks off muttering, "Rude, rude, rude." Soon the curtains open and the MC announces that Alan King will be appearing next week. An old man one table over shakes his head excitedly and says, "Forget it."

Opening for Lawrence is a chanteuse who warms the crowd up with a little Bob Seger sung at a tempo that would put Barry Manilow to sleep. She then segues into a passionate "One Moment in Time" ("Seize that one moment in time / Make it shine"), which must be her anthem.

Then the baldheaded Lawrence comes out, looking like a cross between an aging coke dealer and a real estate syndicator in Newport Beach. He *spritzes*, or lets loose, with the requisite quota of *alter kocker*, old geezer, jokes, including a hilarious send-up of a Yiddish-accented retiree on a CB. Then he launches into a series of Hasidic one-liners. "This is the Hasidic capital here. Right here in the Catskills. Woodbourne, just down the road, has a restaurant called the Glatt Spot and a shop called Mendel the Tzitzis Rebinder. He'll repair them for you, corn row them for you, or make them out of leather so you can flog each other with them. Two T-shirts I bought at the souvenir stand there. One was a Hasid with a revolver. It said 'Make My Day.' The other said 'Lay T'fillin, Not Hookers.'"

After another hour or so it's over, and I follow him backstage. I shake his hand and on my way out overhear him saying that he's been married twice, once to an Italian and the other time to a WASP. Clearly, he's not going to win any awards for promoting Jewish continuity. Even if he is exaggerating, though, Woodbourne sounds intriguing.

The next day I cruise into the town of Woodbourne, which turns out to be a three-block stretch of bustling businesses catering to the summer visitors. There is no Glatt Spot or Mendel the Tzitzis

Rebinder, but there is a Glatt Gourmet, a Netzach Yisrael Take Home Food Store, and a Woodbourne Cholov Yisroel Pizza and Falafel, right down the street from picket fences and colonial houses. There are also two bookstores, one manned by young yeshiva students from New York and the other displaying posters of prominent rebbes for sale in the window like so many baseball stars.

As families push strollers up and down the main strip, I wander into a grocery store and ask an enormous Satmar who could pass as the lead singer for Canned Heat if he could tell me how many bungalow colonies there are in the area. He waves me off and lumbers over to the frozen food section. "You want to know anything, get a Hatzoloh map from the bookstore, it lists everything," he says over his shoulder. Hatzoloh, the nonprofit Hasidic emergency service based in Brooklyn, has ambulances all over the Catskills. It operates with volunteers and does not restrict its services to Jewish clients.

The Jewish bookstore itself, besides having a healthy selection of religious texts, also has on display large numbers of memoirs, including one by an Orthodox former U.S. Army lieutenant who helped liberate Buchenwald. One of his wards was the Klausenberger Rebbe, to whom the lieutenant attributes the most moving sermon he's ever heard.

The rebbe, who lost his wife and all eleven of his children in the war, got up on the pulpit the first Yom Kippur after liberation and listed his sins in the traditional confessional prayer, answering to each of them. We have stolen. But what was there to steal? We have spoken idle words. But we didn't have the energy to speak, only to listen to the orders of our tormentors. We have coveted. Maybe we coveted the slop thrown to pigs when all we had to eat was watery soup. But in the end, we thank God for giving us life and continue to have faith.

I ask the proprietor of the bookstore if he has a Hatzoloh map, and he produces one. Sure enough, it lists over 500 camps, bungalow colonies, resorts, and retreats, ranging from Karnofsky by the Lake to Chai Manor, from Breezy Acres to Zupnick's, spread out comfortably over a twenty-mile radius in and around towns like Hurleyville, Ellenville, Mountaindale, Dairyland, Ulster Heights, and Liberty, to name a few. And as if this cultural dissonance weren't enough, different Hasidic groups that aren't always the best of friends, like the Belzers and the Satmars, are within close proximity to each other, with the modern Orthodox and non-Orthodox European Jews thrown into the mix. Then there are the locals, whose own religious affiliations and ethnic origins span a broad spectrum in their own right. Just outside Woodbourne, for example, is Camp Emunah for Girls and Camp Shearith Hapletah for boys. Not far away, the Woodbourne Reformed Church, established 1802, stoically surveys the whole scene.

Even though Woodbourne is a small town, the influx of Hasidim has given it a congested urban feel. Windows of the Jewish establishments have inimitably Brooklynesque notices clinging to them: "Lice bugging you? We check hair and clean heads for camps, bungalows, and private parties. We are the experts fully equipped to retrieve these pests from your head. Call Avigail and Yehudis" and "Morah Chanie Kinder Palace. Your child will be loved and cared for the way you'd like in a clean, warm, friendly, and Heimishe atmosphere." There is a leaflet advertising the services of the "Mezuzah Doctor. This doctor makes house calls." And a political poster urges the freeing of jailed Jewish settlers. "Shmuel was arrested," it proclaims above the picture of a fierce-looking Israeli in a knitted *yarmulke,* "under administrative detention orders by the Rabin Government. After the present additional three-month detention order, the Rabin government can renew three- to six-month orders over and over. Write to Yitzhak Rabin. Ask him why he releases thousands of convicted Arab terrorists, while Jews who have never been charged or convicted of any crime languish in Israeli jails."

Until the Jewish stores close up shop every year around Labor Day, the town fathers who occupied the original pews of the Woodbourne Reformed Church are probably doing rotisserie turns in their graves. But maybe not. Without the annual influx of Hasidim, the local economy would fall apart.

In the center of town, one of Woodbourne's few African-Americans, whose parents came here years ago to work at the once glamorous but now fading resort of Grossinger's, collars me near a pay phone and asks me if I'm Jewish.

"Yep," I reply.

"But you're not religious. You're like us."

"Pretty much," I tell him.

"You eat pork, don't you?"

I shake my head back and forth. Then I ask him what he thinks of the Hasidim. They're different, he says. Different from the Jews who used to come up here. "But they're okay. They cheap, though. Always wanting something for nothing. You tell the people they cheap. But they're good people."

The founding families would not be the only ones shocked by the transformation that their town has undergone. Early German Jewish settlers who wanted so much to fit in, with formidable names like Baer, Lowenthal, and Lewinsohn, would strongly disapprove of the Eastern European riffraff. Most of their descendants have probably been absorbed into the general population by now, but a few of them are no doubt students at the Ivy League Torah Program I stumble on while driving out of town on Route 42. Situated on a side road called Synagogue Way, the program, run by the French-born Lubavitcher Rabbi Jacob Goldberg, takes in students from all over the world who are taking their first steps toward full observance of the *mitzvot*. Rabbi Goldberg, in his late forties, leads a class in Chassidus, or Chabad mysticism, in a deep Yiddish accent and with no small amount of humor. When I wander into the classroom he urges me to sit down.

"A mitzvah," he is telling the class, "stays with a person always. An *averah*, or sin, if you do repentance, goes away and can be erased." He touches on the notion of *Mitzvah HaBah BeAverah*, or doing a sin in order to perform a mitzvah, and asks for examples. Stealing an *etrog* to use for Sukkot services, someone volunteers. Stealing money to give to charity, another interjects. The teacher nods approvingly. Stealing to perform a mitzvah is worse than stealing to put it in your own pocket, he inveighs.

I decide to try my hand at this. Fresh from Elat Chayyim, I don't lack for possibilities. What about a woman wearing a tallis on Shabbos so she can pray better, I ask. That's okay, he replies, so long as she is wearing clothes underneath. Everyone laughs. How about playing guitar on the Sabbath to heighten the mood? I persist. Where did you hear about this, he demands. Elat Chayyim, I mumble, like Beaver Cleaver finking on Eddie Haskel. And I suppose they use microphones on Shabbos, too? Sure do, I say. He does a passable imitation of a folk singer strumming his guitar to an imaginary woman in a tallis. Everyone cracks up. *This* is a Mitzvah HaBah BeAverah, he proclaims, somewhat pleased by my example. "Playing a guitar on Shabbos, using a microphone—better you don't go to *shul* at all." He hits the table hard with his hand. "What is this Elat Chayyim?" he demands like an inspector administering an interrogation.

"It's Zalman Schachter-Shalomi's institute."

"*Oy a broch.* What a pity. Schachter was a very smart man," he laments.

"*Meshuggeh off's toit!* Crazier than a loon!" a Hasid in a corner of the room bellows out.

"No, not crazy," says Goldberg, "just confused. A Lubavitcher. Ordained by us. He began on the right path. Then he started making changes. First he wanted blue tzitzis fringes, not white. That's okay, some Hasidim have one or two blue strings on their tzitzis. Then he decided his tallis should be multicolored because in the Kabbalah there is the concept of *Tifereth*, the merging of colors. Each color has a different attribute—red is strength, white is love—and a person should balance and mix these attributes together to make a proper combination of them in the *neshuma*, the soul. Schachter took this concept and materialized it. Also okay, but a little strange. Nowhere in the law, mind you, does it say not to do this.

"Then he started descending," Goldberg continues. "First with the finger cymbals during prayer, then mixing Jewish ideas with those of priests, Indians, Japanese. Eventually, he divorced his wife and married, I think, a Chinese girl. He ruined his family. He was a rabbi in Winnipeg and now he's a . . . a . . ." He momentarily loses his thought.

"And what happened to his children?" someone asks.

"I don't know. One became like a *goy*, I think. Another is totally *hefker*." Hefker is the ultimate put-down. It means wild, unruly, outside the fold. Goldberg obviously means it as a sign of pity.

"*Neboch*," a shame, he finally mutters. The dozen or so students, ranging from a recent Columbia graduate to a senior at State University of New York at Binghamton, with a Brazilian and a couple of Californians thrown in for good measure, listen attentively. "Okay, let's get back to work!" he barks. I take this as my cue to exit.

Ten weeks in the Catskills isn't cheap. A simple bungalow runs $2,000 to $3,000, not including food or transportation. And this is just a run-of-the-mill colony. There are luxury resorts like the much-talked-about Vacation Village in Loch Sheldrake, where the families of accountants and diamond merchants languidly push baby carriages along the lake. The accommodations there consist of modern townhouses. Whatever the colony, though, men usually stay in the city and come up for weekends, unless they are employed by one of the local institutions.

I drive over to Monticello, the main city of the Catskills. Off to one side is a road sign in Yiddish pointing the way to the offices of Dr. Tova Rosen. A woman doctor in a Hasidic community is not unheard of, but it is highly unusual—limited to those who have become religious. Her clinic is situated in a modest house on the periphery of a bungalow colony named Fialkoff's, which caters to a non-Hasidic but Orthodox crowd.

Fialkoff's has 110 bungalows and an Olympic-sized swimming pool, which Mrs. Adler, the owner, invites me to visit. It is the end of the men's daily swimming session, and as I walk through the gate a yeshiva student from Detroit, whose parents became religious twenty years ago, blows on a whistle and orders everyone out. In the main part of the resort, families pass their time lounging at picnic tables, reading, laughing, or nibbling at food, while the younger children play in the sand or on swing sets. Across the street from the colony is a kosher pizza stand and a bakery, the latter owned by a Satmar couple who are in their mid-twenties and already have five children.

Dr. Rosen's house at Fialkoff's is a whitewashed double-decker with a modest gate in front. A downstairs window, adjacent to her examining room, also has a sign with her name in Yiddish. It lights up. I walk into the office and find a *balbatische*—a person of healthy proportions—woman in a navy blue denim dress propped on a swivel chair talking on the phone. She motions to me to sit down. After she hangs up, she begins to talk to me as if she's known me all my life. She's a doctor in Williamsburg most of the year, she tells me, but this summer she's experimenting with an office in the Catskills. In the city, most of her customers are Satmars. She herself is a *ba'alat teshuvah,* having become religious in the distinctively unfashionable period of the early sixties when she was barely in junior high school, well before the phenomenon took off later in the decade. She went to live in Brooklyn with some religious grandparents, leaving her nonobservant parents on the Upper West Side behind. After attending Bais Yaakov girl's high school in Boro Park and getting a B.S. from Long Island University, she went to the University of Tampico in Mexico, where she got her medical degree. It was a pigsty, she tells me. The anatomy lab was a cesspool—you'd rather use a fish hook to retrieve organs than to touch them. Then she came back and opened a clinic in Williamsburg.

She praises the Satmars, even though she isn't one. "They're really into *tzedakah,* charity," she says, and when it comes to taking care of the sick, "to strangers they're better than family." As she goes on and on about the Satmars, a Hasidic woman stands in the doorway shaking her head. The phone rings and Tova answers it. "Don't listen to her," the religious woman, apparently a patient, says. "My sister married a Satmar and they treat women like *lochs,* holes. They walk all over them. Into tzedakah?" she asks rhetorically. "They're into screwing the government!" She relates a food stamp counterfeiting scam for which the perpetrator was sentenced to several years in prison but ran off to Israel instead. "Now he sits, he learns, on his $3 million. He's waiting for the—what do you call it—the statute of limitations to run out so he can return."

While the doctor is busy on the phone, she continues. "I never met one who didn't take advantage. Food stamps, ADC, Section 8 housing, you name it—and that's just the millionaires. They own eight houses but they get welfare. Taxes? They don't know the meaning of the word. They put all their assets in one big kitty—a yeshiva fund—and borrow on it. That way they avoid income and inheritance taxes." I'm glad Dr. Rosen is on the telephone, because if she heard this it would no doubt set off a huge verbal conflagration. "They have black Jews—*Schvartzes*, they call them. They're not really black. They're Satmars. Black sheep is what they are. They smash windows, overturn buses."

"How come?"

"Who knows? Who knows what they fight about? They use the black Jews to collect money from each other."

As she finishes off with the dramatic flourish that there is no law in Williamsburg, that Satmar is the law, a delivery man from UPS walks in with some medical equipment and hands it to Tova. She hangs up the phone and thanks him. "You better get ready for the onslaught," he says. "They're expecting 250,000 kids up here next weekend. They say the parking area alone will be twenty-five square miles." Tova assures him that she intends to spend Woodstock weekend in Boro Park.

As he leaves and the woman in the doorway disappears, a well-dressed matriarch in a queenly turban comes into the office and sits down. "Ah, Mrs. Polakoff," Tova greets her. "I have the IV ready." Mrs. Polakoff is here for a vitamin infusion for her Epstein-Barr. Her husband, now retired, was one of the administrators at a Satmar camp up the road. There are four camps, actually, serving thousands of Satmar children. Her camp alone prepares between 2,000 and 3,000 meals each day, four or five times a day.

The children sit and learn from nine to noon and from three to six. Otherwise, they play. "Baseball?" I ask. "Heavens no, maybe the Vishnitzers, but not us. They sit, they swim, there is a creek for fishing." "They fish?" I am somewhat taken aback. "Not exactly," she replies. "They watch the goyim fish." As she is having her IV hooked up, she tells me that camp tuition is according to income, that there are no TVs or radios present, but there is air-conditioning and telephones. Everyone studies: not just the children, but also the staff and visiting parents.

Dr. Rosen talks about the lice problem at the camps. As Mrs. Polakoff sits there, vitamin solution dripping into her hand, blissfully oblivious to my conversation in English with Dr. Rosen, three boys walk in who don't know a word of English either. They won't begin to learn English until they are eight, Tova tells me. They are the children of the Satmar couple that run the bakery across the street.

The doctor treats only women and children. Occasionally, a man comes in, and she's willing to see him, "but most wouldn't see me for more than a hangnail. Something like prostates is out of the question." She does a lot of fertility treatment and deals with communicable diseases that arise from the close proximity of her patients to one another. Hepatitis is a perennial problem, as is salmonella. Eighty or 90 percent of the clients are on Medicaid, but she won't accept their cards. It's too much of a hassle. So she deals mostly with insurance companies. Much of her time is taken up with paperwork because she doesn't even have a nurse or assistant. The season starts on June 28 and everyone goes home on Labor Day, with the exception of some yeshivas in South Fallsburg, Mountaindale, and Woodridge, which are open all year round. After the season, she will go back to Williamsburg, where much of her services are performed on credit, and she has an accounts receivable list that would be the envy of most small businesses. But being a woman has its problems. A male physician tried to bully her into sharing office space with him, and the husbands of some of her patients lean on her to alter invoices, ostensibly to inflate their insurance settlements, but she steadfastly refuses.

Mrs. Polakoff, her treatment complete, gathers her purse and prepares to board a cab back to her camp. I ask her where it is. Outside Ellenville, she says. Ellenville, isn't that where the Nevele is? Oh yes, she replies, but in the forty years she's been at the camp, she's never been to it. "But I do remember one thing. Years ago, thirty, maybe forty, President Johnson and his wife slept there."

On my way out of the mountains and back to New York, I stop in Monsey, the biggest suburban year-round settlement of Hasidim outside the city, a town with perhaps 20,000 Orthodox of every stripe. It started with a single *kollel* in the early fifties. I decide to pay a visit to Rabbi Moshe Tendler, one of the leading figures of modern American Orthodoxy, much criticized in some Hasidic sectors. He is a professor of biology at Yeshiva University, a well-known bacteriologist, a leading bioethicist, and the head of a congregation in Monsey. Taking the shot-in-the-dark approach, I call him from a few blocks away and he agrees to meet me at his home the next day.

When I arrive, his son, a bearded Yale law school graduate, leads me into the basement study. After about ten minutes, Rabbi Tendler appears. I tell him I'm here to gauge the modern Orthodox response to the explosion, both demographically and qualitatively, of Hasidism in this country, and to ascertain, exactly, what is the difference between the two groups. Amid books on the ethics of medical experimentation, euthanasia, and the Talmud, he tells me there is no such thing as modern Orthodoxy. "There are only the halakhically observant and the nonobservant," he says, "and we are just as observant as Hasidim." But, he concedes, "for survival purposes, you can't top the Hasidim." He relates a little-known phenomenon that the only Orthodox in the Soviet Union who retained their practices were the Lubavitchers. "They kept their coats, their hats, their tzitzis. They drank only Cholov Yisroel milk and baked their own bread. Can you imagine doing that for several generations? And you know why they survived?"

"Why?"

"Because people thought they were crazy. Stalin didn't bother with them. The Talmud says not to pay any special attention to a crazy person. And Stalin, *takeh*, for sure, ignored them. So when *perestroika* dawned it turned out that there were several thousand Lubavitchers, all over the Soviet Union, and they came out of the woodwork."

Tendler admits that there are differences between the two, the modern Orthodox and the Hasidim, but they are rooted in custom rather than law. "In the Midrash, it is said that the Jews managed to survive 210 years in Egypt without losing their identity for two reasons: because they didn't change their language and they didn't change their dress. They had portable ghetto walls. Today it's Yiddish and long cloaks."

To Tendler, this is the crux of the difference between the modern Orthodox and their ultra-Orthodox brethren. But what about the study of secular subjects? The modern Orthodox, after all, are perhaps more disproportionately represented in the professions than any other group in America.

"Satmars come to me with ethical questions—issues of fertility, for example. They need professional advice. And I myself asked Rabbi Aharon Kotler just who will fill these roles if the Orthodox won't? We are the doctors, lawyers, and ethicists for the Hasidim."

Yeshiva University offers degrees in the humanities, but relatively few students major in them. For future lawyers, it's political science, for others, it's the physical or biological sciences, or the rabbinate.

"A Hasidic girl will willingly enter into *shiduch* with a boy from Yeshiva University, but only if the boy wears a hat," he says, referring to the black-rimmed Fedoras of the Hasidim, not the knitted yarmulkes of the modern Orthodox. And apparently, more and more of the modern Orthodox are donning this sartorial symbol of unflappable piety. Moreover, only a distinct minority of Yeshiva University students, according to Tendler, go to movies anymore. A decade or two in the past, movies were much more acceptable, as they still are with older modern Orthodox Jews.

Other outward indicators also point to a shift to the right. The wearing of tzitzis by men outside the pants, once a spotty practice among the modern Orthodox, is more common than ever, and wigs among married women are prevalent.

The move to the right is even reflected in a narrowing of disparate birth rates between the Hasidim and the modern Orthodox. Even though a large number of modern Orthodox find birth control pills acceptable–the rationale being that it doesn't involve a blocking of sperm traveling to the egg because with the pill there is no egg–average modern Orthodox family size is climbing steadily. Whereas a generation ago the modern Orthodox would consider it a novelty for an older couple to have, say, thirty grandchildren, today this is far from uncommon–Tendler himself has forty-six, at the relatively tender age of sixty-eight.

What are some of the other differences between the modern Orthodox and Hasidim, aside from the former's involvement in the professional world? I ask.

The real difference, according to Tendler, is of an ethical nature. "When Hasidim get into trouble, when they do something against the law, they hurt all Jews. If you're going to look like a Jew, if you're going to dress like a Jew, then act ethically," he says, assuring me at length that there are plenty of ethical Hasidic businesspeople, but the few rotten ones make everyone look bad.

The other major criticism of Hasidim by the modern Orthodox involves Israel. "Hasidim don't send their children into the army," he complains. "Halakha demands you defend Eretz Yisroel with your life. Israel feeds and protects the Haredim. The aggressive denigration of a country that does this is wrong. Even Rabin and Peres, who are far from being heroes in our eyes, have helped Torah study to flourish. We owe the Israeli government just like we owe the United States."

Tendler has no doubt about the future of Orthodoxy in America—to him it is onward and upward. But as for the rest of American Jewry, the other 90 percent, he is not nearly so optimistic.

"The Reform thought they'd dance on our graves, but sadly, we'll dance on theirs." I express doubt over this, saying that the majority of Jews in America have not been religious for over seventy-five years, yet they have retained their identity. He reminds me that intermarriage poses new obstacles. "The Reform did one thing wrong. They abolished *gittin,* the Jewish divorce. This makes the offspring of all second marriages into *mamzers,* and mamzers and the descendants of mamzers cannot marry Jews who are not mamzers. Everything will be mixed up, we won't know who is who, and the two groups—the Orthodox and the Reform, will be forever separated. They have cut themselves off from the rest of the Jewish people.

"We are not doing enough to bring them back," he exclaims. "There are Jews in the next town, outside Monsey, who don't identify, who don't give to United Jewish Appeal, but they'd send their kids to our yeshiva—not because it's Jewish, but because of the public schools. But the tuition is $4,000 a year. We need a massive infusion of funds for scholarships, because once we have them as students, we have them for life."

When I tell him that it seems to me that the major differences between the two groups of Orthodox are receding and there appears to be a general shift to the right, he begs to differ. "The modern Orthodox will always be separate because we have a strong aversion to the cult of personality that is focused on the *tzaddik.*"

That part may be true, but overall I am not so sure. With the emergence of tzitzis, of an unwillingness to eat even a salad in a nonkosher restaurant, of an aversion to movies and television, the gulf between the two groups is narrowing. Will we live to see the day when the Hasidic juggernaut swallows up the modern Orthodox like so many minnows, and any differences between the two will be strictly superficial? That day, Rabbi Tendler assures me, will never come.

CHAPTER 11

Down on the Farm

KFAR CHABAD AND KOYME MIYUS, ISRAEL

*O*n my first day in Israel, the Satmar Rebbe, Moishe Teitelbaum, delivers a sermon to a throng of 10,000 in Jerusalem on
how the Jews should separate themselves from Zionism the way
they distanced themselves from Korah, the biblical figure who
questioned Moses' leadership. The Satmar Rebbe is here for the
first time, and the Israeli authorities have closed off a main artery
in Jerusalem to accommodate his *tisch,* or festive table, angering
many taxi drivers who feel this is a precedent for future Sabbath
restrictions and setting off a preponderance of shoving matches.

The Satmar Rebbe has cut the lapel of his coat as a sign of
mourning over the destruction of Jerusalem in A.D. 70, and secular
commentators are angrily telling him to open his eyes, Jerusalem
never looked better. Many Israelis see the Haredim, as the ultra-
Orthodox are known here, as afflicted with collective psychosis.
Assailed for running around on hot days in layers of black clothing, they are sometimes referred to as cockroaches, not only for

the color of their attire, but for their seeming ability to survive anything.

A few days later, Menachem Mendel Schneerson, the Lubavitcher Rebbe, dies. A totally different crowd, also numbering 10,000, gathers to watch TV screens set up in Kfar Chabad, the Lubavitch stronghold outside Tel Aviv, depicting the funeral in Brooklyn, courtesy of the satellite network New York 1. There is also a lot of lapel-tearing here. The following day, life goes on. Schools are open and shops have their shingles out, but the streets are empty, like high noon at Black Rock.

When I pull into Kfar Chabad, off the Tel Aviv–Jerusalem road, the pictures of the rebbe are as omnipresent as images of Kim Il Sung in North Korea or Mao in China during the height of the Cultural Revolution. The town center of this 600-family community is nearly deserted except for a lone camera crew filming outside the main synagogue. The experience of cruising into Kfar Chabad the day after the rebbe's funeral is a heady one, like cruising into Tokyo with General MacArthur.

The only sign of life in the city center is a nonreligious Israeli mechanic working studiously away on a little Subaru. Standing beside him is a Hasid who appears to be holding up well, considering the circumstances. Approaching them, I have no idea if the Hasid is going to burst out in tears, start babbling inanely, or tear my head off.

"I've come to see Kfar Chabad," I announce cautiously. "Can you show me around?" To my surprise, and with the openness that characterizes the Lubavitchers, he replies, "My pleasure, if you'll just do me a favor. Follow me to a garage so I can leave my car there."

Ten minutes later, we're in a dusty development town parked in a dilapidated garage with a plethora of resourceful mechanics who know how to do more with wire hangers than an origami specialist knows what to do with paper. As we sit in a dingy waiting room while he's having his car looked at, he introduces himself as Fishel Jacobs, formerly of Vermont, one-time U.S. East Coast karate champion and currently doubly ordained rabbi–not just by Chabad, but by the fabulously exacting standards of the Israeli state certification board.

He invites me back to his house in the treeless subdivision that constitutes the heart of Kfar Chabad. His home, which at first glance resembles most of the other structures in the neighborhood, is huge by Israeli standards, about 3,500 square feet; but it's even larger from a Haredi perspective, where a family of ten crowded into three rooms is more the rule than the exception.

Virtually everything is expensive in Israel, but real estate, particularly in desirable areas, is sky high. The Jewish sector of the Israeli economy, on a per capita basis, is about two-thirds that of the United States, and this leaves the Israeli Haredim that much further behind their American counterparts. But both places have strong safety nets, and well-to-do Hasidim on both sides of the Atlantic are wont to take care of their own.

In Israel, much more so than in the United States, the ultra-Orthodox element vigorously participates in indigenous political life, and at one point or another most Israeli political parties have tried to lure them into being coalition partners. Even the adamantly nonvoting anti-Zionist Neturei Karta is involved in such perennial issues as the closing of quasi-public institutions on the Sabbath and the exemption of *yeshiva* students from the military. But aside from political involvement and marginal economic disparities, Hasidic life in the United States and Israel roughly parallel one another.

Jacobs is the son of a wealthy Vermont real estate developer, all of whose children have become Chabad followers. Jacobs's own children circumnavigate the house on various vehicles, ranging from pogo sticks to two-wheeled scooters. The home itself is bare. There is scarcely any furniture and the walls are blank, but Jacobs and his wife have moved in only six months ago. A house this size could easily cost $1 million in a fashionable section of Tel Aviv, but here the whole thing, land included, cost him less than $250,000.

The neighborhood itself is a neat grid of individual homes separated by small lawns and gravel roads. Dominating the entire colony, on a windy incline, is an architectural clone of Rebbe Schneerson's house in Brooklyn, right down to the brass doorknob. Inside, the table is set with fine china in anticipation of his imminent arrival.

The Rebbe's replica was built for him to use if he ever traveled to Israel. But he never did. In forty-three years, he left New York only once, to visit a suburban community in the Catskills.

Schneerson was a child prodigy in day school, but didn't attend yeshiva. Instead, he studied at the Sorbonne and in Berlin, and became an engineer before becoming the seventh Lubavitcher Rebbe in 1951. He was regarded as a seer, a saint, and a prophet by his followers, and many are convinced he was the Messiah. Truckloads of mail would arrive at his home on 770 Eastern Parkway in Crown Heights, and somehow he found time to answer it all. Before his health deteriorated, he would often receive visitors until three in the morning.

Although Rebbe Schneerson never set foot in Israel, he actively wielded his influence in the political arena there. In April 1990 he undermined the Labor Party from forming a new government by ordering two Knesset members to vote against the Labor leader, Shimon Peres. But most important, he was directly responsible for bringing thousands of people back to Judaism, including the karate expert standing in front of me.

While being a third-degree black belt makes Jacobs stand out in the Chabad movement, it is the ordination by the Israeli rabbinate of someone who scarcely knew a word of Hebrew fifteen years ago that really sets him apart. He takes me into his diploma-strewn office and tosses a Chabad publication at me. It is called *Nefesh: The Jewish Soul Magazine,* a surprisingly slick periodical in the newsweekly mold.

One of the articles is a column by the well-known talmudic scholar Adin Steinsaltz, in which he writes that Jews should define themselves as a family, which is a far more basic tie than that of a nation or a religion:

> To be sure, the family tie is a very primitive way of binding people, but it is probably the most stable one, and the most resistant to outside change and influence. . . . The connections are so very deep that we usually are not aware of them consciously, but they awaken, and sometimes it is as though we feel the clan is calling. And then to our own surprise, we join.
>
> The family feeling is possibly one of the main reasons why Judaism as a religion was never very active in proselytizing—just as a family would never go out into the streets to grab people to join the family, it doesn't mean that Jews feel superior or inferior, it's simply that from the very beginning it has its own pattern and way of living. Even when members of such a family are out of the family house, when they are wandering far away, they follow the lifestyle, theologically, sociologically, behavioristically. Of course, members of the family can be severely chastised and rifts can occur between individuals and groups, but there is really no way of leaving the family. You can even hate it, but you cannot be separated from it. After some time, people, younger or older, come to the conclusion that in fact, they can't get away from it.

This is true, he writes, even if some of us are biologically the children of another people, "because the true father of our family is God." And always, "Whether one hates or loves, whether one is an ardent believer or a convinced heretic, one remains the father's child." Fishel waits patiently while I read this, and then flips the pages to the article he really wants me to see. It is a series of profiles of Lubavitch *ba'alei teshuvah*.

"Name: Jacques," one of the entries begins. "Occupation: Artist. Hometown: Paris, France." Accompanying the text is a photo of what looks like a grizzled Montmartre veteran in the garb of an Orthodox Jew. His story is that of a painter who becomes religious, and it ends with his proclamation that "the only true happiness in life is Jewish life—*mitzvot,* holidays, a *bris,* a bar mitzvah, a wedding. This is the true revolution, because in Judaism, you're finally free. It frees you from your passions—and once you're freed from your passions, you're master of your will. This is true freedom."

"Name: Diane," the next entry begins. "Occupation: Folk Singer. Hometown: Montreal, Canada." Diane's entry describes her busy career as a popular folk singer, performing across the United States. When her music became less meaningful, she turned to religion:

> Now I sing for women only and my songs are better than ever.
>
> Being observant is simply something to count on. We Jews have been around for a long time, and what's kept us alive has been our eternal guideline value system. It's something that belongs to us. We live in times when the rules are changing. The rug is constantly being pulled out from under our feet. It's good to have the Torah, unchanging and steady, for our immediate use.

Finally, I come to Fishel's story. "Name: Fishel. Occupation: Rabbi, third-degree black belt karate champion. Hometown: Bennington, Vermont." Adjacent to the article is a color photo of my host elegantly executing a front kick in full Hasidic regalia. His testimony describes eight hard years of training, which included forty-eight-hour marathon sessions consisting of two hours of punching at 5,000 punches per hour, punctuated by an hour of rest. Then, at some point, he developed a thirst for Judaism and became religious. Why? He doesn't say. But his entire family has "turned black," as the Israelis are wont to call it. His sister is a Lubavitcher psychotherapist in Manhattan.

Jacobs ended up in Kfar Chabad studying with the same dedication he brought to karate, culminating in his ordination by the Chief Rabbinate. To earn the *smicha,* or rabbinical certificate, he had to learn some 40,000 laws and opinions. Just cramming for the exam took him two years of ten-hour days.

> When I took the ordination tests, I got the highest possible
> grade in several areas, passing hundreds of other scholars,
> most of whom had been studying Torah since they were small
> children. But at the basis of it all there are just three things to
> remember: first, there are human beings in the world; second,
> there is an Almighty who created the world; and third, we're
> lucky in that the Almighty gave us a vehicle–the Torah–
> through which he lets us connect to him.

By now I have forgotten that the Lubavitcher Rebbe has just died. Kids are coming in and out of the office with sundry requests, and Fishel's wife is traipsing around doing various chores while munching on a cracker. She turns out to be a formidable scholar in her own right, and an expert on large chunks of scripture. He often defers to her opinion when I ask questions. Unlike her husband, she comes from a religious family and is an Israeli by birth.

The only reminder of the rebbe is a portrait across from Jacobs's desk that seems to be glowing. Also, a child is reading a biography of the rebbe. Anytime Fishel refers to the rebbe, it is in the present tense, which is vaguely eerie. For some reason, I feel awkward about asking the most obvious questions about the future of the Lubavitch movement. It seems inappropriate. Besides, all the newspapers here have been speculating about the rebbe's successor like it's the NBA draft. Some are saying there will never be another rebbe, and the Lubavitcher Hasidim will retain their undivided loyalty to the deceased rebbe, just as the Bratslavers never elected a successor to Nachman. Apparently, no one can fill the rebbe's shoes.

A friend of Fishel's, a Chabad Hasid with an armful of children, drops by to visit. He spent two years studying Chinese medicine in Santa Monica, and within five minutes I have my shirt off and he's analyzing my back.

"Do you know the body has 613 acupressure points?" he asks. "This corresponds to the 613 commandments. And just like the commandments, 248 points are positive and 365 points are negative. The mystical work of Chabad, the Chassidus, written by the first Lubavitcher Rebbe, says that the body is composed of four things: fire, which is desire, arrogance, and pride; water, which is physical pleasure; air, which is frivolity; and earth, which is sloth and melancholy. In opposition to this stands the Godly soul. Your spine is misaligned. Let me tell you about some exercises." All the while, Fishel is on the phone answering the legal questions of a woman planning to get married who has to be absolutely sure, in accordance with the Torah, that she hasn't had any sign of menstruation for at least seven days before the wedding. The problem is, as I understand it, she was misdirected as to when to start counting the seven days.

"Did you take a clean white cloth and check for blood?" Fishel asks. Apparently, the reply is affirmative. "Did you check deep?" Then he puts the phone down and, with the zealous air of a surgeon, goes to his library and pulls out a huge leather-bound book and begins turning the pages frantically. This is the *Mesechta Nid-*

dah, the section of the Gemara dealing with family purity. After he locates the page he is looking for, and following a fair amount of give and take on the telephone, he seems to come to the conclusion that she can go ahead with the wedding.

After he hangs up, he explains that he is writing two books on family purity. One is an overview of *niddah*–or purity–laws, and the other deals with plotting the onset of the next month's menstruation, an important obligation of the husband and wife. This plotting involves recording the dates of every month's menstrual cycle on a piece of paper. Since according to him there has never been a formal chart to facilitate this process, Fishel, with the help of computer graphics, has designed a table that allows women to track their cycle on a day-to-day basis.

Estimating the onset of the next month's menstrual cycle is important because on that day, even if there is no blood, the couple must refrain from sexual relations and the wife must check herself with a cloth. If she is lacking any evidence of menstruation, marital relations–or MR, as Fishel calls it–can resume the next day. On the expected day, however, there can be no intercourse, no kissing, no sleeping in the same bed, no hugging, and no affectionate touching.

This is a veritable Roman orgy compared to the day of actual menstruation. On those days, not only are the aforementioned activities prohibited, but there is an additional arm's-length list of injunctions. For example, the wife is forbidden from singing in the presence of her husband because it might arouse him. The husband and wife are not allowed to pass objects to one another, including plates, pens, paper, foodstuffs, or books. Moreover, if the couple eats at the same table, a Berlin Wall of sorts must be erected between them. This can be any foreign object not normally found on the table, as long as it is the height of a human hand.

Fishel opens a drawer and produces a draft of his other work, his magnum opus, an overview of the laws of family purity. As I begin to peruse the manuscript, he tells me that this is a unique contribution to the Jewish people because nowhere else is all this material easily accessible to the uninitiated. Much of the authority is rather obscure, and Fishel has culled the literature to create this guide.

The subject matter is unavoidably provocative. One chapter begins with a caveat of sorts: "It is not without a fair amount of trepidation that I, with the help of Hashem, approach this chapter, which deals with very personal and sensitive subjects. . . . However, the awareness of the potential benefit possible through the dissemination of this material coupled by the knowledge that this material is entirely based on the eternal wisdom of our holy forebears serves to allay my caution."

The chapter explicitly delineates what is and is not acceptable in the intimate relations of a married couple, with forthright recommendations, such as, "It is advisable for the wife to culminate first," and "It is preferable for them to both be completely undressed, the husband should keep the *yarmulke* on, and the wife should attempt to keep the *tichel* [head scarf] on if easily possible." This last statement is footnoted with a reference to *Siddur Beis Yaakov,* a work of the eighteenth-century Rabbi Yaakov Emden, who suggested that a man's *tzitzis* be kept on during intercourse. Fishel notes that many authorities feel otherwise.

Then there are the injunctions. They read like a collection of do's and don'ts from an expanded version of the Desiderata. It is forbidden in a room where holy books are exposed. In such a room, either the books must be covered with two coverings (for example, two sheets), or a divider must be set up between the couple and the books at least ten *tefachim* (handbreadths) high and four *amos* (arm's lengths) long. If there is a Torah in the house, marital relations are forbidden. There can be no one else in the room, with the exception of a sleeping child. One should contemplate holy thoughts and righteous men during marital relations, since those thoughts will be transformed into the seed and create similarly praiseworthy children. When there is warmth between the father and mother, the seed is influenced and the child born as an outcome will also be warm, his or her warmth bringing with it intellectual sharpness and alacrity. Relations should be avoided if the couple is quarreling, when drunk, when the husband is thinking about another woman, and when the woman is asleep.

Positions are severely circumscribed. The husband below with the wife on top, the husband entering from behind, and the husband and wife lying side by side are not desirable, but not explicitly proscribed. Strangely enough, anal intercourse, according to Fishel, is not prohibited, as long as it is occasional and the husband does not spill seed during the act. A specific section of the Gemara enjoins the husband from engaging in oral sex on his wife, although there is nothing noted with respect to the other way around. But just to be prudent, Fishel advises against it. The bottom line, according to the *Zohar,* is that it's best to stick to the missionary position.

There are other considerations: Rear entry can lead to lame children. Cunnilingus can produce mute children. Looking at the wife's private parts can cause blind children. In addition, the couple should be covered during coitus. Clearly, this is no *Kama Sutra.* There should be no intercourse on the ground, nor while sitting or standing. But kissing is permitted and even encouraged. After the act, the husband should remain engaged until he feels that no more drops of seminal fluid will be emitted. It is proper to sleep at that point, but not before the husband soothes his wife.

After this initiation into the esoterica of Jewish marital relations, I take my leave, stating that I intend to visit a rural Hasidic community, provided one exists in Israel. While Kfar Chabad provides a bucolic setting for the practice of the mitzvot, it really doesn't fit the bill, since almost none of the 5,000 people who live here work the land. I ask for suggestions.

"Koyme Miyus!" is everyone's collective response. "You've got to see Koyme Miyus, a real Hasidic farming community," Fishel's friend, the Chinese medicine expert, tells me. "It's one of the few places like it in the whole country." Sounds intriguing, I reply, and promise to return to Kfar Chabad.

In Israel, a land known for its *kibbutzim* and bronzed farmers, the ultra-Orthodox will take the city over the country. To be fair, this is also true for the population as a whole. But there are a few exceptions and Koyme Miyus is one of them.

Like most places in Israel, Koyme Miyus (or Kommemiyut, in its more conventional Hebrew transliteration) is not too far away. The highway sign outside Beersheva on the way to Koyme Miyus reads "Qomemiyut," in the curiously graceless orthography of Israeli road maps, and if one doesn't pay close attention, it will surely be missed. The main road out of Tel Aviv wends its way through agricultural settlements pockmarked by the occasional truck stop, but the narrow blacktop feeding off the main highway passes only wheat fields. There is one semi-urban exception, a settlement consisting of a cluster of well-maintained buildings dominated by a giant pair of Ten Commandment tablets attached to the roof of a barn. At first glance it's reminiscent of a Bible camp in Arkansas. I take this to be Koyme Miyus, and pull in the main driveway, asking a group of women the way to the main office. They point to a trailer where a polyester-clad manager in a neatly knit yarmulke works purposefully at a computer. *"Shalom,"* I announce, and explain in Yiddish that I've come to see Koyme Miyus, the Hasidic farm community. He doesn't look Hasidic, I observe. Then, eying me quizzically, he replies that he doesn't speak a word of Yiddish, that no one here does, that this is a Sephardic *moshav,* or farm community, and that Koyme Miyus is down the road a ways. Sure enough, turning to the road in front of the moshav, I see a traditionally dressed Hasid peddling away on an antiquated bicycle in the broiling afternoon sun.

I get in my car and drive up to him. "Which way to Koyme Miyus?" I ask. He points straight ahead. Koyme Miyus, I think to myself, what an anomaly. There are but a few agrarian Haredi outposts in Israel, constituting perhaps 1 percent of the total Haredi population. "*Kleinshtayteldik,* provincial," or "*dorfmensch,* village person," my grandmother would derisively call those living outside of metropolitan areas. The country bumpkins in prewar Poland in turn had their own derogatory terms for their cosmopolitan cousins. "*Shtoot shtinkers,*" they cried, roughly translated as city slickers, or "*shmeckzeifels,*" users of fancy perfumed soap. But up until the war, and indeed afterward, the trend was decisively in one direction, and it wasn't rural.

In Israel today there are perhaps ten rural Haredi settlements, including Beit Helkiah, Yesodot, Kibbutz Chofetz Chaim, and a few others. Unlike a kibbutz, where the means of production are owned by all its members, Koyme Miyus is a moshav, a community of privately owned plots worked by individual families.

Koyme Miyus itself turns out to be nothing more than a jumbled collection of stucco houses surrounded by unkempt fields and chicken coops. The whole scene looks frozen in time, as if some laboratory slide's cross-section of life in the Pale—certain districts in czarist Russia where Jews were allowed to live—were being examined under a powerful microscope against the backdrop of modern Israel. But on closer inspection, it is not even that. Instead of a prewar *shtetl* with its surfeit of quaint, albeit austere, charms, it is in reality a remnant of the helter-skelter days surrounding the establishment of the state, when aesthetics were sacrificed at the altar of expediency. In short, Koyme Miyus, with its dilapidated buildings, litter-strewn lawns, and aggressively chirping crickets, makes Li'l Abner's Dogpatch look like Jim Nabors's Hawaiian Hideaway.

Everything seems consciously neglected, as if any nod to the ethos of design is a submission to idolatry. Everything, that is, of a material nature. The *cheder* is brimming with happy and well-fed children. If the line between the realms of equanimity and depression is an elusive one, then Koyme Miyus falls firmly in the former.

It is fully twelve hours before the onset of the Sabbath, and aside from a few lone bicyclists, the only humans visible are some boys from the cheder eating pieces of poppyseed cake by the roadside. Then I look to my left and notice a family lounging on some stools in front of their house. It is a large brood, a couple in their sixties with several grown children and a litter of preschoolers. They flag me over. "Is this Koyme Miyus?" I ask. Sure is, they reply. I tell them I came here to see the moshav that supervises *shmitta* for Israel.

Shmitta is the commandment that the land be left idle every seventh year. Leviticus states that: "When you come to the land that I am giving you, the land must be permitted to rest, a Sabbath to God. For six years you may plant your fields, prune your vineyards, and harvest your crops, but the seventh year is a Sabbatical year for the land. It is God's Sabbath, during which time you may not plant your field, nor prune your vineyard. Do not harvest crops that grow on their own and do not gather the grapes on your unpruned vines, since it is a year of rest for the land."

This is the middle of a shmitta year, a period that imposes innumerable hardships on the farmers of Israel who observe it as a commandment. The family I am with is no different.

"You want shmitta?" one of the sons, a yeshiva student in Jerusalem, says. "Look across the street." With a jerky motion, he points his thumb in the direction of a building that looks like it was at ground zero during a West Bank riot. Surrounded by clumps of noxious weeds, crates of fruit, and broken-down furniture is a small structure with a faded sign that reads *"Vaad Keren Hashviis,"* or Council of the Fund for Shmitta.

This is the nerve center for perpetuating and ensuring the observance of shmitta in Israel. Shmitta itself is a practice that almost fell into complete disuse until some enthusiastic Hasidim at Koyme Miyus took it upon themselves to revive it in the early fifties. None of the secular kibbutzim pay shmitta any heed. To them it is a laughable anachronism, another hoop to jump through in the endless dog-and-pony show that constitutes Haredi life. Even the modern Orthodox have found a way around it, but the Haredim refuse to compromise.

I walk to the building and knock on the door, but much to my chagrin it is locked, closed early for the Sabbath. Upon my return to the family, a steaming cup of coffee is waiting for me, set down on a tree stump by the matriarch. I ask her where she's from, and she replies "Luv." I assume by her Polish-inflected Yiddish that she is referring to Lvov, a town in the Ukraine. I was in Lvov, I tell her, about two years ago. "Not Lvov, Luv! You know Luv, Khaddafi's Luv!" Then I remember that Luv is the Hebrew word for Libya. Twenty-odd years of marriage to her Warsaw-born husband and she sounds like a native Yiddish speaker.

We sit for a few moments in the sun. There isn't all that much to say. Then I formulate a question. "What are some of the *dinim*, the laws, regarding agriculture?" I ask, leaving aside any issues related to shmitta, which I want to find out when I return to Koyme Miyus after the Sabbath.

"There is *b'hor*," the yeshiva student replies intently. "In biblical times, the first calf of a cow owned by a Jew had to be given to a Kohan—a priest—for a sacrificial offering. It couldn't be eaten or used for milk. If the cow, however, belonged in partnership to a

Jew and a gentile, the calf stayed with the owners and could be eaten or milked by the Jew. If it only belonged to a *goy*, the Jew could eat or milk it."

"So this only applied to a Jewish-owned cow?"

"Correct. And today it still applies, but we get around it by selling the cow to a goy just before it gives birth and then buying it back immediately afterward, so it isn't owned by a Jew when the calf is born."

"Who do you sell it to?"

"The *Shabbos goy*. A bedouin."

"How do you know you'll get it back?"

"We have an agreement. He's worked for us for forty years. There is a ceremony called *kinyon suder*, where we pick up a handkerchief. This represents a symbolic selling of the cow. It's conducted in the presence of a rabbi.

"Another commandment is *kelayim*, enjoining improper mixing of crops or animals, including the rule that a horse and ox should not be used together to pull a wagon. This is because the ox is stronger than the horse and will pull the load faster, causing the horse to suffer." There are other restrictions, he tells me, some rooted in compassion, some in common sense, and some more nebulous in purpose.

The father relates to me the history of the settlement. Koyme Miyus was founded in the early fifties by discharged soldiers of the Israeli army, many of whom had served in the War of Independence after surviving Europe. Intent on establishing an agrarian community that kept the mitzvot, they went to an agency that dispersed funds from the Diaspora and petitioned for seed money for such a settlement. They received it, and within a few years more than a hundred families had made their homes here. But like the secular kibbutz movement, you can't keep them down on the farm after they've seen Paris, and the young are steadily trickling away. This gives the place a slightly decrepit aura. But it is still full of children, many bussed in from surrounding towns to attend the cheder here.

Today there are sixty families in Koyme Miyus. One demographic problem that seems endemic to agrarian cultures exists here as well. Instead of rationalizing the means of production and consolidating ownership in a few hands, the families cling to their relatively small plots. When the time comes to divide them up, the plots are only big enough to support one or two of the family offspring. That leaves all the other siblings with the option of remaining landless in Koyme Miyus, or moving on to other opportunities in the big city. Those who stay and do not farm generally work within the community as teachers. Those who leave study in yeshivot and stay on in the city after marriage as students in *kollels*. The women follow their husbands. All of this is relatively nonproductive from a nonreligious standpoint. Indeed, unemployment is leading to increased impoverishment among the Haredim. This is ameliorated by contributions from abroad and transfer payments from the Israeli government, which supplies subventions for families. A family of ten receives about $1,000 per month, enough to get by in a welfare state where health and education is already largely taken care of.

Koyme Miyus is a mixed bag of Hasidic and non-Hasidic ultra-Orthodox—including Belzers, Bobovers, Satmars, Vishnitzers, Bratslavers, and Mitnaggedim—all under the tutelage of the highly respected local chief rabbi, Menachem Mendelson, who is himself a follower of the Gerer Rebbe.

The family I'm with has been here since the beginning, 1951, although the father did not marry until he was well into his forties. Although the facilities here are primitive by modern standards, each of the families has a phone and many have traveled a great deal, some to the United States, to accompany a rebbe or visit a relative at a yeshiva. Most of the agricultural activity is centered on dairy cows and raising turkeys, but some wheat and a variety of vegetables are grown. While it is forbidden to milk a cow on the Sabbath, animals can be fed, as long as the feeding is manual. But they cannot be worked on that day. There is a *schechting* room for fowl. Each of the families owns their own home, a phenomenon that distinguishes a moshav like Koyme Miyus from a kibbutz, where everything is owned collectively.

I am led to the back of the house, which contains an entire dairy operation. Cattle are kept in metal stalls or saunter about under a corrugated roof. At first glance, it seems like a good-sized set up. There is a milking machine and some other equipment. But one of the sons lets me know that it is woefully antiquated and difficult to compete with much larger operations. All milk is sold to the dairy cooperative, Tnuva, and I muse that for this farm and other small operations to be kept in business, the government must provide a subsidy that would be the envy of the American Dairymen's Association.

For some reason, I feel compelled to ask what happens to a cow's carcass. One of the daughters, a stoic Klausenberger, tells me that the animals are either sold to slaughterhouses when they are very old, or their remains are shipped to Safari Park in Ramat Gan, outside Tel Aviv, to be fed to the lions.

From the family's body language, I can tell that they want me to leave because they need to prepare for the Sabbath but are too polite to ask. So I thank them for their hospitality and promise to return.

"Wednesday. Come back Wednesday," one of them says. "Wednesday is a good day to see the workings of the shmitta committee." I promise them that I will.

When I return a few days later, the family is nowhere to be found but the shmitta operation is going full tilt. Inside the ramshackle shmitta building is an office that looks straight out of *Glengarry Glen Ross*. Maps of Israel with pins stuck in them line the wall and computer cables clutter the floors. Outside the window the scene is that of a sleepy little shtetl but inside is a no-nonsense Hasidic hard-sell emporium. Several men are on the phone spitting out orders in Yiddish like drill sergeants, their desks surrounded by cartons of ripe apricots. Women in wigs and scarves stroll in and out and help themselves to the fruit.

After I stand around for about ten minutes like a wallflower at a cotillion dance, one of the Hasidim looks up at me and asks, "*Vus vilst du?* What do you want?"

"Is this the center of the shmitta operation in Israel?"

"One of them—and by far the largest."

"Then perhaps you can show me around."

"Everything you need to know you can ask of Moishe Ziegler. He's an American, like you."

He presses a button and in a few minutes a tall, white-haired gentleman in his seventies appears accompanied by an armed Israeli guard. I am tempted to ask the reason for the guard's presence. Who would make trouble here? There has never been a terrorist attack at Koyme Miyus, and militant secularists—while they consistently make fun of shmitta—would never dream of acting out their anticlerical fantasies, which typically might include shearing the Hasidim clean or inducting them into an Israeli armed forces boot camp. The armed guard exits, apparently after determining I'm not a terrorist, and Mr. Ziegler, a blue-eyed Skverer from upstate New York, launches into a well-honed rap, one no doubt given to many a skeptical *hiloni*, or nonbeliever, in the past.

"The Gemara says that one of the reasons the Jews were forced into exile was because they didn't keep shmitta, the other reasons being idol worship, illicit sexual relations, and murder. The first exile in Babylonia lasted seventy years because shmitta was not kept for seventy shmitta years. If one Jew in the land of Israel doesn't observe shmitta, then it has an effect on the whole country, and if every Jew in Israel keeps it, the Messiah will come.

"Shmitta is one of the toughest mitzvot to keep, because a person who works the land for six years has *parnassah,* a livelihood, from it for those six years and then must stop. He cannot sell fruit that has flowered during shmitta, even if it was planted before the onset of the year; and he cannot, even subsequent to the shmitta year, sell the fruit of plants that were planted during that year. All the fruit that falls to the ground or that remains on trees may be given away to other Jews or gentiles, or used as feed."

While this injunction wreaks havoc on the religious farm economy, it also throws the Haredi urban economy out of kilter, creating shortages, higher prices, a narrower variety of goods, and lower quality of produce. The Israeli press periodically reports on ultra-Orthodox consumers who have gotten sick on vegetables grown in hastily expanded farming operations in the territories that use brackish water or tainted soil.

"The reason for all of this is to show that man is a mere steward, not the owner, of the land. The *Rabenu Shel Olam*–God–is the true owner–and on the seventh year man cannot act like he owns it."

Shmitta must be observed by only those Jews who reside within the bounds of Israel, and it runs from Jewish New Year to Jewish New Year. Any produce, including grains grown by Jews in Israel during that period, is subject to its restrictions. Even animals cannot be fed shmitta-year produce if it has been bought from another Jew. But food grown abroad, even by Jews, or grown domestically by non-Jews, may be purchased. The apricots in the office are an example of shmitta fruit being given away.

There are many other rules. While shmitta lasts from Rosh Hashanah to Rosh Hashanah, fruit-bearing trees cannot be planted less than forty-five days before the Jewish New Year, and vegetables not less than three. Only vegetables that have already sprouted and grains that have reached at least one-third of their normal height before the shmitta year are sellable. Aside from restrictions on sowing, pruning, harvesting, picking, and plowing, there can be no removing stones, spraying pesticides, fertilizing, digging ditches, watering, collecting wood, or trimming. If work is done to prevent a tree from dying, it is permitted, but only in this instance and not to improve the tree or plant.

The modern Orthodox, while acknowledging the rules of shmitta, get around it by selling their land to a non-Jew for the year and then buying it back. This mechanism is called *heter mechira*, and most Haredim see it as a gimmick. A few research institutes specialize in finding ways to farm during shmitta without technically violating the commandment. Since shmitta enjoins working the soil, hydroponics is one touted alternative, and an automatic picking machine another. Moishe Ziegler sneers at this: "Short cuts," he scoffs. Only one plant can be grown during the year without any restrictions, and that is the mushroom, because it gets its nutrition from the air rather than the soil.

The strict adherence to this commandment produces a myriad of financial difficulties, and that is where shmitta central comes in. Koyme Miyus has developed a computer program with files on nearly every observant farmer in Israel. Growers can be called up by name, by region, by size of plot, or by crop, and their files will show, based on a calculation factoring in the number of *dunams,* the type of crop, and the size of their family, how much they are entitled to in compensation for the sacrifice. Checks are issued monthly, and while they do not fully compensate for losses, they soften the blow.

I am taken to a room where a state-of-the-art printer sits on a desk. A woman waves a large pile of bank drafts in my face. These are the monthly payments to the farmers: 3,000 shekels, 2,000 shekels, 600 shekels. These are sent out to shmitta participants throughout the country, and the recipients in turn must send back an affidavit pledging that they have kept the commandment this month. It is this project that takes up much of the energy of Koyme Miyus. Aside from distributing funds, the moshav has taken it upon itself to launch a vigorous lobbying effort for subsidies with the Israeli government and among sympathetic Jews in the Diaspora. It sends out representatives all over Israel to persuade farmers to take up the mitzvah. And although only a small number do, observance continues to grow with each new Sabbatical year.

One problem is determining exactly where the geographic boundaries of shmitta lie. Shmitta is supposed to be kept within the biblical borders of Israel, but no one knows exactly where those are. (This is not only a problem for shmitta, but also for Passover, where two *seders* are celebrated outside the land of Israel but only one within.) Books have been written about the subject, but a clear territorial demarcation is elusive. Is Israel what Moses saw, or what God promised to Abraham, or what Joshua conquered? Even Koyme Miyus is not in all certainty within Israel. So, to be on the safe side, the borders of Israel are given the widest interpretation possible. But this is simply one facet of shmitta open to differences of opinion. Contradictory interpretations riddle the material dealing with the subject.

"Every week the rabbi leads a study group on the laws of shmitta," one of the Hasidim in the office, a potato farmer, tells me.

"Is there much to know?"

"Much to know?" he replies. "You can spend years studying the rules. Mishna, Gemara, commentaries—all deal with it. For example, during the shmitta year, a farmer must not clear his field of stones because then it appears to a passerby that he is preparing to plant. This is *marais ayin,* a principle that runs throughout Jewish law. Marais ayin is all about not giving a wrong impression. If a person sits in the window of a kosher restaurant, eating something that looks like pork, even if it is not, it is forbidden. Why? Because it gives the wrong impression. Likewise, clearing the field of rocks during the shmitta year is forbidden, even if no planting is intended. But what if the farmer needs the stones to build an addition to his house? Ah-ha. Then the farmer may take the larger stones only, as long as he leaves the little ones. That way, nobody will have the impression that he is clearing the field for planting."

"How do you define what is a big stone and what is a little stone?"

"This is where the difference of opinion comes in. One side says that a big stone is one that only two people can carry. This is the more restrictive interpretation. The other says that a stone is big enough to take if it cannot be carried, two at a time, on the shoulders of one person."

Material like this takes up hundreds of dense pages. It is fretted over, argued about, speculated on, and painstakingly deciphered. And every so often, a scholar will come up with a new angle, re-analyze a narrow sliver of it, and write a book on the subject. The number of original works being published by yeshiva scholars is at an all-time high.

The kollel for married students in Koyme Miyus (the unmarried yeshiva students typically go off to Jerusalem or Benei Berak to study) is closed for the afternoon siesta, but I am invited to visit the cheder. I walk through a minefield of litter, navigating around such items as discarded appliances and a rusty red wagon, and climb the stairs to a series of rooms full of young boys squeezed together like matches in a matchbook, their books open to the weekly Torah portion. They're all standing, because the rooms are too small to accommodate them on chairs. As they chant in unison in the stifling heat, I look around and see no totems of contemporary education: no audiovisual equipment, no globe, no chalkboard. Every book looks at least fifty years old. Whenever I look inside a classroom, the children begin to giggle uncontrollably. The teachers stop talking and look at me with barely concealed exasperation. One class is actually learning the laws of shmitta. The language of instruction is Yiddish, although the actual text is in Hebrew. The children seem happy. Many, according to a teacher, have never seen a television set.

I promised Fishel that I'd return to Kfar Chabad for a karate demonstration that night. So I leave the cheder accompanied by the potato farmer, who insists on comparing notes on where our mothers were in Birkenau, and walk to the car.

A few hours later I'm back in Kfar Chabad. I ring Fishel's door, but he is apparently already at the karate exhibition. A pair of boys hanging around on bicycles ask me who I'm looking for. I tell them.

"Fishel Jacobs, a *guter yid,* a good Jew," one says in Yiddish. At the synagogue, they tell me, leaflets have just appeared asserting the Messiah will return with the resurrection of the dead, not before, as is usually supposed.

"This is very important," one of the boys says earnestly, as if uncovering a clue to a mystery. "One Shabbos a few years ago, the rebbe gave an indication that the Moshiach has already been crowned, and that the Moshiach does not have to remain alive until the resurrection. This means that he will come back with the resurrection, not before, as most people think."

"What are you doing with your life?" he asks abruptly. "Join us. Join us, or your grandchildren will be *goyim.*" And with an economy of motion worthy of Georgie Jessel, he flicks his wrist impatiently and walks away.

"Yeah, they will all become goyim," the other says, and ambles off behind him, leaving the bicycles on the ground. Suddenly, I feel like a deeply insulted fourth-grader. Cripes, they sure know how to get to a guy. I can't help but notice a modicum of *schaden-freude*. They don't want the mainstream Jews to assimilate, but on some deep emotional level they do. Hey, I want to say, when we're not around anymore, when all those Sapersteins, Silver-steins, Goldbergs, and Cohens are sitting in their church pews or hot tubs, remember us.

I walk toward the main square. There I see Fishel Jacobs talk-ing to a few people. I take him aside and ask him if it's indeed true that the Messiah has already been crowned.

He gives me a confidential wink. "I got news for you, he's com-ing back soon!"

"How soon?"

"It won't be a year. You see, before the rebbe's death, journal-ists asked a well-known kabbalist when the rebbe would die. He gave the exact date. This upset a whole lot of people because they thought he was immortal. So now some of the rebbe's followers have come back to him and said, 'Okay, wise guy, you were so smart last time, when is he coming back?'"

"And?"

"I told you, it won't be a year. Come with me," he says. "We're going to the auditorium where I'm going to give the demonstration."

We walk to an assembly hall. It is full of high school students from a nearby nonreligious community. Fishel begins to stack slen-der cinderblocks one on top of the other. Then he squirts lighter fluid on the pile and sets a match to it. After a distinctively un-Hasidic grunt, he splits everything in two. The secular kids gasp in collective amazement. After the demonstration, children follow him from the assembly hall like he's the Pied Piper of Hameln.

As Fishel is signing autographs, I make a discreet exit and get in my car. On the passenger seat is an English-language Israeli paper I purchased earlier in the day but hadn't yet had a chance to read. I glance at it briefly and see that on the front page there is an article about the Satmar Rebbe, who is leaving today after a week in Israel. In it he delivers a not-too-subtle parting shot at the recently deceased Lubavitcher Rebbe. "Now we know we have to wait for the real Messiah," he proclaims.

I start the engine and begin the drive out of Kfar Chabad. The radio plays a song popular a few years back, *Moshiach Lo Ba,* the Messiah is not coming. It was not written about the Lubavitcher Rebbe, but it seems a particularly inopportune jab to be playing it now. Perhaps it was unintended.

I come to a fork in the road. To the right is Tel Aviv, home of hedonism and all-night falafel stands. To the left is Jerusalem, with its holy rollers and gun-toting millennialists. I look back in the rearview mirror. There I see groups of children and grandchildren, many brought over from Chernobyl, the offspring of hapless immigrants from the hostile soils of Eastern Europe and North Africa, playing happily in Kfar Chabad's well-groomed streets. Maybe we're not about to enter the Messianic age, I speculate. Maybe it's going to be a long time coming. But I wouldn't want to roll the dice. Because short of paradise, it doesn't get any better than this.

Epilogue

The phoenix-like revival of Hasidism after the Holocaust and the establishment of the State of Israel both represent reasons to rejoice and to infer a mystical sign that the Jewish people are somehow indestructible. Yet despite my immersion in this unique and growing culture, I am unable to divorce myself from my secular upbringing. There has been too much destruction in my family, too much violence inexplicably perpetrated against the innocent, for me to see things otherwise. But for those who are capable of leaping the chasm of disbelief, I extend my heartiest kudos.

Jews of the nonreligious persuasion like myself still represent the vast majority of Jews in this country. But it won't be this way much longer. The once-ascendant Conservative movement, which represents the ritualistic center of the faith, is fast losing its constituency, as intermarriage and a low birth rate continue to take their toll. The still-growing Reform movement, at the liberal end of the spectrum, attracts many intermarrieds but misses many more. It is a well-known generalization of Jewish historians that nonreligious Jews cannot live in an open society for more than three generations without losing their identity. It is my hope that the vast experiment in outreach to unaffiliated Jews the Reform movement is conducting will prove otherwise. Only time will tell.

But one thing is certain: The Hasidic population in America will continue to grow, in number, in confidence, and in economic influence. Fifty or seventy-five years hence, the ultra-Orthodox, along with their modern Orthodox brethren, will represent the majority of Jews in this country. A generation or two later, and they may very well be the only Jews left. What took fifty generations to build will mostly be gone in fifty years. But the Hasidim, against a backdrop of cyberspace, genetic engineering, and new forms of travel, will stand out as a monument to faith and tenacity, and a living memorial to another era. And they will stand erect.

Glossary

apikoros   a nonbeliever who had been brought up to believe
averah   a sin
ba'al teshuvah   a returnee to the faith, newly Orthodox
balebustah (f.)   boss
beit midrash   study hall
bekishe   a long overcoat
boocher   an unmarried young man
boychik (m.)   youth
challah   braided Sabbath bread
chaver   a friend
cheder   day school
daven   to pray
etrog   citrus fruit used for ceremonial purposes on Sukkot, feast of
   Tabernacles
gardle   a belt
Gemara   part of the Talmud

goyim   non-Jews

Halakha   Jewish law

Haredim   the ultra-Orthodox as referred to in Israel

Hasidim   the ultra-Orthodox followers of rebbes or charismatic rabbinic leaders who usually inherit their mantles. Hasidim, along with Mitnaggedim, a smaller group that does not follow rebbes, comprise the whole of ultra-Orthodox Jews.

Haskala   the Enlightenment, when Jews became less observant

hegdesh   a mess

kapoteh   overcoat

Kohan   priest in the Temple in Jerusalem

kollel   an advanced institute of talmudic learning for married students

loshon hora   gossip

lulav   long, pointed plant used for ceremonial purposes on Sukkot

mamzer   a person of illegitimate birth

mashgiach   an inspector of the koshering process

mezuzah   inscription from the scriptures encased in an enclosure on the doorpost

mikveh   ritual bath

mitzvah   commandment

mohel   person who performs circumcision

Moshiach   the Messiah

Mussar   the study of moral and ethical development

neshuma   the soul

parnassah   livelihood

payess   sidelocks

pushke   tin for collecting charitable contributions

rav   a non-Hasidic rabbinic scholar, deferred to by Mitnaggedim

rebbe   a charismatic Hasidic leader who is part of a rabbinic dynasty

sabra a person born in Israel
Schachris morning prayer services
schechting the act of ritual slaughter of animals
schnorr to panhandle or beg
schochet ritual slaughterer of animals
schokling moving back and forth in prayer
sefer a book, often holy
Shabbos Sabbath, Friday sundown to Saturday sundown
shatnes the prohibited mixing of certain fabrics
shiduch an arranged marriage
shtiebl prayer room
shtetl small town in Eastern Europe with a vibrant Jewish community
shtreimel fur hat for the Sabbath
shul synagogue
shmitta the sabbatical year when land is to be given a rest
siddur prayer book
smicha rabbi's ordination
soifer scribe
tallis prayer shawl
t'fillin phylacteries; small leather cases holding scriptures that are bound to the forehead and arms with leather straps during morning prayer
tzaddik a righteous or holy person
tzedakkah charity
tzitzis undergarment with four strands of string
upsherinish the cutting of a boy's hair on his third birthday
yahrzeit annual commemoration of someone's death
yarmulke skullcap
yeshiva seminary for religious studies
yiddishkeit Jewishness
yungerleit young men
zmiros songs sung in unison at the Sabbath table